Architectures of Illusion

From Motion Pictures to Navigable Interactive Environments

Edited by

Maureen Thomas

François Penz

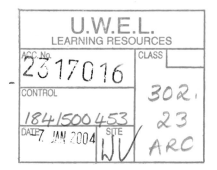
intellect™

Bristol, UK
Portland, OR, USA

First Published in Great Britain in Hardback in 2003 by
Intellect Books, PO Box 862, Bristol BS99 1DE, UK

First Published in USA in 2003 by
Intellect Books, ISBS, 5824 N.E. Hassalo St, Portland, Oregon 97213-3644, USA

Text Editor	Maureen Thomas
Image Editor	François Penz
Consulting Editor:	Robin Beecroft
Cover Design	Martin Robertson
Copy Editor:	Lisa Morris
Proofreader	Holly Spradling

A catalogue record for this book is available from the British Library

ISBN 1-84150-045-3

Printed and bound in Great Britain by Cromwell Press, Trowbridge

Contents

The 'Creative Treatment of Actuality'
Visions and Revisions in Representing Truth
Terence Wright

Historical Note

Cambridge University Moving Image Studio (CUMIS), managed by the Department of Architecture, was established in November 1998,with strong support and encouragement from Professor Peter Carolin, to bring audiovisual digital technologies into the University's pursuit of knowledge, its curating and dissemination, with special care for the Arts and Humanities. CUMIS underpins the Department of Architecture's Digital Studios for Practice-Based Research in Design, Visualisation, Communication and Interactivity, where François Penz (Director of CUMIS) is Head of Research in Spatiality, and Maureen Thomas (Creative Director of CUMIS) is Head of Research in Narrativity. Although in its present form this volume reflects the research focuses of the Digital Studios and CUMIS, it was also inspired by the vision of Henning Camre, Director of the National Film & Television School (NFTS), UK, where, from 1993 to 1998, Maureen Thomas was Head of Screen Studies and began her practice-based research in narrative interactive media. Video artist, animator, film-maker and art critic Brian Ashbee, and visual anthropologist, photographer and researcher in media representation Terence Wright, who both work regularly at CUMIS, were also tutors at the NFTS.

The perception that developments in 3D software and digital production methods would inevitably bring together the architects of the real world and the architects of the illusory world of the screen – a perception reflected in papers delivered at a joint symposium held by the NFTS and Cambridge University, published in the British Film Institute volume *Cinema and Architecture* (ed. Penz & Thomas, BFI 1997) – has proved justified. The digital future was viewed in the 1990s by both architects and film-makers as a great opportunity for innovation and creativity, but a pressing need for collaborative research into its potential, in preparation for a new era of design and production, was identified. In 2003 – the digital present – the Digital Studios Research Group in Design, Visualisation, Communication and Interactivity, supported by CUMIS, provides an environment for the fulfilment of that need. From the vantage point of the Studio, this book offers different but complementary perspectives on the narrative organization of space and the spatial organization of narrative; on the historical cross-pollination between the photographic image, movement, character and animation; and on the relationships between recording, representing and generating screen events in moving-image media from motion pictures through architectural walk-throughs to navigable interactive environments for drama. Its emphasis is on the integration of diversity enabled by creative media technology in the 21st century: tradition and innovation, fiction and fact, observation and creation, animation and live-action, 2D and 3D – in the context of both theory and practice.

Introduction

The buzzword of the 1990s in moving-image-based media was 'convergence'. By the turn of the millennium, with faster and faster, more and more accessible computing and networks constantly speeding up the rate of development, convergence had come to pass. Communications technology (mobile devices, networks, telecoms) and creative media technology (computer graphics, computer-aided design and animation, real-time three-dimensional virtual environments (RT3D) and games design, digital broadcasting and movie-making, e- and d- cinema and digital versatile discs (DVD)) were flourishing in symbiosis in the environment of computer-enabled interactivity. What does this mean for the relationship between traditional design processes, presentation formats, delivery platforms and media production? Crucially, we need to recognise and understand the diverse components which constitute convergence, and integrate them effectively into an inclusive – but not arbitrary – approach. Part of this process is the clear identification of the strengths of traditional media in the context of emerging digital practices, and the creation of an informed awareness of the transformations which need to take place if worthwhile new work is to be produced.

Traditionally, cinema captured 3D reality and transformed it through the medium of film to project moving images on to the 2D screen; television transmitted real-time events from locations and studios, or fiction and factual programmes recorded on film or video, via the small domestic screen; animation created characters and environments from drawings and models for projection in 2D; while architecture created 2D visions on paper to be built in 3D reality. In the 21st century, both architecture and the screen arts use the medium of the computer to capture, manipulate and transmit images via digital video and Webcams, including synthetic imaging for environments and sets, and to create totally simulated, navigable 'virtual' worlds directly in 3D animation – narrating space, design process, experience and information, as well as entertainment, in electronic moving images. The computer as tool and medium has become central to designing buildings as well as sets, simulating 'real' environments as well as staging them for fiction, and creating many different kinds of fictive, scientific and craft-oriented, moving-image presentations – ranging from TV and architectural explorations of houses and gardens through the depiction of landscape and urban environments to instructional, informational, drama and music videos, commercials, games and movies for the cinema.

The effects on 'content production' of the rapid expansion of digital technology – from documentary and real TV through narrative drama and adventure to animation and computer-generated environments – and the proliferation of computer-based methods of origination, production and delivery in all the visual, expressive and creative arts and design disciplines, require contextualizing in history and theory so that they can be assimilated appropriately into practice. Architects modelling buildings and making 'walk-throughs' and other visualizations and presentations require the traditional skills of moving-image communication (including fiction, drama and music) to 'narrate' architectural space – especially populated space – through DV, mixed media and 3D animations. Makers of moving-image material, factual or fictive, need to understand not only the structures and impact of digital effects on the traditional narrative conventions of 2D screenspace, but also the architectural and expressive properties of 3D navigable virtual environments as performance space. Moving-image language is as fundamental to culture in the 21st century as writing and drawing were in the 19th and, in the digital context, wielding it fluently requires spatial as well as temporal, visual and associative understanding.

'Convergence' is a somewhat hazy term, and easily obscures the importance of individual identity and diversity within the environment of digital complementarity. In education and training, as in practice-based research, it can be increasingly hard to find the balance between conceptual clarity, single specialist expertise, multi-skilling, teamwork and individual familiarity with a broad range of aesthetics and craft competences. Digital technologies bring the processes and people involved in production teams throughout the creative design and media world into new relationships. The development of a movie – whether feature-length for the cinema or 30 seconds long for advertising; whether ethnographical, factual or fictional; whether using image capture or synthetic imaging and animation (or all these); whether a 3D animated computer game or an architectural 'fly-through' a virtual building – is not easily divisible into traditional pre-production, production and post-production phases. 'Creatives' are no longer at one end of the process of originating ideas, aesthetics and narrative forms and delivery formats and 'technicians' at the other. In the digital world, what in film was 'post-production' is actually a highly creative 'production' process, where graphic artists, architects, designers, video editors, animators, image manipulators and sound designers make or mar the final product in their computers. As a result, the need for all members of the team to operate from an integrated complementary knowledge base – including narrative, design and aesthetic culture, and not omitting ethical and historical issues – as well as a complementary skills base, grows in proportion to the increasing diversity and equality within the groups united around the computer. Although it cannot tackle all the issues involved, this book offers a range of material to help establish such a focused, but wide-ranging, knowledge base.

At the other extreme both of creative production and practice-based research, the fast computer with plenty of memory and processing power, monitors with high resolution, programs providing tools for most if not all the functions of design, visualization and production, plus rapid, effective connectivity, in theory enable a single well-informed and skilled individual to achieve alone a great deal of what once required a team of experts. However, the passion for multi-skilling evinced in the 1980s and early 1990s cooled somewhat when it became evident that a program with inbuilt formal parameters (the multimedia equivalent of a word processor, which will format letters and adjust style, spelling, grammar and phraseology according to predefined rules) is still no substitute for conceptual education, trained creative talent, professional discipline and experience. Nonetheless, digital technology gives unprecedentedly wide individual access to the means of production. When mass production and distribution of paper and writing instruments make writing accessible to more than a cloistered elite, enormous social, cultural, aesthetic and artistic repercussions ensue. General literacy changes both literature and culture. The same is true of the mass production and widespread availability of digital tools and media, and the music industry experienced many of these changes before the moving-image world.

In the architect's studio, awareness of culture, history, theory, aesthetics, engineering and science have always accompanied design and production practice – and as a research matrix, the architect's studio forms an inspiring model for the digital-media context of the third millennium. Research is a vital locus of integration in the arena of moving-image studies because it leads and informs practice, in an environment where technology develops so fast that conceptual understanding of aesthetic and ethical issues needs continuous scrutiny and revision. The product of an academic institution is not normally a 'thing', a tangible product – it is new knowledge, and scholars qualified to identify and handle that knowledge. If, alongside the optimisation and rapid development of technology, new knowledge about the potential of digital media content is not developed and refined, that content is very unlikely to develop in genuinely innovative, interesting – and marketable – ways. To contextualize and evaluate the contribution of different disciplines to collaborative digital productivity, content-led research is crucial. But more and more in the digital-media universe, that research involves an understanding of, and competence in, practice – and *vice versa*. The ubiquitous availability of digital moving-image production equipment demands a proper understanding not only of its technical use, but also of the historical, cultural, artistic, aesthetic and ethical issues that moving-image-based media grow out of and depend upon, and this book, written by a team whose research is based in practice, aims to help fulfil that need.

Research in Cambridge at the Digital Studios and CUMIS recognizes the necessity of integrating the diverse knowledge sets and perspectives of architecture, animation, and classical and contemporary narrative in movie, video and interactive screen theory and practice – each with their individual histories, characteristics and potentials – in an inclusive studio environment. An integrated environment and practice should not, however, mean loss of individuality, but gain of mutual understanding. Collaborators familiarise each other with differing but complementary outlooks and skills, and contribute together to the development of new knowledge and new practice.

This volume offers a range of complementary perspectives on historical background, theory and specialist practice, illuminating the ways in which tradition can usefully inform transformation and development in the digital era. The book arose in response to the challenge of creating an integrated, inclusive research studio, on the model of the architect's studio, in the digital environment, where the diversity necessary to develop new ideas, new content, new knowledge and new practice could be incorporated in a collaborative forum. The Digital Studios for Design, Visualisation,

Communication and Interactivity and CUMIS bring together conceptual and theoretical approaches to practice-based research and production using digital technology, combining creativity, experiment, historical and cultural debate and intellectual rigour to form a strong research matrix.

The field of spatiality and narrativity – combining place and story – in the electronic era demands an integrated knowledge base ranging from an understanding of the historical and aesthetic relationships between 2D and 3D photographic representation of space and human presence, visual arts, animation and image manipulation, through awareness of the ethical, cultural and aesthetic issues raised by visual ethnography, reportage and reality TV, to a recognition of the special properties of moving-image rhetoric and computer-based interactivity. This book brings together some of the diverse but complementary knowledge, research and ideas whose integration we believe to be necessary for the study, understanding and extension of screen 'architectures of illusion' in the digital era. The angle of approach presents a collection of views informed by an evaluation of the historical and theoretical achievements of a century of endeavour, from the perspectives of contemporary 'content producers' who now work in a shared field in their practice-based research.

Cambridge University Moving Image Studio, Digital Studios for Research in Design, Visualisation, Communication and Interactivity
November 2002

Animation, Art and Digitality
From Termite Terrace to Motion Painting

Brian Ashbee

1. The Escape from Termite Terrace

From being something of a commercial and artistic ghetto, and virtually synonymous (at least in the public mind) with children's cartoons, animation has become, in the 21st century, an essential production tool in the broadcasting, cinema, games and Internet industries. This is largely due to the development of digital technologies, which have facilitated the creation and manipulation of images, making moving-image language accessible to a wider range of practitioners than ever before. It also confirms the profound shift in our culture from the literary to the audio-visual, which had been underway since the middle – perhaps even the beginning – of the 20th century.

Digital technologies enable the transformation of images in real time, and not just in response to predetermined programs; they can respond to the spectator. Digitality thus makes possible new forms of art and entertainment that are genuinely interactive – as the broadcasting and games industries were quick to realise. It unites a wide range of converging technologies – video, film, 3D audio, the Internet and many others – in a way which actively engages the spectator, often outside traditional contexts such as art galleries or cinemas, and creates not only new art forms but new audiences. The possibilities for artists are staggering: suddenly they have within their grasp techniques which could combine the emotional power of narrative forms like cinema, the architectural and spatial possibilities of installation art and sculpture, with the possibilities of music, painting, animation, dance and theatre – and, above all, the capacity for interaction between spectator *and* the work, or between spectator and spectator *within* the work, made possible by technologies such as the Internet and video-conferencing systems.

An instance of some of this potential is the work of Paul Sermon, which uses blue-screen technology (once the exclusive province of broadcasting organisations and film studios) to enable members of the 'audience' to interact with one another, their images being 'cut and pasted' together in startling combinations by cameras hidden in what seems at first like an ordinary domestic environment. Sermon's installation, *There's No Simulation Like Home* (Figure 1), displayed at the Fabrica Gallery, Brighton, in 1999 is:

> ... dependent on electronic technology, and is also, in a sense about electronic technology; but its interest is not limited to technology. Unlike a great deal of multi-media art, it goes beyond mere research to make a penetrating inquiry into our perception of self and others. Our everyday sense of inhabiting a body is replaced with the uncanny realisation

of our bodies as simultaneously real and virtual – as real or unreal as the remote other person with whom one is able to interact, through the monitor. (Ashbee, 2000)

Sermon has spoken of his fascination with being able to perceive the self from outside – to put, as he expressed it, our eyes elsewhere. Electronic technology is being used to

Figure 1. Audiences are amused and intrigued to find themselves sharing virtual spaces in Paul Sermon's installation, There's No Simulation Like Home, Fabrica Gallery, Brighton, 1999.

make possible a kind of self-scrutiny which is not so very different from Rembrandt's, though he used the technology of his day – namely oil paint, costumes and a mirror. But the major difference here is the role of the audience. Sermon's piece is not about the artist: it places the audience centre stage. As the artist has remarked: 'The piece, in a very real sense, is the audience. They are absolutely central to the work.' The work is in effect an open-ended piece of performance art, performed not by the artist but by the spectator. It is public art that captures the public imagination quite differently from the dismal street furniture whose only function seems to be to attract pigeon droppings and local outrage in equal measure. It blurs the boundary between art and entertainment, and as such it is undoubtedly the shape of things to come in the third millennium.

Much multimedia art, like Sermon's, offers elements of interactivity as a means of breaking down the barrier between art and everyday life, between artist and audience, which has been eroding steadily since the 1960s. Outside the sphere of art, interactivity has been the Holy Grail of the broadcasting and the games industries for some time. It is, of course, a defining feature of the Internet. As all of these technologies converge, art, entertainment and indeed much of our daily lives will doubtless continue to change in ways the 20th century would have found hard to imagine.

The meltdown of the barriers that traditionally separated the different art forms, and which separated different media, continues, fuelled by the converging technologies of digitality. Animation is at the heart of this process, because of its protean nature and its ability to absorb all other artistic forms and make them its own. Animation, or the construction of new realities frame by frame, is no longer the exclusive province of a few eccentric draughtsmen but the goal of professionals and enthusiasts across a wide range of disciplines and industries. As a result, animation has experienced the most rapid technical development, transforming both its production processes and bringing into question many of its underlying aesthetic values.

Technological progress has undoubtedly been of benefit to animators, bringing them tools to take much of the drudgery out of the production process, such as programs to colour cells and carry out the 'in-betweening' between key frames, and software to automate perfect lip-synch in any language. Motion-capture technology (magnetic or optical devices that can 'read' and record sensors attached to the moving human body) places the depiction of movement on a new and scientific basis – rendering, it is suggested, the intuitive command of movement which is the hallmark of the great masters of animation increasingly redundant. Such a suggestion is surely excessive. Mechanical devices need not replace the creative artist, although they can provide him with additional tools. And, interestingly, the arguments surrounding the use of such technology are not new. Similar controversy surrounded the use in the 1930s of the rotoscope, a device for transcribing movement filmed by a cine camera, refined (like so many other innovations) by Disney. And there are other echoes of the past: the current aesthetic trend toward computer-generated 3D photorealism, which marks a significant shift away from the graphical inventiveness and economy of 2D animation, could be seen as a resurfacing of the old conflict between realism and fantasy that Disney exemplified so clearly in the middle of the 20th century.

3

The meaning of the term 'animation' underwent a massive change at the turn of the millennium, as it began to be used commonly to denote incorporating moving-image sequences programmed in Flash for the Web, 3D graphics for broadcasting, and computer-generated synthetic imaging for interactive games. In the continuing dissolution of the barriers that once separated the different art forms and the different media, the traditional art of animation must inevitably undergo rapid transformation. The ability to construct reality frame by frame is a cornerstone of the forms of art and entertainment of the 21st-century digital crucible, whose ultimate shape can only be guessed at. But the novelty of developments will never render the traditional skills of animators redundant; on the contrary, they will be needed more urgently than ever.

Most of the developers and users of animation software have not had a training in basic traditional animation skills; they come from a wide range of backgrounds and are often motivated by a problem-solving approach whose goal seems often to be a digitally-constructed world predicated on naive notions of photo-realism. But this approach all too often fails in the basic goal of the traditional painter's art and that of cinema: that of making images *come alive* on a two-dimensional surface.

The clearest example of what *can* be achieved is provided by John Lasseter, whose short films, such as *Knick Knack* (US, 1989) (Figure 2), and later features *Toy Story* and *Toy Story 2* (US, 1995 and 1999) demonstrate the vital part that traditional character animation and storytelling skills continue to play in this brave new digital world. They also suggest that a more fruitful aesthetic for 3D animation may be hyperrealism rather than photorealism: the world of *Toy Story* is one in which colour, texture, movement and form are so perfectly observed and imaginatively recreated as to transform mere fact into poetry. Lasseter is both the guiding spirit behind the production company Pixar, which has led the way in computer animation, and a traditional animator of great skill, trained at the Disney Studios. His example demonstrates that the process of 'giving life', or *animating* in the strict sense of the term, is still as much a magical process as it was for George Méliès at the beginning of the 20th century. It is not likely that any amount of software development will change that.

The Revival of Animation

Thanks in part to the digital revolution, at the end of the 20th century animation emerged from its ghetto. Unlike the animators of the 1940s, buried away in Termite Terrace – the self-deprecating name the Warner Bros. animators gave to their cramped corner of the studio lot – today's animators are more likely to work in an environment devoted to digital imaging. In Angoulême, in France, for example, animators work in what is becoming a city of the digital image, surrounded by companies representing a vast range of technologies, from the most traditional, such as graphic novels and printing, to those of Internet and software developers.

So suddenly, at the beginning of the 21st century, animation came into fashion. Learned journals were founded devoted entirely to its study; international conferences are organised, drawing devotees from all corners of the globe to pick over the disinterred remains of half-forgotten animators. Academics and intellectuals, who for decades have considered animation beneath their notice, have begun to take it

Figure 2. The wit and timing of Chuck Jones inspires the master of computer animation, John Lasseter, and Knick Knack (US, 1989).

seriously. Animators who worked in virtual anonymity for the entirety of their careers within the Hollywood studio system have emerged as 'auteurs' like Hitchcock or Bergman; Tex Avery is compared to Bertold Brecht and the Fleischers to Dali and Buñuel.

Such reassessment was long overdue. But the reasons for the long-standing neglect of animation are not without interest. As evidence of animation's previous marginalisation, one need look no further than the British Film Institute's own book about the cinema, what it describes in its foreword as a 'history of debates in British film culture', *The Cinema Book* (ed. Pam Cook, 1985-1989). Animation does not even appear in its copious index. Walt Disney, who is surely one of the most significant figures in the cultural history of the 20th century and a film producer of some note – he did win more Oscars than any other producer/director of the century – receives just two brief mentions. One is for his early acquisition of Technicolor's three-colour process in the early 1930s, and the second is in connection with ex-Disney employee and live-action film director Frank Tashlin.

This neglect of Disney is not mere perversity on the part of the BFI; it reflects a long-standing blindness on the part of film theorists. Animation has simply not been a part of the main debate over the nature of cinema, which has raged throughout the century. As Gerald Mast has pointed out, in one of the few theoretical studies to give proper centrality to animation (Mast, 1977, 4), animation has simply not been part of the main debate over the nature of cinema, which has raged throughout the century: André Bazin and Siegfried Kracauer, for example, maintain that the essence of film lies in its relationship with reality – its function as a recording medium, its capacity to register the objective, visible world. In this conceptual scheme, animation clearly has no role; animators routinely construct alternative worlds, and whatever animation is, it is not an automatic registering of reality.

But as Mast goes on to show, Bazin and Kracauer are not alone. Film theorists Rudolf Arnheim, Stanley Cavell, Sergei Eisenstein, Christian Metz, Hugo Munsterberg, Erwin Panofsky, Gene Youngblood and others have failed to include animation as a form of cinema and, in order to define cinema, they have developed categories and criteria which are quite incompatible with animation.

There may be more than one explanation for this neglect. It may be that, for most of these theorists, as for Bazin and Kracauer, animation simply did not fit into their conception of cinema. It was an exception. But it might also be the case that animation was simply beyond the pale; film theorists have had a long struggle to show that cinema, which is indisputably a form of popular entertainment, was as worthy of consideration as literature, music and painting – a struggle to show that it is an art, in fact, as well as a business. Even as late as the 1960s, Film Studies in Britain was treated with deep suspicion by the academic establishment, still under the influence of F. R. Leavis, for whom films involve 'surrender, under conditions of hypnotic receptivity, to the cheapest emotional appeals, appeals the more insidious because they are associated with a compellingly vivid illusion of actual life' (FR Leavis, Storey, 1994). According to this view, cinema was 'largely masturbatory' in its appeal, 'cheapening, debasing, distorting' (Q. D. Leavis, 1932:,165). But such sweeping dismissal of what we have come to describe as film culture (to the Leavises, a contradiction in terms) was not characteristic of the political right alone; the left-wing intellectuals of the Frankfurt School, in particular Max Horkeimer and Theodor Adorno, were equally contemptuous: 'film, radio and magazines make up a system which is uniform as a whole and in every part... all mass culture is identical' (Adorno and Horkeimer, 1972, 122-3). However, whereas the Leavises feared that film, and popular culture in general, represented a threat to the cultural authority of 'high art', the Frankfurt School argued that they produced the opposite effect: they maintain social authority by keeping the masses entertained, distracting them from the realities of the class struggle.

Film theorists naturally aspired to academic respectability, and so wished to rescue film from this blanket dismissal as part of a hopelessly debased and corrupted mass culture. And if film as a whole was academically suspect, then animation – or rather, the 'cartoon' – was even more tainted, having been connected since the earliest days of 'trick-film' with commerce and entertainment.

Some gifted animators have fought to raise the status of their art, such as Windsor McCay in the second decade of the 20th century, and Walt Disney in the third. But, paradoxically, Disney was to achieve such an unprecedented level of popular and commercial success with his short films in the 1930s, and his subsequent features, that he forged in the popular and academic minds alike an indissoluble link between animation and kitsch, from which it has never quite recovered. Disney would be mortified to learn that the term 'Mickey Mouse' has become a synonym for cheap, shoddy, mass-produced items. And Disney would not be altogether wrong, since the Mickey Mouse of the 1930s was the fruit of a decade of the most intense technical and artistic development the animation industry has ever seen, at least until the computer-related developments of the 1980s. So Disney, despite his efforts to make animation respectable, must remain in part responsible for the academic neglect from which animation continued to suffer up until the 1980s. Too readily identified as a popular, debased form of commercial entertainment – the fodder of children's television – animation only began to receive the attention it deserves with the breakdown of academic hierarchies separating 'high' and 'low' arts, which coincided with post-structuralist theories of culture.

Within a post-modernist framework, animation was no longer marginalised or excluded from the canons of cinema; on the contrary, it became central to it. Thanks largely to the digital revolution, animation could now be seen to be right at the centre, not just of film practice but of the development of the moving-image language on which depend the multimedia arts and communications industries.

2. A Lexicon of Babel: the Multiple Languages of Animation

Animation does not merely exploit all the other arts; by appropriating their methodologies and media, it interrogates their various languages and, in the most successful works of animation, offers a critique of them as representations of the world. Live-action cinema is itself the most hybrid of art forms, and a melting pot for all the other arts, which it, too, has plundered ruthlessly for its material. Animation goes one better: it encompasses – and illuminates – not only all the other arts but live-action cinema itself.

Animation and Live Action

Since the earliest days of animation, animators have exploited live-action film in order to question notions of cinematic truth and its relation to reality, challenging live-action cinema's claims to authenticity with the opposing claims (to the psychological or otherwise deeper truth) of animation. *Gertie the Dinosaur* (Windsor McCay, US, 1914) was a cartoon character who amazed vaudeville audiences early in the 20th century by apparently interacting with her 'trainer', McCay, in real time, responding to his commands and even carrying him off the stage on her back. In the Fleischer Brothers' series *Out of the Inkwell,* which ran throughout the 1920s, Max the artist finds in each film a different way of introducing the drawn figure of Koko the Clown into live-action film of himself, the artist, in the studio. Sometimes Koko materializes out of an inkblot, or out of Max's pen, and at the end of each film he disappears, again for a wide variety of reasons, back into the inkwell, sometimes taking refuge or falling in by accident. In *Big Chief Koko* (Fleischer, US, 1925), Koko is still wriggling on the drawing board when Max receives a visitor to the studio (in live action, of course) – an Indian trying to sell him some drawings. Koko is furious, seeing the characters in the Indian's drawings as competition to his own star status in Max's studio, and the rest of the film is devoted to his frantic efforts to see off the intruders. Walt Disney took Fleischer's idea and reversed it, putting a real girl into a cartoon world in his series of short films, *Alice's Wonderland* (Walt Disney, US, 1924).

Combining live action with cartoon characters, though too expensive to be a frequent resource, was nevertheless a useful means of collapsing the distinction between reality and fantasy, and was inventively employed in *Anchors Aweigh* (George Sidney, US, 1945), where Gene Kelly dances with the animated mouse, Jerry; and in Disney's *Mary Poppins* (Robert Stevenson, US, 1964), where, among a wide range of fantastic adventures, Dick Van Dyke accompanies the family of children to a world inhabited by animated penguins, who serve them tea. The strategy reached altogether new levels, both in technological sophistication and in conceptual self-reflexivity, in *Who Framed Roger Rabbit?* (Robert Zemeckis, US, 1988) where the segregation of experience into 'fantasy' and 'reality' is undermined by the central plot premise: that cartoon characters 'really' do exist and work alongside 'real' human beings, though segregated into a ghetto known as Toontown and disdained as 'Toons' by human beings. The seamless marrying of animation with live-action performances, so impressive in this film and achieved only with the greatest technical difficulty, became altogether more achievable in the 1990s, with developments in computer imaging. The paradoxical result, however, may be that the animation per *se* became in danger of disappearing, swallowed up in the all-too-plausible surfaces of computer-generated worlds indistinguishable from the 'real'. Gertie the dinosaur's charm lay in the fact that she declared herself both a drawing *and* a real, moving, responsive creature. The function of the dinosaurs of *Jurassic Park* (Steven Spielberg, US, 1993) is not to raise questions about their reality or our reality, but primarily to terrify, and to do so they must appear not as constructs of the human imagination but as real.

Animation and Painting

The relationship between conventional cel animation and painting and drawing is evident. The very word 'cartoon' can apply to a sketch or drawing for a painting (such as Leonardo da Vinci's 'cartoon' in the National Gallery) and to a humorous drawing in a newspaper, as well as to an animated film. Many animators have begun as newspaper cartoonists, from McCay, Disney, Fleischer, Terry and many other early producers, down to Dragc, Miyazaki and Groening. Many others have begun as artists trying to extend their skills from two or three dimensions into four, adding to the perceived dimension of space the extra narrative dimension of time.

Adapting the visual language of art into the medium of animated film raises many interesting problems. Here, as a demonstration of the critical scrutiny that animation can focus on the art of painting, it is useful to consider *Breakfast on the Grass* (Pritt Pjarn, USSR, 1988). This takes as its subject the gulf between art and modern life; the gulf between the perfect, ideal world of an Impressionist painting and the squalor of a modern, industrialized society; and the gap between Western bourgeois values, exemplified by art, and the Communist way of life. Its title and four main characters derive from one of the icons of French 19th-century painting, Manet's *Déjeuner sur l'Herbe*, which caused a scandal when exhibited at the Salon des Réfusés in Paris in 1863. The picture shows two male students, clothed, sitting in a woodland glade outside Paris with two women, one in the background bathing in a pool, the other sitting naked, her head turned to interrogate the spectator.

The Estonian animator imagines these four characters living in the Soviet society of the 1980s and creates a narrative for each one, revealing the privations and fear that dominate society and culminating in the four characters entering a park, adopting the poses of Manet's painting for a brief, ironic meal together. The sequence devoted to Berta, the nude in the foreground of Manet's painting, is particularly revealing. After having a baby, Berta suffers a crisis of identity; she contemplates her image, in the same pose as in Manet's painting, until suddenly she loses her facial features. She attempts to make up a face – in both senses – then, in anger, destroys all the images of women, derived from Western art, which adorn her walls. These *images* of women, Pjarn seems to be saying, no longer accord with reality as it is *experienced* by women. She then sits in despair at a table while the years pass, and the baby pulls at the tablecloth. Through the window, we see the leaves fall from the tree, which is then covered by snow, which melts, replaced by new spring leaves, which fall and are covered by snow... Four seasons pass and the tree is cut down, while simultaneously the child pulls slowly at the tablecloth, until everything crashes to the floor and the baby has become a child of five. This is a remarkable example of the capacity of animation to represent, and distil, temporal processes – here, two different time scales simultaneously. Four years pass while the child pulls at the tablecloth. It would be difficult to imagine a more telling expression of the experience, common to all parents, perhaps, of time's disappearing, swallowed up by the role of parenting. 'How time flies!' laments Berta, waking from her stupor as the breakfast things crash to the floor.

Breakfast on the Grass is a film of enormous visual energy and assurance, combined with considerable narrative complexity, and it derives much of its critical language from its source in Manet's painting. It is unusual in that it explicitly evolves its narrative from a famous painting; although it does not attempt to model its *design* on Manet's work. Much animation, both mainstream and experimental, does however attempt to adopt particular styles from historical sources. The Disney studio has often modelled the design of its features on antique styles, from medieval manuscripts in *Sleeping Beauty* (Clyde Geronimi, US, 1959) to oriental art in *Mulan* (Tony Bancroft and Barry Cook, US, 1998).

Other styles of art offer alternatives to Disney's realism. Abstract Expressionism privileged mark-making of a direct, gestural kind, and it is this spontaneity of expression which often informs 'direct' animation, usually consisting of painting on to clear film or scraping into black leader. Norman McLaren is one of the supreme exponents of this style of animation, and films such as *Fiddle de Dee* (Canada, 1947) and *Boogie Doodle* (Canada, 1940) brought all the spontaneity of soundtracks featuring folk violin and piano boogie respectively to a dance of abstract marks.

Dance and Musical Forms in Animation

Dance is as important an element in expressionist films as is the purely visual. Len Lye, a colleague of McLaren's at the British GPO film unit in the 1930s, before McLaren's move to the Canadian Film Board, believed that the art of so-called primitive cultures, with which they decorated their pottery and buildings, showed a direct expression of primal feeling, and he used batique and stencil as methods of marking film, achieving astonishing density of visual rhythm and texture in films like *Colour Box* (GB, 1932) (Figure 3) and *Trade Tattoo* (GB, 1937).

Like McLaren, Lye uses rhythmical dance music for his soundtracks, emphasising that abstract animation draws as heavily on dance for its inspiration as it does on purely visual arts. McLaren himself believed that every animated film, whether it involved moving people or objects or drawings, was itself a kind of dance.

In her own dance-based animations, Erica Russell, herself inspired by Len Lye, makes this connection explicit. Her *Feet of Song* (GB, 1989) (Figure 4) manipulates semi-abstract forms, derived from the body of a dancer, in complex and compelling rhythmic patterns, to a soundtrack of African-derived dance music.

Russell's work, while powerfully demonstrating the appeal of dance as a model for animation, perhaps also indicates its limitations. Attempting to extend her expressive range in the longer and more ambitious *Triangle* (GB, 1994), with its implied narrative interaction between three dancers, the film seems to exceed what may perhaps be a natural limit in terms of duration. It is perhaps no accident that few popular songs and

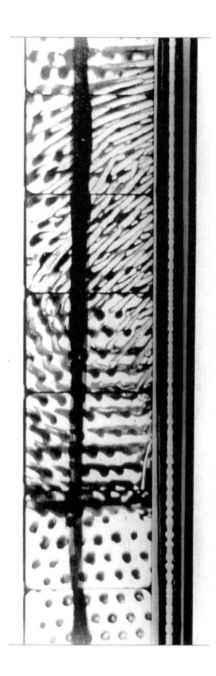

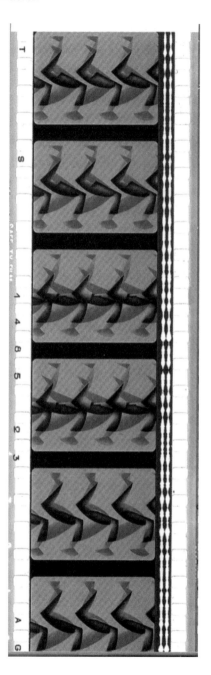

Figure 3. Stencil and batik applied directly to the filmstrip were techniques used by Len Lye in Colour Box (GB, 1932).

Figure 4 Semi-abstract shapes derived from the dancing figure animate Erica Russell's Feet of Song (GB, 1989).

pieces of dance music exceed four minutes in length, and that animated films based on them tend to be similarly concise.

Music and dance do offer larger structures as models for animation, but successful use of these seems rare; Disney's *Fantasia* (US, 1940) offers some supreme examples, as does Bruno Bozzetti's parody of it, *Allegro Non Troppo* (Italy, 1976). In Bozzetti's sequence based on Sibelius' *Sad Waltz*, the musical structure rests on a sombre main theme in the minor key, interspersed with shorter episodes in the major. The minor episodes accompany images of an abandoned cat haunting a derelict house, while in the major episodes the cat dreams of past glories, as its owners reappear, with all the warmth and comfort of human companionship. The film works because a narrative structure has been found which precisely coincides with the musical structure.

Animation and Collage

Cut-out animation employs strategies similar to collage, a medium with strong surrealist connections. The surrealists treasured the juxtaposition of unrelated objects; nothing was more beautiful for André Breton, poet and leader of the movement, than the accidental encounter of an umbrella and a sewing machine on an operating-theatre table. Modern television would have sent them into ecstasies, demonstrating how far surrealist discontinuities have become part of contemporary experience. Collage, which assembles disparate images from various sources, is the surrealist technique *par excellence*, as is evident in the work of Terry Gilliam for the groundbreaking television comedy *Monty Python's Flying Circus* (BBC TV, GB, 1969-1974) (Figure 5a).

Gilliam also draws heavily on the work of Polish animators Jan Lenica and Walerian Borowcyck, from the 1950s and 1960s, though bringing an element of low comedy to their visually nuanced and introspective East European sensibilities. In *Labyrinth* (Poland, 1963), Lenica exploits the strangeness of 19th-century engravings to tell the tale of a man destroyed by monstrous creatures in a deserted city (Figure 5b).

Even more subtly surreal and visually exquisite is the work of French animator Jean-François Laguionie, who uses cut-out with extraordinary skill. His *Crossing the Atlantic in a Rowing Boat* (France, 1978) tells the strange story of a couple who set off securely roped together to cross the ocean in 1908; 40 years later, having passed the sinking Titanic and the haunted hulk of the Marie Celeste, they are showing signs of advanced age but are still at sea. Beautifully designed, in a style reminiscent of 19th-century naive painter Henri Rousseau (a favourite of the surrealists, incidentally), it is not so much a film about a maritime exploit as an allegory of marriage.

Animation and Theatre

Every animator who designs and animates a recognisable human or animal character, whether in two or three dimensions, must of necessity develop the skills of an actor in order to use the body of the character, its movements, voice and its relationship to the surrounding environment, to make clear its character and motivation, and through these engage the audience with the narrative. Of course, the animation medium offers possibilities that go far beyond what any human actor could achieve: the bodies of Wolfie, Bugs Bunny, Tom and Jerry or any other 'stretch 'n' squeeze' characters in the

Figure 5a. Surrealist collage inspired Terry Gilliam's cut-out animations for Monty Python's Flying Circus (GB, 1969-74)

films of Warner Bros. and MGM are infinitely plastic and utterly indestructible, which is the source of much of the wry humour in *Who Framed Roger Rabbit?* (Robert Zemeckis, US, 1988). Nevertheless, all animation, to a greater or lesser extent, whatever the precise medium, involves notions of expressive movement and performance.

Puppetry is one of the traditional arts which has directly inspired animation, especially in Eastern Europe with the work of George Pal and Jiri Trnka, and in Japan, where Kihachiro Kawamoto draws on Noh theatrical traditions in his use of masks.

Figure 5b. 19ᵗʰ-century engravings help to create the urban nightmare of Jan Lenica's Labyrinth (Poland, 1963).

Lotte Reiniger's 1920s paper cut-out animation, most notably her animated feature *The Adventures of Prince Achmed* (Germany, 1923-26), was inspired by Javanese shadow puppets (Figure 6).

The recent work of British animator Barry Purves draws on many of these sources, especially in his *Screen Play* (GB, 1992), a dazzling play on the nature of theatrical and cinematic illusion. The title makes this explicit: *Screen Play*. This is a play (in both senses) on the differences and the common ground between cinema and theatre.

For *Screen Play*, Purves chose an ancient story, which also inspired the willow pattern of oriental porcelain, popular in Europe since the 18th century. Naioki is an aristocratic lady, betrothed to a samurai against her will, who falls in love with Takoko, her father's gardener. He is murdered by the samurai and Naioki commits suicide. In death, their bodies are transformed into birds, whose shapes form the willow pattern of so much oriental porcelain.

The story is told using state-of-the-art puppets on a revolving stage. And stage is the correct term, at least in the first part of the film, as the frame is that of the theatre's proscenium – the fixed camera position that of the audience in a theatre – and the visual style of the action utterly theatrical in the Japanese tradition, using masks and extreme stylisation. But near the end of the tale, shockingly the conventions change from those of the theatre to those of cinema. The camera moves to participate in the action, now much more realistic; we are suddenly plunged into a world of 'real' blood rather than the red paper streamers that had represented blood earlier in the film. But this cinematic realism, so forceful and convincing, is itself still only a fabrication, an illusion, as the final seconds of the film demonstrate, pulling back to show the camera, then the framing device of the animator's log book, with the hand of the animator

[Figure 6. Javanese shadow puppets inspired the exquisite paper cut-outs of the first ever animation feature film, The Adventures of Prince Achmed (Lotte Reiniger, Germany, 1923-26].

himself ticking off the sheet recording the photographing of the final frame of the film. Both the stage and the screen are the arena of performance, Purves seems to be saying; theatre and cinema are both forms of illusion.

Not only does three-dimensional animation borrow from puppetry; it also draws its vocabulary from the arts of model-making and sculpture, often exploiting the expressive nature of their materials in startling new contexts. There is literally no limit to the materials that may be used – plasticine or clay is relatively neutral, but other materials range from glass, paper, card and textiles to metal, and these can be powerfully expressive. In her film dealing with child abuse, *Daddy's Little Bit of Dresden China* (GB, 1988) (Figure 7), Karen Watson constructed the abusing father out of a variety of materials, including razor blades for lips and glass for the head. The mother was constructed out of dried flowers with a wooden spoon for an arm,

Figure 7. Dried flowers and razor blades become gender signifiers in Karen Watson's film about child abuse: Daddy's Little Bit of Dresden China (GB, 1988).

the abused daughter from feathers and bandages, with a china vase for a head. The materials are used here not solely for their visual qualities but also for their symbolic associations – a strategy familiar from the work of pioneering puppet animator George Pal, who, in his *Tulips Shall Grow* (GB, 1942), opposed a little girl puppet with marching Nazis represented as bombs with screws for necks. Again, the origins of this technique may lie further back, in the ferocious collages of John Heartfield, who opposed the rise of Hitler with his communist magazine covers of the 1930s.

Sometimes the materials chosen for 3D animation affect the images in quite unexpected ways. Czech animator Jiri Barta, for his feature *Pied Piper* (Czechoslovakia/West Germany, 1985) (Figure 8), carved 16 puppets and 170 sets in walnut, giving his images the hard-edged, grotesque quality of gothic woodcuts. The visual/tactile qualities of the materials in this film, from the curved metal hands and the hard, polished wooden faces of the corrupt burghers of Hamlyn, to the soiled and squalid pelts of the animated rats, are powerfully expressive.

Literary Forms in Animation

A wide variety of literary forms have inspired animated films, ranging from poetry and fairy tales to short stories and novels. Halas and Batchelor's *Animal Farm* (GB, 1954), based on the novel of the same name by George Orwell, and the Fleischers' *Gulliver's Travels* (US, 1939), based on the novel of the same name by Jonathan Swift, are both realistic depictions of their sources and heavily influenced by the Disney model. More innovative is Caroline Leaf's short film *The Street* (Canada, 1976), based on Mordecai Richler's novel of the same name about growing up in a Jewish family, which shows how adept the medium of animation is (here finger-painting in oil

Figure 8. Carved walnut figures and sets, reminiscent of Gothic woodcuts, in Jiri Barta's Pied Piper (Czechoslovakia, 1985).

directly on to the glass stage of the animation-camera) at creating fluid transitions between frames, and creating a moving viewpoint travelling through constantly evolving space.

Literary language creates a psychological space in the reader's mind, composed of images, memories, sounds and voices, all impregnated with emotion conveyed by the narrator's voice. This verbal space is quite different from physical space, which is usually represented, in Disney, for example, by means of classical perspective.

Caroline Leaf's films (most notably *The Metamorphosis of Mr. Samsa* (Canada, 1977) (Figure 9), her treatment of Kafka's story of a man's transformation into a giant insect, demonstrate how well animation can model the stuff of which that psychological space is composed. Her viewpoint is as mobile and responsive to every nuance as is the constantly evolving present in a 'stream of consciousness' novel.

Given this 'poetic' quality of animation, it is perhaps surprising that so few animated films use poetry, or poetic forms of speech, in their soundtracks. Or perhaps not: as Hitchcock is famously said to have remarked, if the image and the soundtrack are doing the same thing, then one of them is redundant. What at first sight looks like an interesting exception is the collaboration between English animator David Anderson

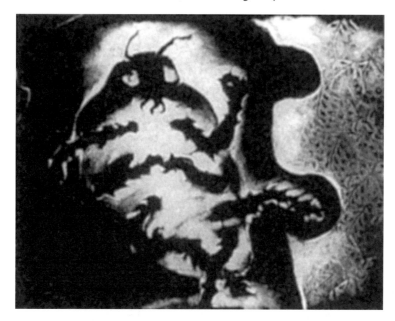

Figure 9. Drawing in sand, frame by frame, is the remarkable technique used by Caroline Leaf in The Metamorphosis of Mr. Samsa (Canada, 1977).

and the American writer Russell Hoban. Animation, according to Hoban, lends itself to interesting word/picture combinations. 'With animation, you can write with complete freedom, as if you're writing a poem, a fragment, a short burst of ideas' (Russell Hoban, *Fourmations: Deadtime Stories for Big Folk*, Channel 4 Television, 1994). This obviously presents something of a challenge both to the viewer and to the animator, who has to construct a visual narrative out of verbal fragments, often of a highly ambiguous nature.

Hoban's later work is particularly challenging as, in novels like *Riddley Walker* (GB, 1980), set in a post-nuclear holocaust society, he writes in a language which has itself mutated, or rather degenerated, into a poetic but ungrammatical stream of consciousness.

In *Door* (GB, 1991), Anderson rises to the challenge, providing the text with a visual accompaniment which does not illustrate it but complements it with a visual poetry all of its own. As in *Riddley Walker*, the text deals with the idea of (nuclear?) apocalypse. The door of the title seems to be the door through which we would have to go to turn the nuclear key, before obliterating the world. That, as Anderson explains, is his reading of Hoban's script; but in his imagery, the animator has tried to bring a more personal element into the story, locating it as much on the level of human relations as on cosmic disaster. So here we have a curious example of two collaborators, writer and animator, each allowing free rein to their imaginations without altogether coinciding in their interpretation of the material.

The Animated Fairy Tale

The fairy tale has come to occupy a privileged place in the output of the Disney Studios but other, less realistic, versions of the genre suggest that animation is particularly suited to the expression of the darker, more irrational aspects of these tales. One factor they both have in common, according to Marina Warner, is metamorphosis

> Shape-shifting is one of the fairy tale's dominant and characteristic wonders: hands are cut off, found and reattached, babies' throats are slit, but they are later restored to life... the slattern in the filthy donkeyskin turns into a golden-haired princess. More so than the presence of fairies (or)...the happy ending...metamorphosis defines the fairy tale. (Warner, 1994, xv):

It is also a key feature in the animated fairy tales of the Fleischer Brothers and Tex Avery, most notably their treatments of the story of Little Red Riding Hood. Fleischer's *Dizzy Red Riding Hood* (US, 1931), in which the cartoon character Betty Boop takes the part of the heroine, makes clear in its voice-over prologue, apparently addressed to children, that we are in a world where innocence may mask adult desires:

- 'Listen my children and you shall hear
- An exciting story of a little dear.
- There's lots of rumours of Riding Hood -
- Some are bad and some are good.
- Why do they pick on the poor little kid?
- Some say she didn't, and some say she did;
- You've surely heard the story before,
- When she tried to keep the wolf from the door.
- How really true can a story be?
- Well watch, my dears, and you'll hear and see.'

The film begins with Betty Boop going to the larder, whose handle is oddly flaccid; it's a sausage, the first of a string of them, somehow stuck in the keyhole. Betty pulls them through, then finds a fish, which advises her of its suitability as a present for grandma. Bimbo, a humanised dog of nondescript appearance, is enamoured of Betty and asks to accompany her; and although told that 'Grandma wouldn't like it', does so – after making short work of the sausages.

Betty enters the wood, unperturbed by the trees that lean over to warn her that there's a wolf in the forest. Soon the wolf accosts her, performing circus tricks, then suggesting she take some flowers to Granny and helping her plant flower seeds by pulling a magic worm (labelled 'hole digger') from his basket, which dives into the soil, emerging, diving, re-emerging and making a series of neat holes into which Betty drops the wolf's seeds while he stands behind her, laughing sinisterly. He makes his intention clear by sharpening a knife against a fork, testing its readiness by a nifty piece of self-decapitation, instantly mended, singing (somewhat illogically), 'Tell her not to wait for you, for you're not coming home!' In the nick of time, Bimbo arrives, thrashes the wolf (to the instant applause of the flowers emerging in chorus from their holes) and disappears with him into a nearby tree, from which the wolf's skeleton shortly makes its escape, followed by Bimbo with a rolled-up carpet under his arm. This is unrolled to disclose the wolf's skin and head, which Bimbo dons as a disguise, with the explanation that 'she loves wolves'. Bimbo now helps Betty pick the flowers, movements – including those of the flowers (which grow lips to kiss Betty) – animated to the song on the soundtrack, in walking tempo.

The song continues throughout the following sequence: Betty strides off, the viewpoint moving closer so that her legs and skimpy skirt fill the frame, disclosing her garter slipping to the ground, then skipping along to keep up with her. She leans down to replace it (her skirt clinging miraculously to preserve modesty) and as she does so, the other garter falls – a sequence repeated several times – while Bimbo looks on, hiding behind a wooden pole supporting a washing line, and quivering with lust so apparent that the pole produces an indignant face, then, with a wink at the audience, pulls down a lacy item from the clothes line to cover Bimbo's eyes. Bimbo is then hoisted up on to the washing line, which acts like a pulley, and is sent by the pole toward the upstairs window of Grandma's house (to which we now discover the washing line is attached), the window turning into a face to inform us that Grandma has gone to the firemen's ball, then morphing back into a window in time to open and admit Bimbo.

When Betty arrives at Grandma's bed, Bimbo (still disguised as the wolf) seizes her, one paw around each breast, and pulls her to him, the wolf disguise falling away and the pupils of his eyes emitting heart shapes. In the final shot, Bimbo and Betty are in a hammock in the moonlight, swung backwards and forwards by the trees to which the hammock is attached, their rhythm echoed by other trees in the forest, which sway in time to the music.

As the prologue makes clear, Betty is a girl with a reputation ('Some say she didn't, and some say she did') who (and this during the time of the US Depression of the 1930s) has to cut corners 'to keep the wolf from the door'. Betty's world, and that of the fairy tale in general before its Disneyfication, is alive with carnal appetites, hunger and desire, here personified by the ravenous wolf and the love-struck Bimbo. But Bimbo's lascivious inclinations, and by implication our own, have to be dissembled; too frank an enjoyment of Betty's charms is to be discouraged (the pole covers Bimbo's eyes) while simultaneously indulged (the pole gives us, equally voyeuristically engaged with Betty, a knowing wink.)

How far the Fleischers' business with limp sausages and worms digging holes for seeds derives from a knowingness or naivety toward their (to us) thinly disguised sexual symbolism is very much an open question. Awareness of Freud, or indeed of the European surrealism he partly inspired, is not appreciable in the New York animation industry before the influx of European refugees following the rise of Hitler. The Fleischers were, of course, playing upon Betty Boop's innocent(?) sexuality, which was her main, indeed her only, characteristic, ever since the early film in which her boss tries, and fails, to take away her – 'Boop-oop-a-doop'. Until the much stricter censorship restrictions imposed on film producers by a new Production Code in 1934, when the Motion Pictures Producers and Distributors of America bowed to pressure from the Legion of Decency, and Mae West and Betty Boop alike were both obliged to clean up their acts, it is sexuality which impregnates the whole physical universe of her films, stirring into lascivious life anything from trees and flowers to prehistoric fossils; and it is animation's capacity for metamorphosis, so intrinsic to the medium, that makes it such a perfect vehicle for the expression of this sexuality.

The Red Riding Hood story held great appeal for Tex Avery, for very similar reasons. Avery did much to keep alive the anarchic and erotic content of the short cartoon in the 1940s and 1950s. Even more than Fleischer, Avery allowed his characters free rein to express their primal desires and irrational urges, showing not just the external effect but something of how it feels to experience ungovernable lust or surprise, as in his celebrated double-takes, where characters sprout multiple heads like hydras in surprise, their eyes leap from their sockets or their jaws clang like anvils to the floor. In his treatment of Red Riding Hood, in his films *Red Hot Riding Hood* (US, 1943) or *Little Rural Riding Hood* (US, 1949), the character ('Red') becomes a sophisticated nightclub singer, fully able to exploit her sexuality, and the wolf's carnal appetites are firmly relocated to the domain of sexual desire. Avery's depictions of the wolf's sexual response to Red's performance were extreme: the character eats his hands, pounds himself on the head with a sledgehammer and lights his nose with a cigarette. Sometimes the wolf's reactions were so explicit as to get into trouble with the censor – such as when he sprang, stiff as a board, into mid-air – but it was assuredly this direct appeal to (and parody of) masculine arousal that helped these films achieve a popularity with American GIs serving abroad, and with the public at home, which MGM achieved with no other films.

The films of Avery and the Fleischers demonstrate that the animation medium is the supreme vehicle for more or less coded expressions of the unconscious fantasy and erotic desire which lie within the fairy-tale form. Viewed through the lens of feminism, however, the patriarchal assumptions of the form acquire a distinctly ironic gloss, which was amply exploited by late 20th–century female animators.

In Karen Watson's film, *Daddy's Little Bit of Dresden China,* discussed above, the mother, father and daughter relationship is presented in a prologue as the story of the King, Queen and Snow White. But the voice-over concludes, 'Unfortunately for Snow White, no one ever questioned the King's love for her. The mother was blamed, the father forgiven, and the daughter silenced.' The film later uses the real testimony of victims of child abuse, as well as the voices of men, demonstrating their ignorance of the issue and lack of self-awareness, edited to images of collaged photographs, presenting women in their mass-media role as sexual objects and commodities for male consumption.

A similar use of fairy-story conventions occurs in *The Decision* (GB, 1981) (Figure 10) by Vera Neubauer, where it is also intercut with other styles of animation – notably, live action. The brutal realism of live action here is apparent at the beginning of the film with the opening caption: 'THIS IS WHERE EVERYTHING BEGINS', followed by a shot of female baby genitalia, 'AND' (followed by a shot of same smeared with excrement) 'ENDS'. In this remarkable work, the childhood dreams of a princess in a fairy tale (expressed in childlike drawings) collide with the ugliness of the real world (in live action). The childlike drawing style seems to be taking animation back to its

The animation industry of 1920s New York, where Disney began, was far from being a repository of 'family values'. It echoed the slapstick of many live-action shorts, but added to it a subversive element of sex, violence and outrageous fantasy. Cartoons routinely outraged the laws of physics along with those of society and good taste.

Not surprisingly, cartoons were not highly regarded. Paul Terry, producer of Terrytoons, tells of trying to sell his first cartoon film to eminent producer Lewis J. Selznick, who offered him one dollar per foot of cartoon film. Terry protested that it had cost him more than that to make. Selznick replied that he could pay him more for the film stock if he hadn't 'gone and put them damn drawings on it'. Terry said later he never knew if Selznick was joking or not (Maltin 1980, 126). Selznick's attitude was typical: cartoons were not much respected by the viewing public, nor by cinema managers, who used them as a device to empty cinemas before the next showing of the main feature, nor by the critics or the trade press and not even by the producers and animators who made them. In the words of perhaps the first great American animator, Windsor McCay, speaking at a dinner in his honour given by the industry at the end of 1920s: 'Animation should be an art, but what you fellas have done with it is make it into a trade. Bad Luck' (Maltin, 1980, 126).

McCay had been an inspiration for early animators; he liked to call himself the 'inventor' of animated cartoons. This was an exaggeration: Emile Cohl (1857-1938) in France and J. Stuart Blackton (1868-1941) in the US had made films from genuine animated drawings, though neither had the enormous popular success that McCay enjoyed.

McCay began as a newspaper cartoonist, like many producers of animated cartoons, including his contemporaries Disney, Fleischer, Terry and many others, down to Dragc, Miyazaki and Groening. But McCay was an artist of real distinction as well as a gifted storyteller. His newspaper comic strip *Little Nemo in Slumberland* is generally considered the high point of pre-war comic-strip art. He used his popular character, Little Nemo, for his first foray into animation, laboriously producing 4,000 drawings over four years, then colouring by hand the 35mm footage, finishing the film in 1911. But his most celebrated cartoon character was Gertie (*Gertie the Dinosaur*, US, 1914) (Figure 11).

McCay initially drew film of Gertie not to be shown in cinemas but as part of a vaudeville stage act, in which he appeared on stage as Gertie's trainer and talked to her.

Gertie apparently obeys his commands, reacts to his remarks and even bursts into tears when scolded, then catches a pumpkin when it is thrown at her. For the climax, McCay appeared to walk right on to the screen and was apparently carried away on Gertie's back.

McCay was here opening a debate about reality and cinematic illusion which runs throughout the century, and which took on new relevance with the development of digital animation, and its capacity seamlessly and invisibly to merge with live-action film. It is possible to read McCay's contribution to this debate as a plea in favour of fantasy, undermining the claims to realism of the photographic image:

Figure 11. The first of many cartoon animals to captive the public: Windsor McCay's Gertie the Dinosaur (US, 1914).

> It is as if the early animators wanted to constantly expose the limitations of representing 'reality' on film and insist upon the domain of 'fantasy' as: first, the most appropriate mode of expression for the cinematic form and, most specifically, the animated form; second, as the most versatile model by which to create amusement and illusion; and third, as the most expressive vocabulary by which to interrogate the complexities of the human condition. (Wells, 1998, 16)

This perhaps underestimates the drive toward realism in McCay; his aim was, after all, to astonish audiences with the reality of Gertie, to convince the spectator that her size, her apparent weight and her movements were those of a real creature. His vaudeville interactions with her were to enhance this reality, to show that he and she inhabited the same narrative space. He played on this in the advertisements for his act: 'Windsor McCay and his wonderful trained dinosaurus GERTIE: She eats, drinks and breathes.

She laughs and cries. Dances the tango. Answers questions and obeys every command. Yet she lived millions of years before man inhabited the earth and has never been seen since!'

McCay's vaudeville act is not recorded but what does survive is the one-reel film that he distributed in 1914. For this, 10,000 drawings had been made on paper, with the entire frame, Gertie and background, redrawn for each frame of film. McCay himself drew Gertie, while his assistant drew the landscape. The film begins with the cartoonist accepting a bet with friends that he can make a dinosaur come to life. In live action, we see the drawings being made, piled into towering stacks, with burlesque scenes such as McCay's assistant struggling with them and dropping them. Then, at a dinner party with the friends, we see the animation of Gertie, intercut with title cards giving McCay's stage dialogue with her.

McCay's achievement is considerable. He created convincing 3D movement, in perspective, and above all he succeeded in giving Gertie personality. It is hardly surprising that for years *Gertie the Dinosaur* was named in film histories as the first animated cartoon.

Following McCay the animation industry developed rapidly, based largely in New York in the form of small factories which produced what were essentially animated versions of newspaper comic strips. These were shown in cinemas, between screenings of the main feature. Characters and backgrounds were rendered in simple black lines inked on to white paper. Movement was spare, dialogue was written in comic-strip balloons, and cinematic innovations were few.

By the 1920s a number of studios were established, including the Fleischer brothers', featuring Koko the Clown in the *Out of the Inkwell* series, John R. Bray producing *Krazy Kat*, Paul Terry's *Aesop's Fables*, and Otto Messmer's *Felix the Cat*.

Terry's output is of interest because it had an influence on Disney, who said that even as late as 1930, his ambition was to make cartoons as good as Terry's *Aesop's Fables*. This is a remarkable admission, because in looking at Terry's work today, one can readily understand the low status of the cartoon. The films suffered from stereotypical animal characters, which all tend to look alike, whether cats, bears or mice; graphically stylised, simplistic drawing and limited movement, often dismissed as 'rubber hose' animation; and poor or non-existent plot-lines that are basically successions of ill-timed gags.

Terry's was essentially a factory product. His small studio of four or five animators produced one film per week for more than eight years – a total of 400 films. To make a six-minute film, each animator had to produce 500 feet of film in four weeks. This offers a revealing comparison with Disney, whose animators in the 1930s were required to produce just five feet of good quality character animation per week. Terry's product makes abundantly clear how much of Windsor McCay's achievement had been forgotten and what remained to be reinvented by Disney.

During Disney's early career, the business environment was viciously competitive. His first company quickly went bankrupt. His second was achieving some success with a character called Oswald the Lucky Rabbit, drawn by Ubbe Iwerks, when his distributor, Charles Mintz, stole the character from Disney, along with virtually all his animators. But Iwerks came up with a new character, Mortimer Mouse, soon rechristened Mickey. The first two Mickey Mouse films found difficulty in getting a distributor. But when *The Jazz Singer* (Alan Crosland, US, 1927) came out, Disney was quick to see the potential of the new medium and fitted up Mickey's third film, *Steamboat Willy* (Walt Disney, Ubbe Iwerks, US, 1928), with a rhythmical music-and-effects track that achieved extraordinary impact throughout the entire film industry, and gave Disney's rhythmic combination of sound effects and music the name 'mickey mousing'.

Not even Disney himself could have suspected, in 1928, that The Mouse would subsequently become one of the most significant and ubiquitous icons of the 20th century. At the time, Mickey was just one among a host of animal stars, by the turn of the 20th century largely forgotten. Like Messmer's Felix the Cat, Mickey borrowed many of the characteristics of the live-action star, Charlie Chaplin; Disney described Mickey as 'a little fella trying to do his best'. He also had a lot of Disney himself in him – including Disney's own voice. Disney always knew what his character would do in any given situation – 'Mickey would never do that', he would say – and he never let gags take precedence over character.

The Mickey Mouse films were Disney's first great public and critical success, to the extent that within two years, the Mickey Mouse Club had a million members. Merchandising soon followed, with Disney's brother and business manager skilfully exploiting the studio product's mass appeal; two million Mickey Mouse watches were sold in two years.

Throughout the 1930s, the Disney studios transformed the animation industry with a remarkable series of technological innovations. After sound came colour. Although Technicolor's three-negative colour process was still not ready for live action, Disney persuaded Technicolor to give him two years' exclusive use of the process, which was first tried in *Flowers and Trees* (Burt Gillett, US, 1932). This was one of the 'Silly Symphonies' – one-off animations which enabled Disney's animators to explore new ground, beyond the limitations imposed by the stable of characters that had developed around Mickey.

Throughout the 1930s, Disney was constantly striving to improve the quality of his short films. This has sometimes been described as primarily a struggle toward commercial stability; but if that had been Disney's main goal, he would not, constantly throughout his career, have jeopardized the financial future of his studio in order to produce what he felt were artistically or technically better films. He brought in new talent, improved staff drawing skills with life-drawing classes, and introduced storyboards and line-tests – two innovations soon adopted throughout the industry. Disney passed another milestone with *Three Little Pigs* (Burt Gillett, US, 1933), which became the most successful cartoon to date and which even got billing above the main feature in cinemas all over the country. Its theme song, 'Who's Afraid of the Big, Bad Wolf?' became a popular favourite, a symbol of resistance to the Depression.

By the mid-1930s, Disney's short films had attained a level of technical and artistic perfection that left all the other studios far behind. This success was not achieved without cost, however. Much of the subversive and fantastic quality of early animation was being lost, and this loss is one of the main reasons why later animators have such an ambivalent attitude toward Disney.

Subjugating the Unruly

Its capacity for unbridled fantasy is one of the essential qualities of the animation medium, distinguishing it from the realism implicit in live-action cinema. Animation offers a space for unlimited kinetic exuberance, erotic spectacle disguised as innocent play, metamorphosis of figures moving freely between animate and inanimate forms – all perhaps characteristics of the unconscious mind, released by the animation medium from social constraints into a world of fantasy.

It was this liberation which attracted Sergei Eisenstein to early Disney, and which the Russian film-maker identified with a personal and ideological liberty, so difficult to sustain, he thought, in the mercilessly conformist and mechanistic capitalist system. 'Plasmaticness' was the name Eisenstein gave to the ability of cartoon figures to assume any form, animate or inanimate, in the pursuit of their liberation from social constraint and the fulfilment of personal desire. Eisenstein applauded the ability of Disney's early work to create characters which behave 'like the primal protoplasm, not yet possessing a stable form, but capable of assuming any form and which, skipping along the rungs of the evolutionary ladder, attaches itself to any and all forms of animal existence' (Leyda, 1988,21).

But every innovation introduced by Disney increased the realism of his figures and the physical and narrative spaces they inhabited, making the 'play of free lines and surfaces' increasingly difficult to achieve. Some writers have seen this development in unambiguously negative terms, and have lamented the fact that Disney 'moved further away from the plastic flexibility of many of the early Silly Symphonies and coerced the animated form into a neo-realist practice' (Wells, 1998, 16).

Nevertheless, an examination of two small masterpieces from the middle of the 1930s, *Clock Cleaners* (Ben Sharpsteen, US, 1937) and *Alpine Climbers* (David Hand, US, 1936) suggests that the gains in the mastery of space and the fluency of the figure-drawing are every bit as apparent as any loss in spontaneity. The manipulation of the figures in three-dimensional space is inventive and exhilarating, and it is achieved without sacrificing any of the kinetic energy of the earlier films. The assurance with which Mickey, Pluto and Donald move in these films – their sense of rhythm and timing – is astonishing. In both films Disney gave his animators the challenge of hurtling his characters into free fall, in dizzying displays of their technical skills. By now, and not without reason, Disney's animators felt they could do anything.

What is undeniable, though, is that some of the subversive quality of earlier animation – its sheer, creative anarchy (especially where it dealt with sexual or socially transgressive elements) – was being bowdlerized, or squeezed into a progressively narrower space within an increasingly realistic narrative framework. Disney wanted to impose order on these unruly elements, which for him were too reminiscent of animation's scurrilous beginnings. He wanted recognizable and likeable characters, with consistent personalities and understandable motivations, pursuing recognizable goals throughout well-constructed narratives enclosed within classically constructed perspective spaces. These characteristics were, and are, those of live-action fiction, and it was an entirely logical development for Disney to move toward the animated feature.

In 1934, Disney began planning what soon became known throughout Hollywood as 'Disney's Folly'- his first cartoon feature, *Snow White*. How far he was excluding the subversive and anarchic from the new world of Disney features is indicated by comparing his treatment of the fairy tale with the Fleischer Brothers' version, made just the year before Disney's adaptation went into production.

The Fleischers' *Snow White* (US, 1933) exploits to the full the surreal and sinister elements in the fairy tale. Metamorphosis, one of their favourite devices, is employed liberally, often without any narrative justification, giving the sense of a threateningly unstable moral and physical environment. Snow White herself is played by the highly sexualised Betty Boop, toward whom the entire physical universe of the Fleischers' films seems to harbour erotic desires. The film begins with the ugly Queen interrogating her magic mirror (complete with tiny hands and a black face) to confirm her role as 'fairest in the land'. Betty Boop arrives at the palace to see her stepmama the Queen, and is immediately befriended by armoured sentries Koko and Bimbo from the Fleischer stable of characters. Less enamoured of Betty than they, however, the Queen's scowling face turns into a frying pan with eggs for eyes and she orders Betty's execution, with a cry of 'Cut off her head!' accompanied by a gesture in which two of her fingers, like a pair of scissors, cut off a third. Koko and Bimbo reluctantly prepare for the execution outside in the snow, with Koko sharpening his axe so enthusiastically he grinds it into nothing. They throw a tree into the grave intended for Betty, but fall in and knock themselves unconscious instead. Betty, tied to a tree, is lifted to freedom by the tree's own branches coming alive. She walks away but falls into a snowball, which rolls downhill into an icy lake, from where it emerges as a transparent coffin then slides into a cottage labelled 'The Seven Dwarves'. Without hesitation, the dwarves lift it on to their shoulders and ski off with it to the Mystery Cave.

Koko, knocked awake by the pursuing Queen, suddenly bursts into song – 'The St. James Infirmary Blues'. This was pre-recorded by Cab Calloway, whose rotoscoped, dancing figure was the model for the animation of Koko, and who is turned by the Queen's magic mirror into a ghost but continues to sing and dance through a series of extraordinary transformations against a backdrop of the cave, itself transforming in response to the lyrics of the song. When Koko sings 'Hey, boy, hand me another shot of that booze', his head morphs into a bottle, from which he pours liquid into a glass and thence down his own headless throat. The Queen finally explodes into a fearsome dragon and chases the three out of the cave, until Bimbo turns and pulls the dragon's tongue so vigorously that he pulls the monster inside out, causing it to run off in the opposite direction and leaving the three victorious in the snow.

The Fleischers' *Snow White* probably distils more anarchy and surrealistic invention into six minutes than any other of their films; it also emphasizes how disciplined Disney's employment of fantasy was in his own *Snow White,* where it is never released from a precise narrative function. In the work of Disney, as in the Fleischers', the inanimate world can suddenly come alive, as it does when the trees of the forest transform into monsters, and pluck at Snow White's clothes as she flees from the huntsman/executioner; but this is not as a gratuitous invention – the animation mirrors the terror Snow White is feeling. Disney's Queen transforms herself, but into an old hag, again for a narrative purpose, this time of disguise. Disney knew that to sustain the story through 80 minutes he needed to develop a totally different strategy from the free-wheeling anarchy of the Fleischers' film.

To shift a small studio, geared to the production of six-minute cartoons, to the production of feature films was a perilous undertaking, and not just in terms of the massive staff recruitment and extension of facilities it necessitated. It also meant a radical extension of the skills of Disney's artists and animators, because a feature demands quite different skills from those of a short film. Disney knew that a feature had to engage the audience on a much deeper emotional level and involve a wide variety of contrasting characters and moods, each with its appropriate visual style.

All Disney's staff had to grapple with new problems. The seven dwarves presented a typical challenge. Whereas in the Fleischers' *Snow White* the dwarves were indistinguishable one from another, Disney saw that these characters presented great comic opportunities. Disney's *Three Little Pigs* had achieved immense success by creating three distinct animal characters and synchronizing their individual movements with the music track. With the dwarves in *Snow White*, Disney created not three but seven distinct personalities. While this brought immense benefits to the film as a piece of storytelling, it posed problems for the animators. Shamus Cullhane, who animated the dwarves' march home to the song 'Hi Ho', recalls:

> I worked six months on that goddam thing and I don't think it's a whole minute in the film... In the first place... each dwarf had a different style of walk. They were always in a row, and they had to stay even. And they often walked in perspective, sharp perspective in some cases, which meant that you had to sit down and map out every damn walk with a blue pencil and a ruler. In perspective you would diminish these steps so that everybody diminished properly, even if they had a different step – with Dopey out of step! I had two assistants and one in-betweener and we all worked about six months. There was that much work. (Maltin 1980, 54)

Bill Tytla told his staff:

> We are trying to get an entirely different type of drawing into the characters than in the shorts. In the shorts, everything is based more or less on a ball, and when it is inked everything has a sharp, hard, incisive line without any feeling of texture... The problem with this stuff is to try to get the feeling of various kinds of texture – texture of the flesh, the jowls of the dwarves, the eyes, the mouth and the texture of the hair and of old cloth, so that it feels heavy, unwashed for a couple of hundred years, according to the story. (Maltin 1980, 55)

The biggest challenge lay in animating the human figure. Snow White herself was designed and animated by Grim Natwick, who had already achieved celebrity in 1930 by creating Betty Boop for Max Fleischer. Natwick was the only one of Fleischers' animators with the skills necessary to create even a remotely realistic female body. It was clear that Betty Boop was far from the convincing female figure that Snow White needed to be. She was also unashamedly erotic in a way that Disney could never countenance. To help, a Los Angeles dancer, Marjorie Belcher, was filmed walking and dancing, and then rotoscoped. But the tracings of the live-action footage were of limited value. Natwick said later:

> I remember one scene I had where there were 101 rotoscoped tracings; that would mean they traced every second frame of the film. I used drawing one and drawing one hundred and one, and I filled in the rest, because there wasn't enough in it to give me anything to animate. (Maltin 1980, 56)

In the industry, it was widely assumed that the human figures were merely rotoscoping, but Natwick denies this: 'We went way beyond the rotoscope. And even when we took a rotoscope drawing, her chin came almost as far down as the bosom would be so we had to reconstruct the entire body' (Maltin 1980, 56).

In fact, the proportions of Snow White were midway between those of a child and those of a woman – a feature she shares with Betty Boop, though without any of the latter's sexuality. Critics at the time found the animation of the human figures, especially the Prince, the weakest element of the film, and the animators have since admitted that a number of technical problems were only satisfactorily solved in subsequent features. Nevertheless, the amount of pioneering work in *Snow White* was enormous. Great strides were made both technically and artistically. Disney's staff worked with missionary zeal and the budget soared to six times its initial quarter-of-a-million dollars. When it was released in 1937, *Snow White* was a worldwide success, taking eight million dollars in its first release and enabling Disney to pay off all his many debts and build a new studio at Buena Vista Street in Burbank, California. It was clear that the studio's future lay in features rather than shorts.

Snow White had taken three years to complete, so in order to release one feature per year, Disney saw it was necessary to have three features in production at any one time – which again required a massive expansion of staff and facilities. Within months of *Snow White's* success, Disney had three new features in production: *Pinocchio* (Hamilton Luske, Ben Sharpsteen, US, 1940), *Bambi* (David Hand, US, 1942) and *Fantasia* (James Algar, Samuel Armstrong, US, 1940). His staff had numbered six in 1927; by 1934, it had grown to 187; by1940, it was over a thousand. In effect, the success of *Snow White* gave Disney the confidence and the resources to aspire to make his studio the research and development laboratory for the entire animation industry.

Fantasy and Reality

Fantasy continued to play a role in Disney's later features, but was always subservient to the realist narrative, in which it sometimes struggled to find a place. *Dumbo* (Ben Sharpsteen, US, 1941), for example, contains one of the most famous fantasy episodes in Disney – the 'Pink Elephants on Parade' sequence – but it is inserted into the narrative in much the same way as a dream sequence in a live-action film.

Indulging in the pleasure of fantasy has always been one of the principal pleasures of movie-going. (It may even be one of the principal motives for movie-making.) But this indulgence has to be carefully negotiated by the film-maker. It requires a carefully constructed space within which the private can be made public, and the imagery of the unconscious, with its explicit expression of infantile or sexual drives, can be revealed without shame or embarrassment.

Live-action film, even when realist in style, is often a vehicle for fantasy, but the fantasy is generally safely packaged within a realistic framework. Fantasy disrupts the realistic narrative in two common ways: either as a 'dream sequence' which presents the motivations, fears or memories of the protagonists in a subjective fashion, 'as if in a dream'; or else in 'the trip' – that is, through subjective imagery supposedly induced by drugs or alcohol. This is the device used by Disney. To negotiate the step from the three-dimensional, solid 'reality' of Dumbo's circus to the two-dimensional world of metamorphosing coloured elephants, Disney exploits the realist strategy of 'the trip': baby Dumbo accidentally drinks some wine and gets drunk. What the Fleischers' *Snow White* demonstrated was that the medium of animation was itself a perfect vehicle for fantasy, the natural beneficiary of the Méliès heritage, permitting a variety of techniques such as metamorphosis and the elision of time and space which were impossible or at least difficult in the live-action film. Disney's realism meant that such potentialities of the medium were relegated to those areas where the narrative permitted realistically-drawn characters to possess some magical ability. In other words, the potentiality for magic lies in the characters and not in the medium itself.

This has continued to be the pattern of Disney features. In late 20th-century features such as *Aladdin* (Ron Clements, John Musker, US, 1992), for example, it is only the supernatural powers of the Genie which enable him, once summoned from the magic lamp within which he has been imprisoned, to release into a realistic world the shift-shaping and anarchic humour that was once the animated form's natural style. Disney claimed, in a speech delivered to the Society of Motion Picture Engineers in 1940:

> The first duty of the cartoon is not to... duplicate real action... but to give a caricature of life and action... To picture on the screen dream fantasies... to caricature life as it is today. But we cannot do the fantastic things... unless we first know the real. Comedy, to be appreciated, must have contact with the audience... (it must be) something based on an imaginative experience or on a direct life connection. Thus the true interpretation of caricature is the exaggeration of an illusion of the actual, possible or probable. (Maltin, 1980, 35)

In other words, fantasy must be founded on knowledge of the real world. To come alive, characters, their personalities and their physiques must not be copied slavishly from the real world, they must be caricatured; but this caricature must be based on close observation and understanding. In practice, this meant that Disney's artists and animators scrutinized the world with a quite unprecedented intensity.

The film which best exemplifies this drive toward realism is *Bambi*. Based on a novel by Felix Saltern (published in Austria in 1923, with the first English translation appearing in the US in 1928), it deals with the coming of age of a deer in the forest. The theme is a serious ecological one – something quite unprecedented in animation – concerning the destructive effects of man on the natural world. The animal characters are realistic, presenting a real challenge to Disney's animators.

To meet this challenge, a noted animal painter was hired, a cameraman was sent to Maine to shoot thousands of feet of forest, snowfalls, spiderwebs and other natural phenomena, and two live fawns were brought into the studio and sketched and photographed as they grew, along with rabbits, ducks, skunks and owls – all known collectively as Disney's zoo.

This realistic observation helps to give the backgrounds and landscapes of *Bambi* an authenticity that goes way beyond the stereotyped landscapes of *Snow White*. But where animal characters were concerned, realistic observation was only the first step. It was essential to design characters which could engage an audience's sympathies, which could evoke pathos as well as laughter – in fact, express the full gamut of human emotions. In reality, an animal's facial structure is not designed to show human emotion at all; but if it is to engage our sympathies for a full 90 minutes, it is essential that it should do so. In a very revealing interview in *The South Bank Show:* 'The Art of Walt Disney' (London Weekend Television, 25/09/88), *Bambi* designer Marc Davis *describes* how he has altered the natural skull formation of a deer's head to incorporate the features of a human child, clearly demonstrating the anthropomorphism which is a striking feature of Disney's style. Ward Kimball, in another interview in the same programme, shows the same processes applied to the character design of Jiminy Cricket in *Pinocchio*. The character began with recognizable insect characteristics, such as sawtooth legs and an extended lower abdomen. At the end of the process, he is a little man with a round head. Kimball concludes: 'He's a cricket because we *call* him a cricket.'

Anthropomorphism is at the heart of the process which is sometimes called 'Disneyfication', implying a tendency to omit the darker or more challenging elements in a story and emphasise the sweeter ones, plus a cloyingly sentimental approach to characterisation. Disney is often regarded as the purveyor of a homespun, sentimental view of American history and values, and the maker of sugary fairy stories from which adult emotions have been rigorously excluded, rendering them suitable only for young children.

But few animators would dismiss Disney in this way. Richard Williams is typical of many later animators in his attitude to Disney:

> When I saw *Bambi* for the first time I was seven years old and I was crazy about it, I was just bowled over... Then when I was 22 I started my first animated film, and I finished it when I was 25, and I happened to see *Bambi* right towards the end; I thought, 'what a lot of sugary, sentimental mush' – the young intellectual's reaction. Then I became kind of conscious of my shortcomings as an animator... I began to catch on that I didn't know too much. About three years after that, I saw *Bambi* again, and I came out on my hands and

knees. I thought, how did they do that? – how did they animate those creatures with dignity? Four-legged creatures appearing with human emotions! Extraordinary! (*The South Bank Show*: 'Walt Disney')

Contrary to what is often assumed of Disney, his early features did, in fact, deal with many negative emotions and fears, which gave them an appeal to adult audiences as strong as to younger ones. Many mothers protested that the Queen in *Snow White*, with her transformation into a witch, was too frightening for young children. In *Pinocchio*, characters like the fox, the cat and the puppet master convey more menace than humour, and the sequence on Pleasure Island, where the boys are punished by being transformed into donkeys, remains disturbing to this day. The final section of *Fantasia*, 'Night on Bare Mountain', where the shape of the mountain transforms into an image of the Devil calling the souls of the dead from their graves, is a superb visualisation of a nightmare (and furnishes, incidentally, what must surely be the only example of bare female breasts, with red-painted nipples, in the Disney *oeuvre*). The famous sequence in *Bambi*, where the young deer's mother is shot dead by hunters, must rank as one of the most powerfully affecting pieces of animation ever made. Confronting the death of the mother, and through that the spectator's own eventual death, is a disturbing theme. In this scene, the landscape is transformed by the tranquil snowfall obliterating everything, translating the emotions of loss and distress into images of an almost abstract grandeur, expressing the beauty and the indifference of the natural world in the face of individual suffering.

If *Bambi* marks a high point in one kind of animated realism, Disney was simultaneously attempting to keep abreast of avant-garde developments in European animation, and in particular to build on his early innovations in the use of music. In *Fantasia*, the third film in production alongside *Bambi* and *Pinocchio*, Disney tried to extend the boundaries by animating pieces of popular classical music in a wide variety of animation styles. The film was released with the studio's own newly-devised stereo sound system in a number of cinemas, but its success was at most partial.

There were several reasons for this. Disney's drive for innovation and improvement sent *Bambi*, *Pinocchio* and *Fantasia* all vastly over budget. Their critical reception on release was mixed, and receipts from foreign sales were now reduced by the onset of World War II. To later animation history, these three films, along with the feature that followed, *Dumbo*, appear as (occasionally flawed) masterpieces.

Disney's post-war films failed to reach the artistic heights he had scaled with his first five features. After a while, he lost interest in animation, and although the studio turned out one feature per year throughout the decades that followed, the studio's financial situation remained perilous until his diversification into live-action adventure movies, nature documentaries and television (the potential of which, astonishingly, Disney was the only major Hollywood producer to see).

The amusement park, Disneyland, became a personal obsession; not as a money-making venture but as an outlet for the restless creative imagination that had found its earlier expression in cartoons – Disney was never interested in money except as a means of realizing his fantasies. When Disneyland proved a success, contrary to the expectations of all his advisors and financial backers, it put the studio on a solid financial base for the first time in its 30-year history. Theme parks proved viable in a way that animated films never had.

Retrospectively, however, theme parks have done a good deal to reduce Disney's stature as a producer of animated films -they, and the media conglomerate that the name Disney became after his death. But if one compares the films produced under Disney's leadership with the output of the studio since his death, it is clear what is missing. The single, guiding intelligence has gone. Later Disney features look as though they have been made by committee – as indeed they have. They are of course fully scripted, whereas in Disney's time, although they were storyboarded, the script existed only in Disney's head. And Disney was a supreme storyteller and actor, with a great producer's talent for exploiting other people's skills. One example will suffice.

One afternoon in 1934, Disney gave all his creative staff 50 cents to buy a meal, asking them to assemble on the sound stage at 7.30pm. They returned to find a darkened stage, lit by a single spot. Disney then entered that spot and proceeded to tell the story of *Snow White*, acting out each part in turn, explaining, describing, dramatizing the story for them, doing the voices of all the characters and their actions. When he finished, some two hours later, the audience of industry-hardened animators had tears in their eyes. They'd been sold on *Snow White*. This was not an isolated instance (Bob Thomas, 1977, 99). Any animator who had difficulty in visualising or animating a character could ask Walt, who would act out the movement and voice and bring the character alive.

Disney's influence on animation has been profound. His short films of the 1930s and the first five feature films set standards against which other studios could rarely compete. They also created enduring links in the public mind between animation and realism, and animation and family entertainment, which have tended to marginalize other kinds of animation, certainly until the beginning of the 21st century, when so-called 'experimental' animation was still usually relegated to late-night television slots or specialist festivals.

No other animation studio of the time was able to match Disney on his own ground. It was only in the 1950s that the more simplified and angular style of U.P.A. (United Productions of America), based more on the square and the triangle than the circle, offered an alternative to the pictorial realism of Disney, showing a way of escape from its extremely expensive and laborious production process. However, it is in the subsidised film industry of the USSR that the Disney aesthetic of pictorial realism has been developed and extended.

Pictorial Space in Disney

An essential element in Disney's realism is his use of space. It is space based on traditional linear perspective, as evolved in Europe during the Renaissance.

As is well known, the essence of the perspective system of drawing is that it uses converging lines to create a single vanishing point, which defines the spectator's precise position in space in relation to the image. It places the viewer at a single viewpoint in front of the picture, as if he were a locked-off camera framing the image in its viewfinder.

As Panofsky has demonstrated, this way of viewing the world corresponds historically to the emergence of the idea of the 'I', the subject, separate from the world as object. Such an approach led to the scientific investigation of the physical world, establishing the laws of physics and optics, which in turn led (logically enough) to the discovery of photography and the camera (Panofsky, 1924-1997). It is often assumed that this is the way the world is, that objective reality accords with the way a camera sees it. But we do not actually experience the world like this; instead we move around in the physical environment, touching things, sensing them in other ways, penetrating space rather than simply observing it.

There are other ways of representing space which take account of these other ways of experiencing the world. As a way of representing pictorial space, linear perspective dominated European art from the Renaissance to the middle of the 19th century, when Impressionism began to replace it with a more tactile, intuitive space. Cézanne (1839-1906) began to incorporate into his pictures his own movement in relation to the image. In Cubism, Picasso (1881-1973) and Braque (1882-1963) combined completely different views of the same object into a single image. Braque explained that what pushed him to Cubism was the need to bring the object nearer, to within arm's length, to make it touchable on the canvas (Richardson, 1996). In other words, to break down the distance between subject and object, the distance that linear perspective creates between the observer and the world observed.

These developments in the world of art were of little interest to Disney. He was not a particularly cultured individual. He understood the lowbrow tastes of the general American public because he shared them. His favourite writer was Mark Twain (1835-1910) – best remembered for *The Adventures of Tom Sawyer* (1876) and its sequel, *The Adventures of Huckleberry Finn* (1885) – because Twain's world was a fictionalised version of the one Disney had grown up in during his formative years, living on a farm in the Midwest. The climate in the Disney studio was basically anti-intellectual and the visual style of the films owes more to 19th- and 20th-century illustration than to 'high art'. *Fantasia* did mark an attempt by Disney to incorporate into his film elements of 'high culture', such as classical music, ballet and abstract art, but the results frequently ring false. His animators seem most at home when treating the arts with gentle mockery, as they do in the sublime parody of classical ballet in the penultimate sequence of *Fantasia*, where a troupe of hippos, ostriches and crocodiles interpret – with total seriousness – 'The Dance of the Hours'. Jules Engels, who animated the 'Chinese Dance' sequence in Tchaikovsky's *Nutcracker Suite* (the little dancing mushrooms) remarks that 'the people who were working on the material had never seen a ballet in their life, and I don't think they ever went to the theatre (Maltin, 1980, 61).

Fantasia dabbles in more advanced styles of art, but only very superficially. Oscar Fischinger, brought over to work on it because of his pioneering work in abstract film, left the studio deeply unhappy. The styles of popular illustration, rather than high art, remained the studio's terms of reference, and have done so since. Disney's drive toward realism expressed itself by trying to make traditional linear perspective *more* real – a more convincing model of the three-dimensional world. In this he was ignoring the direction taken by 19th- and 20th-century painting, which was motivated by a desire to destroy linear perspective as a model of the world.

Disney's treatment of perspective is made clear in his development of the multi-plane camera. When a character walks from left to right against a background, the background naturally moves from right to left. If the background is painted on to a single plane, all the objects painted on the plane will move at the same pace: a nearby tree, a distant hilltop and the moon in the sky will move as one. In the real world, of course, the displacement of these objects depends on their distance; the nearby tree is quickly passed, while the moon seems stationary in the sky. The multi-plane camera enabled Disney to put foreground figure, tree, hilltop and moon all on different planes, so that the camera could move through the three-dimensional pictorial space as a painted equivalent of the real world. Disney's animators used this new tool to great effect in *Pinocchio,* where, on the morning of Pinocchio's first day at school, the camera starts above the level of the church spire then swoops down past the rooftops to end in a close-up on Geppeto's door. This type of shot quickly became a staple in the studio's repertoire, allowing a freedom of movement through space which recent 3D programmes vastly extends, as in *The Hunchback of Notre Dame* (Gary Tousdale, Kirk Wise, US, 1998), for example, where it enables a free movement over the exterior facade or through the interior space of the cathedral that would be beyond even the most flexible camera crane in live-action cinema. Nevertheless, it is clearly the three-dimensional space of live-action cinema that the multi-plane camera enables animation to imitate.

Alternative Forms of Realism

There are many ways of representing space in art, and other animators since Disney have explored alternative ways of representing space in their work. One of the most interesting is the Russian, Yuri Norstein.

Norstein's work, like much Russian animation, has in common with Disney's a fondness for tales based on animals, and a character design which is equally anthropomorphic, though rather less inclined to cuteness. Norstein uses a variety of animation techniques, including cut-out, and he makes extensive use of the multi-plane camera, though to rather different ends.

In *The Hedgehog in the Fog* (USSR, 1975), Norstein tells the story of a hedgehog who is on the way to visit his friend the Bear when he gets lost in the fog. Fog dissolves all spatial certainties, bringing the hedgehog into close confrontation with other creatures both real (owl, bat, horse and dog) and perhaps imagined (an elephant... or is it a mammoth?). The hedgehog is forced to rely not on the sense of sight but on the sense of touch, feeling his way by the aid of a stick. His relationship to the world is transformed : objects like a leaf or a tree become images of great beauty and power. He suffers misadventures: losing his bag, falling into the river, abandoning himself to death by drowning. But the mysterious fog hides forces of salvation as well as revelation.

Norstein's most celebrated film is the *Tale of Tales* (USSR, 1980), which takes his exploration of space a stage further. In this film, space becomes a metaphor for memory. In *The Hedgehog in the Fog,* when a snail disappears toward the top-left corner of the frame, fading from view, we read this as a form vanishing because of the fog. In the *Tale of Tales*, precisely the same effect is used with the figures of the soldiers, as they are plucked from the arms of their wives and girlfriends and sent off to the front. Their disappearance, their slow fade from the frame, is a metaphor for their disappearance from the collective memory.

The Animated Feature in the 21st Century: No Escape from Disneyland?

Fox's *Anastasia* (Don Bluth, Gary Goldman, US, 1997) and Disney's *Pocahontas* (Mike Gabriel, Eric Goldberg, US, 1995) suggest a new impetus toward realism in animated features nearing the end of the 20th century. Dealing with genuine historical characters raises the possibility of engaging with social and political issues in an altogether new way. But neither film, however successful in their treatment of the personal stories of their protagonists, begins to address the ideological issues raised by their stories. *Anastasia,* whose heroine's moving personal story begins with the murder of the Romanov dynasty, even sidesteps any depiction of the events of the Russian Revolution, still less the social and political causes from which it sprang. And in *Pocahontas*, the love story sits uneasily in the context of the clash between Native American and white immigrant cultures. The fact that Pocahontas actually travelled to England and died in Gravesend is excised from the film in order to permit a simplistic final sequence of lovers separated for ever by 2,000 miles of water, rather than confront the issue of the cultural divide, which must have been a great deal more difficult to cross than the Atlantic.

In both films, it is clear that the animated feature is still struggling with ideological limitations as severe as those imposed by Walt Disney. A scene in *Pocahontas* in which John Smith, naked to the waist, enveloped the heroine in a passionate embrace, was removed from the final cut as though Walt was still haunting the viewing theatre.

While animation for television has rediscovered some of the subversive quality of early animation in programmes such as *The Simpsons* (Matt Groening, US, 1989-) and *South Park* (Trey Parker, US, 1999-) it seems that the ambition and scope of the animated feature is still limited by its continuing to address audiences containing young children. In spite of Ralph Bakshi's 'adult' features of the 1970s, such as *Fritz the Cat* (US, 1972), Disney's legacy endures, ensuring that the animated feature remains linked to 'family entertainment'.

In the meantime, the subversive quality of animation – the surrealism, the sexual fantasy, the exuberant departures from social and physical laws alike, which played such a powerful part in early animation and even in early Disney – is largely absent from the animated feature by the end of the 20th century. Where it is present, it is relegated to subsidiary roles, typically the animal friends or the magical allies of the main protagonist – roles such as that of the Genie in *Aladdin* (Ron Clements, John Musker, US, 1992) or the dragon in *Mulan* (Tony Bancroft, Barry Croft, US, 1998); 'magical' characters who, endowed with the subversive energies of 'voice artists' – in this case, well-known and popular screen actors Robin Williams and Eddie Murphy – keep alive the anarchic impulses of the magical medium that is animation, while the narratives of the main character adhere to realist conventions familiar from live-action cinema.

4. Animation and Documentary

When the Cunard passenger liner the *Lusitania* was sunk in 1915, Windsor McCay, like the American public generally, was so incensed that he produced an animated and (literally) graphic reconstruction of the event, as propaganda against the German military machine and putting the case for American entry into World War I.

This film is the first piece of widely known animation based on an actual event. In it, as in *Gertie the Dinosaur*, McCay does not attempt to hide the mechanics of the animation process. In the earlier film, he had made great play of showing the piles of drawings; in this film, he photographs himself interviewing the eyewitnesses of the disaster, to give authenticity to the account that is to follow. McCay is not, however, striving for objectivity; he constructs a narrative in which the villain is clearly identified – and vilified – as the Hun, and the innocent victims are typified by the Madonna-like mother, clutching her child, who sinks like a statue under the waves in the final shot of the film.

The strengths of *The Sinking of the Lusitania* (US, 1918) lie less in its narrative qualities than in its graphic and pictorial ones. There were, in fact, no photographic or film records of the event; the ship sank in just 15 minutes after being hit by German torpedoes. McCay studied news reports and eyewitness accounts, then visualized the scene from a number of dramatic viewpoints, joining these views together in a way reminiscent of the then developing grammar of live-action film.

The intertitles and their violently anti-German message are somewhat disruptive of the flow of the narrative, and on occasion one wishes for the animation sequences to be longer and the intertitles shorter. But what really impresses is the pictorial quality of the images: the power of the drawing.

McCay used the full tonal range of black and white film exquisitely, with dense blacks, a good range of greys and bright, clear whites, exploiting to the full the visual possibilities offered by the explosions and the smoke that pours from the stricken ship, and the bubbles that rise afterwards from the wreck. The human actors do play a part in the tragedy, though that part is mainly to drop from the sinking ship like leaves from a tree; but the main player is the *Lusitania*, the ship herself, from whom McCay coaxes a superb performance (Figure 12).

At first sight, *The Sinking of the Lusitania* may appear as an isolated oddity. Since World War II, the photographic record, whether still photo, movie film or video, has been regarded as the essential component of any worthwhile journalistic enterprise. It is inconceivable that a journalist or even a serious writer (if the two are not quite the same) could be dispatched to a war zone or to a natural disaster without the means to take photographs. We would instinctively (and wrongly) suppose the writer's text to be a personal, subjective reaction to the events, and the photographic records to be just

Figure 12. The first animated documentary, Windsor McCay's The Sinking of the Lusitania (US, 1918).

that, a *record*, with the connotations of a neutral, disinterested registering of the objective truth.

Set beside this notion of the documentary truth of the photographic image, McCay's artistic reconstruction of the event seems quaint. It is subjective, artistic and aesthetic – notions far from the documentary norm, indeed it seems rather odd to call it a 'documentary' at all. But if this is the case, perhaps the notion of documentary needs closer examination.

Live-action film is conventionally classified as 'fiction' or 'documentary'. It is supposed, intuitively, that documentary lies closer to the truth of the real world, whereas fiction is a fabrication or at least a construction. Animated film, which is of all kinds of film the *most* constructed, must necessarily belong to fiction, and lie at the furthest extreme from the 'raw truth' of the documentary form. But if we accept this simple view, we are faced by an awkward fact: the animated documentary. If our intuitive model were correct, the animated documentary could not exist; but it does, so something must be wrong with the model.

First, the assumption that documentary is closer to the real world than is fiction is questionable. Both forms are necessarily constructed. Documentary material can be edited in different ways, to disclose radically different meanings. Even without obtrusive editorialising devices such as voice-over or captions, 'raw footage' can be shaped in different ways so that the constructed narrative seems to say quite different things. But even the notion of 'raw footage' is suspect. The idea that this can provide an unmediated, objective recording of the real world may be difficult to sustain in practice.

The camera can only provide one, partial view of an event; and where the camera is placed, as every director and cinematographer knows, has a crucial impact on the meaning of the shot. Furthermore, as soon as a camera is taken into a social situation, that situation is changed. Photojournalists and film-makers have discovered, to their chagrin, that the mere glimpse of a camera stimulates crowds and terrorist groups to produce acts of violence *for the camera.* The camera cannot be a neutral recording device because it influences its subject; people behave differently in front of it.

In physics, it was discovered in the early years of the century that complete objective truth at the subatomic level was impossible: you can never measure both the exact weight and the exact position of a subatomic particle because the act of measuring it changes it. This is known as Heisenberg's Uncertainty Principle. Something similar pertains to the moving-image medium: you can never make a completely objective record of the world because the act of filming it changes it. Reality remains essentially unknowable. All we have is *opinion.* A movie, whether documentary or fiction, is a constructed, subjective statement – an opinion.

Of course, there are methods in documentary to minimize this obtrusiveness of the camera and camera crew. The camera can be hidden; it can slip into the domestic environment like a 'fly on the wall' to give an illusion of invisibility. But it *is* an illusion. Paul Watson, the maker of many such documentaries, claims that the family becomes quickly habituated to the presence of a camera crew, and soon acts as if it wasn't there. You may or may not find this argument convincing, but the point is, how could you ever know how the family behaves when you are not there? Does the fridge light go out after the door is closed? The Uncertainty Principle again.

There are also types of raw footage – film or video – which are much less mediated, or constructed, than most documentary film. The images recorded by security cameras, for example, or military surveillance aircraft. These, perhaps, represent the most 'objective' kinds of recording conceivable. When, by accident, they record events of great personal tragedy, the coldness of the medium can, paradoxically, produce images of extraordinary power. An example would be the shot, recorded by a security camera, of Jamie Bulger, the small boy led off to his death by two, only slightly older boys (discussed by Terence Wright in 'The Creative Treatment of Actuality' in this volume). But such a shot is no longer raw, unmediated footage: it has been *selected* from many hours, indeed weeks of material, and the very act of selection, and editorial decisions about where to begin and end the shot, and how to contextualize it, inevitably affect its meaning.

Images like the Bulger one represent one extreme of the documentary form, which is inevitably and inescapably an editorialised construct. And seen in this way, as a constructed view of the world, the documentary genre can indeed include animation. *The Sinking of the Lusitania* is far from being a freak documentary, just because it is not masquerading as an objective, photographic record; as a self-declared construct, it is a paradigm of the documentary form.

Another film which foregrounds the question of photographic truth takes as its starting point the footage (shot on video) of a London square. In *Soho Square* (GB, 1992), Mario Cavalli began with an analysis of human movement and gesture, shot in the course of one summer, then recreated it with actors, and finally purged it of all extraneous detail to present it in fields of saturated colour. It is a film that transforms raw documentary fact with theatrical performance and expressive colour – a remarkable combination of documentary, theatre and painting (Figure 13).

Cavalli was initially inspired by the paintings of Milton Avery, typically landscapes with figures in which superfluous detail such as facial expressions are stripped away, leaving only body language, rendered in pure fields of saturated colour. He began with a camcorder, shooting hours of material in Soho Square, just like a tourist. From this 40 hours of material, he compiled a storyboard. The painter Ashley Potter prepared background sketches to represent different times of day. Choreographer Jane Turner rehearsed actor/dancers in movements specified by the storyboard, who were then put into baggy costumes and filmed. The resultant footage was electronically voided of colour, which was then added by the animator, using the electronic brush of the Quantel Paintbox. This footage is transformed – there is no attempt to claim the film as an objective record, as the images are processed into flat areas of brilliant colour, reminiscent of the painterly qualities of artists' lithographs or screen prints. The people passing through or lingering in the square; the drunks, the bag-ladies and the joggers occupy the space like actors on a stage, animating it with their various gestures, which the animator has carefully manipulated to emphasize their rhythm, their theatrical or

[Figure 13. Documentary reality is illuminated by theatre and painting in Mario Cavalli's Soho Square (GB, 1992).

ritualistic quality. Policemen move through the space like ballet dancers, their movements as stylised as those of the t'ai chi. The comment springs to mind of Yuri Norstein, the great Russian animator, that animation is superior to live action because it can give the true weight, the true meaning to human gesture (Noake 1988:, 72). There are no narrative events in this film, just the space of Soho Square, its grass and flowers acting as a brilliant backdrop for its human protagonists, whose individual dramas we glimpse.

Soho Square is a film based on photographic record – on real events, in one particular place. But that objective record is transformed by the painterly sensibility of the animator, seeking to elevate a specific mundane reality into a dazzlingly choreographed ballet of colour and gesture.

Sound, rather than abstraction and choreography, can also be used to structure documentary. In recent years, the documentary element in much animation has been contained in the soundtrack. The use of naturalistic, documentary sound has become a trademark of the work of Peter Lord and David Sproxton, founder members of Aardman Animation. In a series of films they have used location sound-recording to provide the raw materials for various documentary investigations. This raw material is edited down to make a final soundtrack, and plasticine characters are then designed and animated to fit ('claymation'). The visual aspects of these films is distinctly at odds with the soundtrack: our ears can easily discriminate between unscripted dialogue recorded on location and the dramatic representation of even the very best actors, so we quickly realize that the soundtrack is made from recordings of real people in a real social situation. The naturalism of the soundtrack thus produces a real shock alongside the patently fabricated images: visual narrative functions as an ironic or comic commentary on the soundtrack.

In some of the Aardman films, the character design and animation are themselves in a naturalistic style. In *On Probation* (Peter Lord, David Sproxton, GB, 1984) there is no attempt to deceive us into accepting the plasticine people as real – we can see that they are animated clay figures. But their design, behaviour and movements are all closely modelled on observation: there is no attempt at gags, or even the caricature that is usually part of character animation. These are plasticine people, but – and this is what produces the shock – they behave just like us. They dress just like us, they talk just like us – and they indulge in the petty social rituals and struggle for power the film-makers observed during the meeting of probation officers and ex-prisoners.

On Probation poses interesting questions: first, about how appropriate naturalism is as an aesthetic for animation (would live action be a more appropriate medium for this subject?) and second, what is it exactly that these images add to the aural narrative comprised by the soundtrack? But an attempt to make the film using live-action techniques would have encountered difficulties. A film crew would have been far more intrusive than a tape recorder, and a single camera would have been unable to film the range of set-ups that the animation medium allows. But above all, the animation medium calls attention to the language of physical gesture, by selecting and isolating its most revealing manifestations; recreating the minutiae of social interaction in such an alienating medium as plasticine creates a remarkable intensity of focus. Once again, the comment of Yuri Norstein is applicable: animation is superior to live action because it can give the true weight, the true meaning to human gesture.

War Story (Peter Lord, GB, 1989) makes an interesting comparison with *On Probation*. In it, the character design and animation are more inclined toward caricature and gags, which makes the film fit more easily with traditional notions of animation.

In Nick Park's short film *Creature Comforts* (GB, 1989), he played brilliantly on the ambiguity inherent in the relationship between naturalistic sound and animated images (Figure 14).

Talking animals have been a constant resource of the animation industry since the invention of the sound film, and they seem to lie at the furthest extreme away from notions of documentary realism. But that is precisely what the voices on the soundtrack of *Creature Comforts* suggest: for example, the South American voice whose complaints about English food, weather and lack of wide, open spaces Park put into the mouth of a plasticine panther imprisoned in the zoo. The discomfort of real people removed from their natural habitat or confined in unsatisfactory housing, voiced on the soundtrack, is depicted in claymation, with gentle irony, as the sufferings of the animals transported from their natural habitat and caged in the zoo. The result can be read as a plea for the abolition of zoos, or of inhuman housing projects, or homes for the elderly or all of these -or simply as an amusing piece of character-based animation, which communicates very directly, without any explicit propaganda.

A number of animators have taken up the challenge of illustrating the stories of people interviewed on tape. *Some Protection* (GB, 1989), the story of a juvenile delinquent, is interpreted with great visual flair and energy by animator Marjut

Figure 14. Real documentary voices emerge from the mouths of animated animals in Nick Park's Creature Comforts (GB, 1989).

Rimminen. The graphic style is not far from that of comics and strip-cartoon, especially the True-Life Crime Story of cheap popular fiction. It's an appropriate style for O'Dwyer's story of institutionalised violence and despair: the extreme contrasts of light and dark of the prison interiors accord well with a moral world, where the choices are stark – fight violence with violence or go under (Figure 15).

Josie O'Dwyer's story is, of course, filmable in conventional live action, as fiction or documentary. What the animation brings to her account is not a heightening of its claim to be objective fact, but rather the opposite: the appeal to our emotions and our senses through the graphic language of popular fiction. But the goal is to communicate – while protecting the original subject from unwelcome exposure – the personal experiences of someone whose voice is not normally heard in mainstream media; a member of the criminal underclass.

Another attempt to communicate the subjective experience of a disadvantaged minority is Tim Webb's *A is for Autism* (GB, 1992), a film that combines formal inventiveness and striking design with a serious didactic purpose, in a way difficult to attempt in the conventional, live-action documentary form. The film uses a wide variety of techniques, including animated drawings by autistic children, live-action sequences, pixillation and object animation, to penetrate the under-examined world of autistic children, and allow us to experience their particular preoccupations, obsessions and fears. A fascination with numbers, calendars and the passing of time, with spinning records and coins, with trains and roads, is powerfully evident. The recorded voices of the children tell of their difficulties in managing interactions in the everyday world of shops and streets, while the drawings convey the threatening or distorted spaces they inhabit. With its visual playfulness, its engaging and striking use of the medium's full range of techniques, *A is for Autism* powerfully demonstrates the versatility of the animated documentary as a form.

In some of the animated forms of documentary mentioned above, the animator is visualizing a reality that is unfilmable. The *Lusitania* sank without leaving any visual record, but with a massive effort of the imagination, Windor McCay constructed his own. In a 1995 film by American animator Paul Vestor, the events depicted are also probably unfilmable, not just because they occur in the absence of any camera, but because they are, in all probability, unreal: they belong to the world of subjective fantasy. Or perhaps not. That is the question posed by *Abductees* (US, 1995). This film is based on interviews with the victims of alien abduction: people who believe that they have been taken off to alien spacecraft and subjected to strange experiments. The sincerity of these people is not in doubt. Their stories are animated without recourse to jokes or gags; there is no obvious irony intended. As a result, the film stands as a strangely disturbing document of what may be an out-of-this-world experience, or may be a delusion. It is situated, like the animated documentary form itself, somewhere between objective fact and private fantasy, declaring itself a constructed, invented view, a visualisation of what is ultimately, perhaps, unknowable.

5. Motion Painting

The digital revolution and, in particular, the growth of digital video has profound

Figure 15. The real-life story of a 'juvenile delinquent' is animated in Marjut Rimminen's Some Protection (GB, 1989).

implications for cinema. By 2000, it was clear that the days of celluloid as a medium were, like those of vinyl discs, almost certainly numbered. This idea is a cause of regret to many, if only for one curious reason: looking at streams of digital data on a tape or a hard disk tells us much less about the nature of audiovisual media than does the experience of handling a piece of old-fashioned film.

A strip of film is a remarkable thing. A child would notice lots of pictures in a row, each one almost the same as the one next to it. Sometimes they are the same. But usually, there's a change, however slight, between frames. And sometimes there's a complete change: one frame has nothing in common with the next.

A single frame of film is a 'still' photograph. As such, it obeys a logic worked out over a century and a half of photography – a logic comprising answers to questions like 'Where do I put the camera?', 'Do I light the subject, and if so how?', 'Do I pose the subject or surprise it?'. Considered as a still picture, the single frame of film also obeys the logic of the Fine Arts or Graphic Arts. This includes the artist's answers to many of the questions posed by the still photographer, such as 'How do I compose the picture?', 'Do I emphasize horizontals and verticals, or diagonals?', 'Do I wish to create space or negate it? To produce an illusion of movement or an impression of stillness?', 'Do I want a painterly rhythm of light and dark, or an overall evenness of illumination?'.

The image contained by the single frame of film follows the logic of two-dimensional art forms – still photography, drawing and painting. These art forms are, of course, timeless, creating static, unchanging images. But in the cinema the single frame only exists on screen for a fraction of a second; it only exists as a metaphysical idea, in fact, because it is not perceived. Watching a 90-minute film, we spend more than 45 minutes sitting in complete darkness – the darkness that separates each frame as it is projected on to the screen. What we actually perceive on the screen is not the single frame but the difference between frames; the movement of the image. Project a film of an unmoving object, taken with a static camera, and what the eye sees is the differences between the frames: the slight jiggling of the image caused by the imperfect registration of the film in the gate, the other imperfections like dirt and dust, scratches, variations in film emulsion, marks left by the development process, and so on. When Andy Warhol filmed the Empire State Building for 24 hours, he drew attention to these elements: the drama of the medium itself, in particular its temporal nature.

While the single frame of film relates the medium to timeless art forms like painting and photography, the temporal nature of film – the fact that all those frames relate to each other, one after the other, 24 per second – relates it to the other temporal arts. These include performance arts such as music and dance, and narrative arts like folk tales, poems, stories and the novel.

But film is nonetheless unique. One could think of atomising a novel down through its constituent parts and finally calling a word its basic unit. In the same way, one could call a note the basic constituent of a piece of music. But these still exist in time: even a word and a note need time to exist at all. Film, on the other hand, is composed of elements that exist out of time – still pictures. It is only the physiological fact of the 'persistence of vision' which unites them into moving images when projected.

So what the physical strip of film demonstrates is a conflict, a paradox: film is an art of time and motion, but its building blocks are timeless, still pictures. This paradox affects all kinds of film, but it affects animation more than any other, for three reasons. The first is that animators daily confront this paradox in the making of animated films, because unlike the makers of live-action film, animators consciously construct moving films out of still frames. The second is that animators often come to film with skills acquired in the 2D arts and have to confront the fact that these skills, though essential to animators, are not in themselves enough – the secret of animation, as Norman McLaren remarked, is what happens *between* the frames of film (Nelmes, 1996, 194). The third reason is that animated films are frequently based upon existing styles of art, styles built upon the authority of the timeless, still image.

A good example of such a style is Russian icon painting – a style deeply rooted in 2,000 years of Eastern Orthodox religion, a style which is immobile in various senses: static, unbending and impersonal. It is clearly not a style easily suited to the fluid, kinetic nature of the film medium. But Andrei Khrzhanovski and Yuri Norstein accepted this challenge and used the style of Russian icons to animate a famous battle from Russian history in their film *The Battle of Kerzhenets* (USSR, 1971). Evident throughout the film is the clash of two opposing conventions: stylised human figures, with strong, linear, two-dimensional forms, and the animation, which moves these flat, curved forms as though they inhabited real three-dimensional space. The putative realism of the movement in space serves only to emphasis the unreality, the stylisation of the forms. The effect is bizarre, awkward, even slightly comic. The paradox lies not necessarily in the style of art chosen, but rather in animating that style, transgressing its fundamental aesthetic of out-of-time stillness by making it move.

Contrast this film with another animator's use of a style even more ancient than Russian icons: ancient Egyptian art. In her trilogy, *Ra, Path of the Sun God* (GB, 1990), Leslie Keen does not attempt to animate the figures realistically but has adopted an equally stylised and linear form of animation. Her figures remain in the flat, two dimensional other world in which the ancient Egyptian artists inscribed them. But it could equally be argued that Keen's divinities, however beautifully articulated, fail to engage us emotionally, perhaps in part because of their failure to engage with the physical three-dimensional space which we mortals inhabit; and that Khrzhanovski and Norstein, in wresting their icons out of the flatland of medieval iconography, run the risk of some awkwardness but nevertheless exploit much more powerfully the dramatic potential of the medium.

Choice of style is one that faces the animator today in a painfully self-conscious way, as the options available are no less than the entire history of the visual arts. Erica Russell has said that:

> Animation, because it is the one medium that uses all the other media, is intrinsically post modern. To me, the post modern is dipping randomly into art movement, dance styles and music cultures and finding new juxtapositions and outrageous couplings: something evocative and challenging because of its new relationship... Though some argue that the post modern is a Western concept, by its very nature it allows the eclectic borrowing of any global art form. (Russell, 1997)

The style of art which is perhaps most characteristic of the 20th century is abstraction. Many artists who became interested in film between the two World Wars were artists who were interested in abstract art. They thought of film as a means of extending their abstract images in time: motion painting.

From the vantage point of the 21st century, abstraction seems empty, decorative and familiar. But for artists in the early 1900s, this was not the case. Abstract forms were charged with a mysterious power. Kandinsky, the Russian painter and first theoretician of abstraction, developed a complex, pseudo-scientific theory which ascribed precise psychological and spiritual meanings to geometrical shapes and colours. Kandinsky famously asserted that a triangle touching a circle possessed all the spiritual and visual power of Michelangelo's Adam, touched by the finger of God on the Sistine ceiling (Kandinsky, 1911).

While that may have seemed a plausible view in 1911, when geometrical forms, in their startling purity, had previously not been seen as the subject of art, further on in history it may seem like wishful thinking. Circles and triangle and other abstract forms are the devalued currency of the applied and decorative arts, and are handed down to their posterity stripped of all magic, indeed virtually empty of meaning.

The art which, above all, inspired Kandinsky and other abstractionists was music, which they perceived as completely abstract, speaking directly to our emotions. It seemed to offer to artists the model of a non-representational art impinging directly on the psychological state of the listener.

In Germany, where Kandinsky taught in the 1920s, a number of artists were interested in linking music and painting, trying to create the total work of art that would include all others – an idea that had motivated the dramatic composer Wagner in the 19th century. In the 1920s, the recently born medium of film was clearly a candidate for this new, all-inclusive art form, and a number of artists produced experimental, abstract films clearly inspired by music – among them Viking Eggeling's film *Diagonal Symphony* (Germany, 1921) and Hans Richter with his series *Rhythms* (Germany, 1921). But these film experiments, unlike most 'silent' movies, were projected without a live orchestra or pianist, and it was some years before Oscar Fischinger began to use records to be played along with his films – his *Study No.5* (Germany, 1928) is charcoal-drawn animation to a jazz score, while *Study No.7* (Germany, 1931) is accompanied by a Brahms Hungarian dance. When synchronised sound became a reality, Fischinger was quick to explore the possibilities of moving abstract forms to music. His films became popular both in Europe and the United States, where they exerted an influence even on Walt Disney, leading eventually to Fischinger's moving to the States and working (briefly and unhappily) on Disney's *Fantasia* (US, 1940).

Fischinger's *Composition in Blue* (Germany, 1935) raises interesting questions about the effects of very close synchronization of music and image. When Fischinger's red circles or blue cubes grow and shrink following the increases or decreases in the volume of the music, a powerful illusion is created, to the effect that these abstract forms seem to be performing a musical ballet on a three-dimensional theatre set. This effect is at times bizarre and rather comic. But so compelling is the illusion that one can readily understand Disney's compulsion to push this realistic effect a stage further, and endow the abstract shapes with identifiable personalities – so that in Disney's *Fantasia*, glittering points, for example, transform into fairies.

Frame and Sequence

The starting point for this discussion of animation was the paradox between the static nature of the single frame of film and the temporal nature of film as sequence. This paradox is most acute for animation, and especially for abstract animation because the abstract image in itself carries no narrative content whatsoever – no implications for temporal development. A circle is a circle is a circle: there is no inherent reason why it should grow larger or dwindle into a dot or transform into a square. It can do anything with equal validity. This freedom is the attraction of abstraction. But it is also its weakness: when all things are equally possible, it may be that everything is equally meaningless. Meaning only emerges when some possibilities are excluded, when some form of logic demands that choices be made. When Fischinger's red cubes grow or shrink in response to crescendos or diminuendos in the soundtrack, it is clear that the image is following the logic of the soundtrack: the film-maker is animating to the music. Whether this is enough to convince us of the logical coherence of the whole experience is an open question.

Len Lye's work in the second half of the 1930s takes up Fischinger's approach and explores the kinetic possibilities of abstract marks in a still more fluid and painterly way. Lye's film *Colour Box* (GB, 1935) is generally thought to be the first piece of direct animation – that is, made without use of the camera. Lye used freehand marks, as well as stencils through which he sprayed, painted and scratched directly on to the film. These stencils were cut specially to achieve particular rhythms, and found objects, such as sheets of perforated metal or saw-blades, were chosen for the rhythmic potential of their regular patterns. Direct animation, interestingly, makes it clear that the fundamental technical component of the cinematic experience is not the camera, which can be dispensed with, but the film projector. What makes Lye's films work so well is rhythm – musical rhythm: the logic here is that of the physiological imperative of the dance. Erica Russell, much influenced by Lye, takes dance explicitly as her subject in *Feet of Song* (GB, 1989), discussed in section 2.

Popular song, with its verse-and-chorus structure and its lyrics, can also provide a rationale for the development of abstract images. In Norman McLaren's *Le Merle* (Canada, 1958) the play is upon abstract marks which compose and decompose the recognisable image of the blackbird in response to the lyrics of the folk song. The film works by playing with the gap between abstraction and recognisable forms (Figure 16).

Much the same might be said of the work of artist Robert Breer, who makes experimental handmade films from images freely drawn on to small pieces of card. Only one of his films has achieved any real popularity, a short film entitled *Man and Dog Out for Air* (US, 1951), whose success derives in part from the sense that these abstract, moving lines, drawn with real artistic sensibility, are progressing toward meaning, which they achieve only in the final moments of the film.

Figure 16. Lines dancing between abstraction and the form of a bird: Norman McLaren's Le Merle (The Blackbird) (Canada. 1958).

Abstract film has continued to develop, influenced since the 1960s by the computer. The Witney brothers in California have been especially influential. As early as 1968, John Witney called for a future of 'small, fast and cheap computers to aid artists in the task of exploring the elements of a structural system of images as complex and ordered as language or music' (Noake, 1988, 124).

By 2000, many varieties of such computers existed, and were within the grasp of animators with moderate resources, though whether a truly 'structural system' of abstract images has been created, or *could* be created, is open to question. Can any moving-image work dispense with either narrative development or formal structure without degenerating into meaninglessness? 'Narrative' and 'formal structure' are by no means the same: Michael Snow's *Wavelength* (US, 1967), for example, consisting as it does of one, extremely long zoom, benefits from a strict, formal structure without implying narrative at all. It is particularly difficult to achieve in abstract works that sense of closure which implies that a visual idea has found its appropriate form, and pursued the temporal development of that idea for just the right length of time, and no longer. Without that, it is hard to escape the suspicion that image follows image arbitrarily or, to put it crudely, that it is 'just one thing after another'.

To pose the question less colloquially: just how *can* abstract images be composed into 'a structural system as complex and ordered as that of language and music'? And how can such a system offer us more than the simple visual pleasures of moving colour and form offered, say, by a tank of tropical fish? How is such a system to be organised and, above all, how is it to be made meaningful? As an abstract painter myself, I am certainly not hostile to abstraction, but it is my suspicion that abstract images lack something which might enable them to develop from within themselves a logical extension in time. It is possibly for this reason that most abstract film seems dependent on temporal forms such as music, dance and song to provide a narrative structure.

Language (spoken or written) and music both exist in time, and both lead naturally to expressive narratives, having their origins and their power to move us emotionally in the cadences of the human voice, speaking or singing. Will abstract images ever be as capable of moving us and holding us in their own developing formal narratives, as powerfully as the masterpieces of the novel and the narrative film? The computer Witney had wished for in 1968 had already become ubiquitous, and yet that was a question still waiting to be answered at the turn of the second millennium.

Beyond Digitality: Cinema, Console Games and Screen Language
The Spatial Organisation of Narrative

Maureen Thomas

The protean nature of the computer is such that it can act like a machine or like a language to be shaped and exploited. It is a medium that can dynamically simulate the details of any other medium, including media that cannot exist physically. It is not a tool, although it can act like many tools. It is the first metamedium, and as such it has degrees of freedom for representation and expression never before encountered and as yet barely investigated. (Alan Kay, 'Computer Software', *Scientific American*, Vol. 251, No. 3 [September 1984], 52-59.)

1. Console Games and Storytelling

At the end of the 20th century, media production went through a period of extraordinarily rapid transformation with the transition from the world of film and analogue media to the domain of digital multimedia. In the age of the Internet, the home computer, cable networks, non-real-time integrated services, digital broadcasting, electronic and digital cinema, and interactive entertainment consoles, do traditional standards of excellence apply? Or does the merging of virtual architectural and story space mean that we must identify new criteria by which to evaluate and make contemporary moving-image entertainment art?

Although some attempts have been made to experiment with interactive cinema in the movie theatre, these have been few and not very encouraging. However, in 1995 Nicholas Negroponte predicted that by the turn of the millennium the computer would be the means by which screen entertainment reached the widest audience, probably in a domestic situation, whether in the form of video on demand, digitally broadcast TV, the Internet, DVD or other as yet unrevealed kinds of production and distribution (Negroponte, US/GB, 1995). His vision has been confirmed in a number of areas, though not in all. By the beginning of 2000, the BBC was investing heavily in digital broadcasting, including interactive programme-making, and Cable TV became Cable Interactive. In 2001 Channel 4 launched C4 e, and in January 2002 'BBC i' went live. Telcos the world over are proactive in the infotainment era, and the manufacturers of set-top boxes have created multipurpose digital interactive entertainment centres, some networked and with Internet connections. Digital production and dissemination not only affect traditional moving-image arts and sciences – they generate fresh ones. How do these digital creations improve upon their predecessors?

Traditional film-makers – including those like James Cameron, Steven Spielberg, George Lucas, Ridley Scott and John Lasseter, who deploy digital techniques to create cinema films – use well tried and developed strategies to engage their audiences, not only to tell them stories but also to *involve* them – touch them, move them. The rhetoric they use was developed in the cinema for a century, in television for half a century. How far can, and should, interactive story-based screen entertainment deploy these tried-and-tested techniques?

By 2000, computer-supported interactive narrative was predominantly represented by PC or console games, frequently based on violence and mayhem. Console games were a comparatively new phenomenon in terms of the medium itself, but they undoubtedly represent a continuation of the tradition of domestic screen entertainment. It took only three years (from the birth of the Sony PlayStation in 1995) for console games to overtake PC games in popularity by a long head. Their success was due not only to an effective marketing strategy, but also to the fact that they exploit forms of entertainment already familiar to the entertainment-seeking public, while adding new dimensions of their own.

By the beginning of the 21st century the phenomenon of television – of an entertainment box located in a place where you like to relax – was familiar worldwide. The domestic TV environment is relaxing and comfortable; often the lighting levels can be adjusted, so you can enable yourself to enter a semi-hypnotised state of almost-sleep – you can even go to bed – while you enjoy your programme, video, or DVD of a film on the domestic screen. Throughout the late-20th century, computers, on the other hand, tended to be identified with a workplace – with a desk or table alignment rather than a sofa or bed. The computer screen is associated with mental, often exhausting, activity; with word-processing or spreadsheets, with nerve-wracking trips into the imperfectly mapped and signposted Internet, requiring concentration of a very different type from that with which we enjoy drama or fiction. The kind of games supplied with office computers for relaxation between working hours tend to be repetitive – chance- or skills-based, a distraction as opposed to a focus.

By the beginning of the 21st century this was changing, and changes ever more rapidly as digital broadcasting develops and as computers become the receivers and display mechanisms for much more than was available on the Web at the turn of the 20th century. The shape and size of screens will respond to new media demands, and designers will rethink our relationship to them. Mice and keyboards give place to a variety of interfaces, from touch screens and styluses to physical and tangible interfaces embedded in everyday, or not so everyday, things.

Games consoles that plug into the TV and use joysticks or joypads are perhaps to be seen as a way-station on the border between the analogue and digital worlds, situated at the turn of the second millennium. To what extent does the interactive console platform inherit the drama, and what does it offer to narrativity?

The Content of Adventure Games

This investigation is based round interactive titles developed for the Sony PlayStation, which proved to be a blockbusting success of the 20th century and a pathfinder for the highly lucrative interactive adventure games industry (chronicled by Steven Poole in his book *Trigger Happy,* GB, 2000). Poole quotes (p. 24) US analyst Datometer as suggesting that by 2003, EU and US sales of games consoles and software products would 'generate over $17 billion worth of business'. The period from PlayStation 1 (1995) to PlayStation 2 (2001) defines an era of great change: in 1996, Lara Croft, protagonist of *Tomb Raider*, was born a 3D animated adventure hero, negotiating a 3D navigable world; in 2001, she appears on the big screen, incarnated by movie star Angelina Jolie. Between lies a phenomenal, high-profile career for Lara in gaming – and advertising.

In 1995, Disney released *Pocahontas*, an animated feature with a dainty (though resilient), lyrical, nature-loving heroine, who canoes through digitally-generated waters singing to the wilds and her animal friends, finally sacrificing romance in order to lead her people. Kathryn Bigelow's *Strange Days*, a meditation on screen violence, reality and the nature of immersion in 'entertainment', starring Ralph Fiennes, Angela Bassett and Juliet Lewin, hit the big screen. And John Lasseter's *Toy Story* made history as the first 3D animated feature to fully engage audiences. In 1996, the British Lara Croft (Eidos/HardCore) swept attributes of all these together – adding the new ingredient of interactivity. Alan Jones' *Lara Croft – Tomb Raider Official Film Companion* (2001) bears the proud banner: 'There is a place and a time in the Universe for everything. This is the time of Lara Croft.'

What is special about an interactive adventure? A PlayStation title can easily take 70 hours of game-time to explore to the end – roughly what it takes to read seven 500-page novels, attend around 20 plays or opera performances, see about 40 feature films, or watch some 120 episodes of a soap. The original PlayStation plugged into the television and cost about the same as seven or eight professionally recorded video-cassettes of movies, while PlayStation 2 (2001) cost about as much as a dozen professionally recorded DVDs. A typical game cost around the price of a couple of hardbacked novels, three or four movie videos, a couple of prerecorded DVDs, four or five visits to a cinema, or two cheaper/one expensive capital-city theatre-ticket; but could be hired, or, if bought, traded in against new versions or new games. PlayStation 2 could also play linear movies on DVD.

The target audience for console games at the turn of the second millennium was overwhelmingly adolescent males, though some attempts have been made to extend it, and by 2000 some girls and women were buying console games (Poole, 2000, 22). The Interactive Digital Software Association's 1998 *Video and PC Games Industry Trends Survey* puts 29 per cent of US videogamers over the age of 36 (Poole, 2000, 20). Many students entering undergraduate programmes from 1998 onward – in creative media, computing, architecture or literary and screen studies among other humanities subjects – had progressed from *Space Invaders* (Toshihiro Nishikado, Taito, Japan 1978) through PC games to owning gaming consoles such as the Sony PlayStation. They found the screen, the mouse, the joystick, the joypad and the joygun more familiar than the printed page, much more familiar than the stage, and certainly as familiar as television or cinema.

The choice of console-game titles examined here has been dictated partly by the popularity of the games, partly by their relationship to traditional narrative and dramatic forms.

The digital domain has already, since the computer game *Myst* (Rand and Robyn Miller, US, 1993), firmly established a tradition of fairy-tale-like dramatic fictions, many fundamentally inspired – like contemporary role-playing games – by JRR Tolkien's novel *The Lord of the Rings* (GB, 1954/5), which Peter Jackson began filming for the big screen in 2001. The book itself is based on the traditional poetry and tales of Old Norse, Celtic and Anglo-Saxon.

In his study of the power of the fairy tale, *The Uses of Enchantment* (GB, 1976, Penguin ed. 1991) – a book which makes no reference to Vladimir Propp's better-known *Morphology of the Folktale* (US/GB, 1968, trans. Laurence Scott) – Bruno Bettelheim points out that:

> Prevalent parental belief is that children must be diverted from what troubles them most: their formless, nameless anxieties, and their chaotic, angry and even violent fantasies. Many parents believe that only conscious reality or pleasant and wish-fulfilling images should be presented to children – that they should be exposed only to the sunny side of things. But such one-sided fare nourishes the mind only in a one-sided way, and real life is not all sunny. (Bettelheim, 1976, 7)

Parents in 2000 were more likely to feel anxieties about violent fantasies in the context of console and online games than in that of fairy tales. Bettelheim continues:

> Contrary to what takes place in many modern children's stories, in fairy tales evil is as omnipresent as virtue. In practically every fairy tale good and evil are given body in the form of some figures and their actions, as good and evil are omnipresent in life and the propensities for both are present in every human being. It is this duality which poses the moral problem, and requires the struggle to solve it. (Bettelheim, 1976, 8-9) (*I have silently substituted plural forms for singular – children ... their for child... his and human being for man, in order to avoid Bettelheim's androcentric language.*)

This assessment of Bettelheim's, like his comment on the function of violence, can be applied to most console games, where the hero is constantly attacked by monstrous enemies, not necessarily for any obvious reason; but is empowered, if the player is agile enough, to destroy them. Bettelheim is convinced – like psychoanalyst and theorist CG Jung – that the active imagination, enabled through fiction, is a powerful tool, essential to the full health of human beings.

In this respect, immersive Virtual Reality (VR), where you physically exclude normal perceptions in favour of those generated by a computer, is perhaps even closer to the notion of an 'imagination machine' – in fact, it has been likened to the dream (fantasizing) process itself. Michael Heim, author of *Virtual Realism* (GB/US, 1998), comments:

> Some Jungian psychiatrists make a direct correlation between inner and outer technologies, between dream analysis and VR, as I learned from a discussion with Dr. Robert Romanyshyn, author of *Technology as Symptom and Dream* (US, 1989). In the glossary to *The Metaphysics of Virtual Reality* (Michael Heim, US, 1993), under the entry 'virtual reality' I once wrote the following: 'Virtual Reality convinces the participant that he or she is actually in another place, by substituting the normal sensory input received by the participant with information produced by a computer' (p. 180). Reading this passage closely, Romanyshyn wrote me that my definition could be slightly altered to make an alchemical point. All we need do is substitute two phrases: 'Dreams [instead of VR] convince the participant that he or she is actually in another place, by substituting the normal sensory input received by the participant with unconscious wishes and desires [instead of information produced by the computer].' In other words, VR parallels the functions of dream life. Both are profound forms of visualization that blend inner vision and outer scenes. (Heim, 1998, 93)

The distinction between the obligatory sensory, fantasy-environment generation of immersive VR and engagement in a console or computer game mediated by the screen is an important one. Although in gaming some of the adventures and archetypal situations and characters bear a relationship to dream imagery, the activity of watching a screen while you experience the adventure via a control mechanism is much closer to the feeling of watching television, where you submerge yourself in the dramatic material through an act of imagination, than to immersive VR, where digitally generated input is substituted for sensory input. From the outset, it should be clear that this investigation is concerned with screen entertainment and art, not with fully immersive VR – though many of the general conclusions it draws can be applied to VR as well as 3D animated interactive adventure/drama.

In his discussion of the impact and function of fairy tale, Bettelheim continues:

> Today children no longer grow up within the security of an extended family, or of a well-integrated community. Therefore, even more than at the times fairy tales were invented, it is important to provide the modern child with images of heroes who have to go out into the world all by themselves and who, although originally ignorant of the ultimate things, find secure places in the world by following their right way with deep inner confidence...
>
> The fairy-tale hero proceeds for a time in isolation, as the modern child often feels isolated... The fate of these heroes convinces children that, like them, they may feel outcast and abandoned by the world, groping in the dark, but, like them, in the course of life they will be guided step by step, and given help when it is needed (p. 11). This is... the message that fairy tales get across to the child in manifold form: that a struggle against severe difficulties in life is unavoidable, is an intrinsic part of human existence – but that if one does not shy away, but steadfastly meets unexpected and often unjust hardships, one masters all obstacles and at the end emerges victorious. (Bettelheim, 1976, 8)

Most of the interactive titles examined here, whether or not they are ostensibly set in a fairy-tale world, exhibit the characteristics Bettelheim ascribes to fairy tales. Perhaps in the third millennium, these games perform a similar function to such tales in an oral storytelling environment.

The features Bettelheim mentions also, of course, appear in a number of highly successful films, obvious late-20th-century examples being *2001: A Space Odyssey* (Stanley Kubrick, UK, 1968), *Blade Runner* (Ridley Scott, US, 1982), *Conan the Barbarian* (John Milius, US, 1982), *ET* (Steven Spielberg, US, 1982), *Indiana Jones and the Last Crusade* (Steven Spielberg, US, 1989), *Terminator* (James Cameron, US, 1984), the *Star Wars* trilogy (George Lucas et al, US, 1977-1997), *Toy Story* (John Lasseter, US, 1995), *The Fifth Element* (Luc Besson, France, 1997), *Sleepy Hollow* (Tim Burton, US, 1999) and *The Matrix* (Wachowski Brothers, US, 1999). Bettelheim might have been writing of any of them when he adds:

> It is characteristic of fairy tales to state an existential dilemma briefly and pointedly. This permits the child to come to grips with the problem in its most essential form, where a more complex plot would confuse matters... The fairy tale simplifies all situations. Its figures are clearly drawn; and details, unless very important, are eliminated. All characters are typical rather than unique. (Bettelheim, 8)

Adventure, Fantasy and Exploration

If Bettelheim's contention is correct, the power of 'fantasy' adventure films as well as console games may be of more real value to children – and adults – than much contemporary screen drama, which offers imitative naturalism or realism in fiction format, whether in the shape of television soaps such as the British *EastEnders*, *Coronation Street* and *Brookside* or character-based dramatic film fiction such as *The English Patient* (Anthony Mingella, US/GB, 1997), *The Idiots* (Lars von Trier, Denmark, 1999), *Billy Elliott* (Stephen Daldry, GB, 2000), *Chocolat* (Lasse Hallstrom, GB/US, 2000) and *Erin Brockovich* (Steven Soderbergh, US, 2000). Console games, with their emphasis on solo heroism, personal empowerment through control of the central figure, overcoming obstacles and solving puzzles, rather than social realism or the Hollywood happy-ending, feelgood phenomenon, surely owe some of their popularity – like fairy tales – to their powerful function of reassurance: the player *can* win through, no matter what the odds.

The classification under which console games are generally sold is: Action, Adventure, Beat-'em-up, Puzzle, Racing, Shoot-'em-up, Simulation, and Sport. For the purposes of this study, however, the 35 titles considered here have been considered in three main categories, one of which is the product of interactivity and two of which correspond with traditional movie formats – Skills Game, Goal-oriented Adventure and Mystery.

Of course there are crossovers, and where these are strong the games are included in all relevant categories.

Skills Games

Bust A Groove (Enix/SCEE 1998) – compete as a hip-hop, disco, techno or house dance -star!
Colony Wars (see below)

Final Fantasy VII & VIII (see below)

Jedi Masters (LucasArts/LucasArts 1998) – fight hand to hand in the personas of your favourite *Return of the Jedi* characters!

Jedi Power Battles (LucasArts/LucasArts 2000) – as the Chosen One, save the planet Naboo with the aid of a friend by fighting allcomers!

NHL '98 (Electronic Arts/Electronic Arts 1997) – play top-league ice-hockey!

Oddworld: Abe's Oddysee, Abe's Exoddus (see below)

Parappa The Rapper (SCEI/SCEE 1997) – learn to learn, with rap, rhythm and bright colours!

Tekken 2/3 (Namco/SCEE 1995, 1996, 1998) – be a great martial arts exponent! Fight against a friend or the computer.

Tenchu: Stealth Assassins (see below)

Tomb Raider I, II, III, IV and Last Chronicles (see below)

Wipeout (Psygnosis/SCEE 1997) – drive a superspacecraft against others at superspeeds!

Goal-Oriented Adventures

Alien Trilogy (Probe/Acclaim Entertainment 1996) – shoot the aliens!

Broken Sword II (Revolution Software/SCEE 1997) – save the kidnapped girl!

Colony Wars (Psygnosis/Psygnosis 1997) – redeem freedom from the (Earth Empire) oppressors by destroying the warships and weapons of the tyrants and repairing the assets of the colonies! Discover the identity of 'The Father' who leads the revolution .

Dark Forces (LucasArts/CTO SpA 1997) – destroy the attackers and discover the truth1

Discworld 2 (Perfect Entertainment/Psygnosis 1997) – locate Death, who has gone missing somewhere in the colourful Multiverse of the Discworld!

Discworld Noir (Perfect Entertainment/GT Interactive 2001) – find out what has happened to the missing lover of the *femme fatale* in the dark and dangerous city of Ankh Morpork by questioning its unsavoury wisecracking denizens!

Excalibur (Tempest Software/Telstar Electronic Studios 1997) – find the Sword of King Arthur!

Final Fantasy VII (Squaresoft/SCEE 1997) – fight to save the planet! Discover how the life-cycle functions and how heroes and superheroes/divinities relate.

Final Fantasy VIII (Squaresoft/Squaresoft 1999) – follow Squall Leonhart through his training and missions as a 'seed' mercenary, find out about his comrade, Seifer, and improve your battle skills!

Lost Vikings (Beam Software/Melbourne House 1997) – get the Viking-age team home from the time zone where they have lost themselves!

Machine Hunter (Eurocom Entertainment/MGM/UA Home Entertainment 1997) – shoot the captors and rescue the prisoners!

Metal Gear Solid (Konami/Konami 1999) – infiltrate the terrorist group Foxhound and complete your mission by extreme stealth!

Nuclear Strike (3DO/3DO 1997) – learn about military hardware and zap the Indo-Chinese!

Oddworld: Abe's Oddysee (Oddworld/GT Interactive Software 1997) – rescue the slaves from Rupture Farms, the biggest meat-processing plant in Oddworld. (And maybe save the universe. Discover who the Chosen One is and how morality relates to cosmic justice.

Oddworld: Abe's Exoddus (Oddworld/GT Interactive Software 1988) – rescue the slaves whose tears, extracted by electronic torture, flavour the factory's best-selling brew!

Resident Evil (Capcom/Virgin Interactive Entertainment), *Resident Evil: Director's Cut* (3DO/3DO 1997), *Resident Evil 2* (Capcom/Virgin Interactive Entertainment 1998), *Resident Evil: Survivor* (Capcom/Eidos Interactive) – find your missing companions, explore the chilling mystery of the Haunted House/demon-possessed Town (Hall of Justice/Police Station) and discover the history and effects of the ghastly Death Viruses.(es)!

Silent Hill (Konami/Konami 1999) – search for your lost daughter and try to see the truth through the mist of evil!

Space Hulk (The Spice Factory/Electronic Arts 1996) – rid the space hulks (abandoned spacecraft drifting in space) of their evil inhabitants and make them safe!

Tenchu Assassins (Stealth Tenchu Assassins) (Acquire/Activision 1998) – as a ninja assassin, complete your mission by stealth and cunning against brute force and aggression!

Tomb Raider (Core Design/Eidos Interactive 1996) – explore the tombs of vanished civilisations, find the parts of the mysterious talisman and pit your wits and agility against the tomb-protectors, the rival-seekers, and anything else that needs tackling!

Tomb Raider II: Dagger Of Xian (Core Design/Eidos Interactive 1997) – get the Dagger of Xian before someone else does!

Tomb Raider III: Adventures Of Lara Croft (Core Design/Eidos Interactive 1998) – travel through London, the South Pacific and the Antarctic wastes to find the lost artefact that will explain the mystery of the gene-altering rock and the frozen sailor!

Tomb Raider IV: The Last Revelation (CoreDesign/Eidos Interactive 1999) – discover how to put Egyptian death-god Set to rest, and escape the vengeance of your past enemy!

Tomb Raider Chronicles (Core Design/Eidos Interactive 2000) – navigate four past adventures of hero Lara Croft's that introduce her enemies and friends!

Mysteries

Colony Wars (see above)
Dark Forces (see above)
Discworld (Psygnosis/Psygnosis 1995) – solve the puzzles and explore a zany world!
Discworld 2 (Perfect Entertainment/Psygnosis 1997) (see above)
Discworld Noir (Perfect Entertainment/GT Interactive 2001) (see above)
Final Fantasy VII (see above)
Final Fantasy VIII (see above)
Metal Gear Solid (see above)
Oddworld: Abe's Oddysee, Oddworld: Abe's Exoddus (see above)
Over Blood (Electronic Arts/Electronic Arts 1997) – discover who you are, where you are, and why you are awakening from cryogenic sleep...
Resident Evil, Resident Evil II & III (see above)
Silent Hill (see above)
Tomb Raider I, II, III, IV, and *Chronicles* (see above)

Since the focus of this study is to find out how traditional moving-image storytelling and interactive games design relate to each other, the emphasis is finally on the titles which have features in common with movies. Of these, *Final Fantasy*, *Oddworld* and *Tomb Raider* fall into all three study categories, and it is perhaps not surprising that these are also the top best-sellers. *Discworld, Metal Gear Solid, Resident Evil, Silent Hill* and *Tenchu Assassins* fall into two out of three categories and also sell steadily. *Metal Gear Solid, Resident Evil, Silent Hill, Tenchu Assassins and Tomb Raider* are all played in Real Time 3D (RT3D) navigable environments – that is, animated environments where the character(s) can move freely around the virtual location, steered by the player. *Final Fantasy* uses a mixture of 2D animation backgrounds and 3D figures and environments, *Oddworld* uses 2 1/2 D characters, animated with a model-animation look, moving across background screens, and *Discworld* uses 2D animated characters which can be steered around 2D painted sets.

Analysis focuses on how the relationships between plot, presentation, characters and player work, and how these correspond with more traditional dramatic adventure structures and rhetoric.

Figure 1. Final Fantasy VII (Squaresoft/Squaresoft 1999).

Final Fantasy VII – *fight to save the planet!*

Final Fantasy VII is an interactive, fighting fantasy drama, where the player controls first Cloud Strife, a former soldier turned rebel, then, as they join his mission to save the planet by toppling the tyrannical corporation Shinra, a chosen member or members of a team of helpers, each of whom has different combat skills. Cloud Strife seeks Sephiroth, his mentor, the greatest of all martial artists (who is apparently in the grips of dementia and destroying all he touches) in order finally to overcome the Shinra, who are draining the Mako life-energy of the planet so as to supply power for the Metropolis-like city of Midgar. *Mako* is the natural force created by the returning spirits of the dead completing the cycle of being, and sustaining the planet.

The characters inhabit a rich and varied storyscape, incorporating elements of Fritz Lang's *Metropolis* (Germany, 1926) and '80s, hard-edged science fiction design (*Blade Runner,* Ridley Scott, US, 1982; *Terminator,* James Cameron, US, 1984) with overtones of Japanese *Manga* video (for example, *Akira* [Otomo Katsuhiro, Japan, 1987], *Armitage III* [Hiroyuki Ochi, Japan, 1995]) alongside elements of pastel fairy tale, fantasy and sword-and-sorcery landscape. The episodes of story, between highly abstract and complicated interactive combats with monsters of all kinds, are rendered through prerecorded animated dramatic action and dialogue sequences (text and spoken word) using digital versions of both live action and animated (2D) film storytelling techniques and approaches. The prerecorded story sequences are triggered through choices of dialogue response made by the player on behalf of the characters inhabiting the storyworld.

"I'm looking for someone.
I can't be on the dance floor alone."

Figure 2. Final Fantasy VIII (Squaresoft/Squaresoft 1999).

The player can control (directly, using a control device) the direction Cloud Strife goes in to find these characters, or the line of enquiry he and his companions pursue when they have the answer to a question (by selecting dialogue boxes from a menu in the margin of the story screen). Otherwise, player interaction consists of participating in the fight sequences.

Final Fantasy VIII
Final Fantasy VIII is an interactive fighting fantasy drama, where the player controls Squall Leonhart, a 'lone wolf' at the top of his training class (along with equally talented but undisciplined Seifer Almasy) as a 'Gardens' mercenary, on the 'Seed' program. A pre-cut scene (Full Motion Video, FMV) of Squall and Seifer in a training sword-fight ends with Squall receiving a cut on the face from Seifer, setting the game-tone for fierce rivalry between the two. However, through dialogue (grey text on white) with other characters, and private thoughts (text on transparent background) or asides (text, visible to the player but not the other characters), it slowly becomes clear in the course of the action that while everyone else sees Seifer only as a show-off and troublemaker, Squall identifies with him to some extent, respecting his ability, drive and ambition if not his methods.

Training missions and fighting missions involve up to three additional characters in a team, set against the rest of the world, where the number of cities to visit and exercises to work on can appear convincingly limitless. Costume, hair, look and manner of speech are close to the Japanese Manga/Anime futuristic action style, and FMV graphics – like the character animation – are relatively smoothly integrated with in-game graphics. You navigate your characters across screens, and enter environments via a 3D interface. Personality and background are also suggested through graphic-novel or chat-room-style textual ' idioms' such as 'dunno' for 'don't know', 's'up' for 'what's up', 'bout' for 'about' in the speech of some characters.

The game involves a good deal of dialogue, and takes a relatively long time to play, moving slowly compared with adrenaline-driven skills or beat-'em-up and shoot-'em-up titles. Dialogue scenes are the means of revealing both plot and character, as they are in movies or novels, and like these traditional media the plotlines function as essentially linear, though they lead to interactive combat scenes, as they do in *Final Fantasy VII*. The experience seems to flow more like a novel than a movie or adrenaline-driven game, with a similar sense of pace and ramified plot. However, the characters lack the depth of novel characters, being closer to fairy-tale, comic-book or graphic-novel tradition. The four most central characters show some development – as the adventure progresses, they reveal a variety of moods and aspects via reflective (textual) exposition and social interaction, through adversity, victory and emotional conflict.

Final Fantasy VIII relies more on the fantasy-pulp-novel tradition than *Final Fantasy VII*, which seems to have emerged from the world of Japanese 2D animation. The game is comparatively low on puzzles. The predominance of printed text as storytelling medium coupled with the heavy reliance on dialogue to sustain interest/suspense accentuates kinship with the experience of reading fiction, rather than cinematic engagement, while the combat feature functions like an 'add-on' to what is essentially an extended animated graphic novel. Active combat is the reward for negotiating the rather slow and static dialogue scenes.

Oddworld: Abe's Oddysee – *rescue the slaves from Rupture Farms, the biggest meat-processing plant in Oddworld! (And maybe save the universe.)*

In *Abe's Oddysee* the player takes control of Abe, who has discovered that now all the cattle have been used up, he and his fellow Mudokan factory slaves are next on the list of pie ingredients. The player, Abe – unarmed and vulnerable – has to use cunning, athletic skill and precise timing to outwit vicious predatory half-crocodilian guards who gloat every time they inflict harm, while bringing his stupefied and passive brother-slaves to safety as best he can. The player can cause Abe to communicate with the Mudokans in a variety of simple but effective ways (familiar from 2D animation). Abe uses voice only, no text, in the tradition of 'Loony Tunes' Mel Blanc characterisation. To his limited but adequate range of laconic remarks, the slaves respond in apathetic or listless but appealing tones, as they obey Abe's injunctions to follow him.

The interactions between characters employ a wide range of traditional 2D animation techniques, from characterisation through movement and voice, to effects (such as the wreath of circling, warbling birds, which symbolises the gate to freedom, or the reassembling featheriness and little joyful chord which herald Abe's rebirth whenever he 'loses a life') against expertly realised, moody, colour-rich, varied backgrounds. The plot thickens when Abe discovers he is 'the chosen one' and has to make moral choices on which he is judged when he faces final extinction or resurrection at the end of the game. The drama also features transformation of identity – Abe discovers he can take over, and take on, the persona of the guards, turning their own weapons on his enemies. The presentation to the 'audience'/player is left-to-right motion across a fixed stage-like screen; when Abe reaches the right-hand edge or goes through a door, the screen changes to the next 'set', which he traverses in turn. He can retrace his steps, in which case he returns to the previous screen. However, each screen contains independently animated elements, so the background remains lively. Abe tells his own story in flashback in (verse) voice-over between action sections.

Resident Evil/Resident Evil 2

In *Resident Evil*, the player takes the role of either Jill Valentine or Chris Redfield, members of a special-forces squad alpha team. In search of the lost Bravo helicopter troop, they enter an apparently deserted lonely mansion. In the role of Jill or Chris, plagued by the almost unkillable zombies that inhabit the mansion, you explore the gothic environment and discover, bit by bit, through scraps of diaries and hidden notes from an unwilling scientist, what happened to the previous incumbents: they have been caught in a complex genetic engineering experiment. Your quest is to find your

Figure 3. Oddworld: Abe's Oddysee (Oddworld/GT Interactive Software 1997).

missing squad members, and escape the house of horrors – but the plot thickens when you discover that squad leader Albert Wesker is in fact in league with the experimenters, and that you have become a part of their perverted mission to develop and test new combat skills. The player controls the character's combat prowess and can direct her or him to have (prerecorded) conversations (involving dramatized scenes) with the occasional people they meet in the house (voice only, no text). The virtual camera hovers at a consistently very high angle, which shows the character the player is controlling in the environment she or he is traversing. The virtual camera strategy does not correspond with the conventions of normal action cinematography, and figures pass from one 'set' to another through abstract doors. The camera normally remains at ceiling level looking down, and jumps into medium close-up, over-the-shoulder shots for combats with zombies and other monsters.

In *Resident Evil 2* the player takes the role either of Claire Redfield, Chris's sister, who is searching for her brother, or Leon, a new recruit to the police force of the town neighbouring the terrible house of *Resident Evil*. The town is now overrun with zombies – the question is, are they suffering from the ghastly 'T' virus which has somehow spread, or is this the new 'G' strain? If so, what are its effects? What has happened to Chris and Jill? This time round, the characters are realized through much more impressive synthetic acting techniques, modelled on live action with some graphic novel/comic book qualities in the mise en scène – a style not unlike that of *Batman* (Tim Burton, US, 1989), *Dick Tracy* (Warren Beatty, US, 1990), *Bram Stoker's Dracula* (Francis Ford Coppola, US, 1992), *The Flash* (Robert Iscove, US, 1995), or *Judge Dredd* (Danny Cannon, US, 1996) – and great attention is paid to the small and convincing detail, while the virtual camera adopts some of the conventions of normal action- and suspense-film shooting strategies, as, for example, exploited in *Jurassic Park* (Steven Spielberg, US, 1993). The angles vary considerably and show the character moving through three dimensions – forward into the screen, out toward the spectator and across the set.

There is a soundtrack, which exploits some of the possibilities of film music. The sets, like the mise en scène (staging for the camera), tend away from graphic-novel style toward classic '50s interior Hollywood film design (particularly the marble hall of Orson Welles's *Citizen Kane* (US, 1941), coupled with '70s, '80s and '90s New York 'mean streets' exteriors e.g. Martin Scorsese's *Mean Streets* (US, 1973) *Taxi Driver* (US, 1976), *After Hours* (US, 1985), *Raging Bull* (US, 1990) and David Fincher's *Seven* (US, 1997), with a slight Midwest small-town feel to the layout. The style of shooting and editing is of the traditional continuity kind, familiar from classic Westerns – for example *The Searchers* (John Ford, US, 1957), and thriller drama/melodrama and its descendants – for example, *Sunset Boulevard* (Billy Wilder, US, 1950), *North by Northwest* (Alfred Hitchcock, US, 1959) and *The Haunting* (Robert Wise, GB, 1963).

Resident Evil: Survivor

As Vincent, you find yourself emerging alone, with no memory of why you are here or even who you are, from the wreckage of a crashed helicopter. As you navigate the Midwest township you find out that the population has been infected by the T-virus – which, it turns out, you released in an act of vengeance. Like *Resident Evil* and *Resident Evil II, Resident Evil: Survivor* is built on the structure of exploration of a 'house (or township) of horrors', long popular in Gothic novels from Horace Walpole's *Castle of Otranto* (GB 1764), Ann Radcliffe's *Mysteries of Udolpho* (GB, 1794) and Jane Austen's spoof' on them, *Northanger Abbey* (GB, 1818), through Daphne du Maurier's *Rebecca* (GB, 1938), quickly filmed by Alfred Hitchcock (starring Laurence Olivier and Joan Fontaine, US, 1940), and onward. The genre has continued popular in the cinema, with such examples as William Castle's *House on Haunted Hill* (US, 1958) featuring 'Energo', the illuminated skeleton-on-wires who swept out from the proscenium and over the heads of the audience during the show, Robert Wise's *Haunting* (GB, 1963), John Carpenter's *Hallowe'en* (US, 1978), or Tim Burton's *Edward Scissor-Hands* (US, 1990) and *Sleepy Hollow* (US, 1999), which take the audience through an environment peppered with shocks, predators, the supernatural and the unexpected. The camera strategies and cinematic approaches of the earlier *Resident Evil* titles are applied, though the urban environment has more detail and more complex lighting effects.

Tomb Raider- explore the tombs of vanished civilisations, find the parts of the mysterious talisman and pit your wits and agility against the tomb-protectors, the rival seekers, and any other surprise that needs tackling!

The player controls Lara Croft, British athlete and amateur investigator extraordinaire, who undertakes – just for the sport of it – to enter a series of increasingly puzzle-ridden, maze-like tomb environments populated by very aggressive creatures, in order to recover – with her outstanding agility, puzzle-solving and sharp-shooting skills – a talisman for Jacqueline Natla of Napa Valley. Lara has such manoeuvrability, and she moves at such speed, that the player first needs to get to know her in her huge stately home and learn how to work with her. Here Lara addresses the player directly (spoken voice only) – a ploy that facilitates smooth fictionalisation and identification. Lara helps the player learn the manual skills necessary to deploy all her powers, in a setting which projects the personality of a young English gentlewoman scholar/athlete who is serious about her music and library as well as her swimming pool and gym.

The tomb-raiding adventure is preceded by prerecorded pseudo-widescreen computer-animated video sequences, where Lara is invited to take on the challenge, and where she treks through the mountains to her first mysterious tomb (whose mouth looks very like the rock-wall entrance to the Sanctuary of the Grail in Steven Spielberg's movie *Indiana Jones and the Last Crusade* (US, 1989). Lara, unlike other adventurers (such as Beth in *Excalibur* – see below), does not walk; she runs everywhere, unless the player chooses to exert the slowing-down function on the joypad. Each tomb setting is different from the last – much in the style of *Journal Tintin* strip-illustrated adventures (such as Rosinski/Van Hamme's *Thorgal* series, 1985-).

The locations, all underground, are complex, detailed and exciting to explore, not just because they are populated by attackers, but also because they function like imaginative, varied and colourful filmsets in the tradition of *Conan the Barbarian* (John Milius, US, 1982) or *Indiana Jones and the Temple of Doom* (Steven Spielberg, US, 1984) – themselves drawing on the adventures of heroes such as Captain Marvel (such as *The Scorpion*, Republic Pictures, US, 1941) and his descendants. The emphasis is on the mythic quality of the environment, and the features that contribute to the drama and tension, rather than on realism or naturalism. As Samsel & Wimberley, in their book, *Writing for Interactive Media*, point out:

> Interactive presentations, just as other media, gain their appeal as much by the ways in
> which they depart from reality as by the ways in which they mimic it... The technophile

who believes that full-motion video and the holodeck are natural progressions of an aesthetic principle that demands the reproduction of reality misunderstands what it is that makes make-believe different from reality. A technology that perfectly mimics reality cannot be satisfying as a storytelling form...The differences between the story world and the real world are crucial to the participating experience of all media. Radio, novels, plays, and films, all failing in some respect of mimesis, require their audiences to use imagination. Future storytelling technologies will require the same. (Samsel & Wimberley, 1988: 155)

In *Tomb Raider*, Lara (the player) has to fathom how to negotiate the architecture and rockscapes themselves in order not only to pursue her quest but also to get herself out of these dangerous subterranean realms. Between levels/tombs, prerecorded video sequences show how Lara reaches the next stage of her adventure, and provide new information for the plot she is uncovering. It transpires that Natla's motives are dubious, and there are many hidden agendas, which Lara has to penetrate in order to preserve her integrity and her life.

Lara is normally viewed in full figure but extreme close-up from behind, moving away into the screen (an angle rarely maintained long in traditional film), but the player can choose to switch to Lara's POV (Point Of View) and to survey her surroundings through 360 degrees. The player can also tilt and pan the virtual camera by using the buttons on the front of the joypad (operating the camera does not preclude controlling Lara's complex athletic moves). There are no human characters to talk to in the tombs, though Lara's (male) rivals occasionally appear and have to be gunned down. The soundtrack features Lara's footsteps plus music, which grows appropriately dramatic as the pace quickens or the plot thickens, in the tradition of Bernard Herrmann's score for *Vertigo* (Alfred Hitchcock, US, 1958), Basil Polidouris' composition for *Conan the Barbarian* (John Milius, US, 1982), Jerry Goldsmith's *Planet of the Apes* music (Franklin Schaffer, US, 1968) or Ron Grainer's *Dr Who* radiophonic work (BBC TV series, GB 1963-1997).

Tomb Raider II – *get the Dagger of Xian before someone else does!*
In the sequel to *Tomb Raider*, the player controls Lara Croft, who has updated her house by adding an outdoor commando course, as she traverses a wide variety of real-world locations (such as Venice) and underwater environments (such as a sunken cruiser), seeking out the Dagger of Xian. She has human rivals, with whom she does not speak but whom she has to kill, often to gain their weapons as well as defend herself. (In *Tomb Raider I* Providence left weapons and medipacs here and there in the underground environments themselves.) Lara can now use flares to illuminate scary, dark areas and she has acquired a few useful new moves – such as climbing up and down ladders or scaling walls.

The environments she traverses have meticulous detail (individual volumes in the library in Venice) and now include daylight, with skies and horizons – though they are more like precision architectural drawings than dramatic film-sets. Lara is still seen mainly from behind, moving away into the screen, but the virtual camera is distanced a little further from her, so the detail of her surroundings is more visible, but the connection of the viewer/player to Lara herself is not so intimate. The speed of the game is even faster than *Tomb Raider,* but there is virtually no characterisation or story – it is assumed that players will have got to know Lara in *Tomb Raider I*. On the whole, the aesthetic moves a few degrees toward naturalism, a few degrees away from fantasy and drama.

Tomb Raider III: The Dagger Of Xian – *travel through London, the South Pacific and the Antarctic wastes to find the lost artefact that will explain the mystery of the gene-altering rock and the frozen sailor!*

In *Tomb Raider III*, you steer Lara Croft, whose repertoire of athletic skills and moves has increased still farther, through a panorama of five exotic landscapes and cities, solving more and more intricate and mentally challenging puzzles as you fight back attackers and dodge pursuit, commandeering a series of vehicles – kayak, quad-bike, mine-car – to help you. After the second location (India) the other three can be tackled in any order, offering a new sense of freedom and variety. Although the plot is thicker than in *Tomb Raider II*, and there is a past relationship of enmity between Lara and her main pursuer, she is still a lonely character in a hostile landscape, seeking the talisman and using her (your) intelligence, speed and stamina to outwit her enemies. The environments are increasingly complex and architecturally detailed, once more edging further toward an imitation of the 'real' world rather than exploiting the expressive qualities of set design. Lara's theme music, familiar since *Tomb Raider*, still pervades the experience, and cinematic music is used to signal dramatic moments and intensify them.

Tomb Raider IV: The Last Revelation – *discover how to put Egyptian death-god Set to rest, and escape the vengeance of your past enemy!*

The Last Revelation draws even more obviously on adventure-movie conventions like the *Indiana Jones* series and its TV and video sequels and prequels (Steven Spielberg, US 1984 -) than its predecessors, with regard to plot structure and set. This title also motivates Lara more clearly than its predecessors through plot development from level to level – she begins by accidentally releasing the Death God Set, and must therefore undo her own rash deed before she can achieve her goal of finding the talismans. These levels are all located in the macabre setting which first gave Lara her soubriquet 'Tomb Raider' – in underground Egyptian burial chambers.

The effect is to concentrate attention and imaginative focus more on action and atmosphere than in *Tomb Raider II* and *III*, where the eagerness to offer a diversity of surroundings and demonstrate technical skill in rendering detail in real-time 3D animation (RT3D) detracted from the possibilities of atmospheric set design and optimum flow immersion in the narrative afforded by the unity of place, time and action.

In *The Last Revelation*, music and sound-effects are also used with an increased filmic consciousness, enhancing drama and encouraging the storyseeker/player to positively enjoy the aesthetics of the visuals and the sound. However, the quality of the graphics is comparatively rough, hardly doing justice to the potential of the rich

Figure 4. Tomb Raider (Core Design/Eidos Interactive 1996-2000).

set design itself. This is Lara's fourth adventure, and it observes the conventions the previous three have set up for themselves – somewhat more emphasis on energy and ingenuity than run 'n' gun, plus puzzles that challenge inventiveness and concentration as well as speed. Lara's character was established in *Tomb Raider I*, and she remains the intrepid and eccentric British adventurer, in the literary tradition of H Rider Haggard's heroes (*King Solomon's Mines, GB, 1885; She, GB,*

1887) and Arthur Conan Doyle's Professor Challenger (*The Lost World, GB, 1912; The Poison Belt, GB, 1913; The Land of Mist*, GB, 1926) – though with the difference that Lara is a young female. Camerawork includes cinematic anticipation aided by film - music – as Lara approaches a danger zone, the mise en scène allows the camera to anxiously scan the direction from which the danger is likely to come as the heroine enters it.

Tomb Raider Chronicles – *navigate four past adventures of hero Lara Croft's that introduce her enemies and friends!*
These shorter 'chronicles' are variations on the talisman-seeking theme, which take Lara through some familiar and some unfamiliar environments, calling upon her to solve a variety of puzzles and destroy a host of predatory attackers.
   Oddworld: Abe's Oddyssey, Resident Evil and *Tomb Raider* use a number of strategies both in storytelling and mise en scène developed for more traditional screen narrative/drama, as indicated by the references to film-titles above. Others, however, equally important and powerful, they fail to utilise.

2. Tradition and Innovation – Drama, Narrative and Narration on the Film, TV and Interactive Screen
In his book, *The Art and Science of Screenwriting* (GB, 1998), Philip Parker – who is approaching his subject from the angle of a practitioner as well as a tutor, not only as a scholar or theorist – summarises the most common types of screen narrative: 'linear', 'episodic', 'associative' and 'circular':

Structure
There are four basic structures available within screen narratives:

Linear
All the events of the narrative take place in chronological order, as if the camera had merely followed the action in real life, and the narrative was the edited highlights. This is the dominant form of screen narratives from *Fawlty Towers* to *The Lost World*, from *The Bicycle Thieves* to *Das Boot*. However, it has two distinct types:
• The simple linear narrative, in which all stories run in parallel in the same time frame as the main narrative story, e.g. *Gandhi*, *Speed*.
• The complex linear narrative in which a secondary story develops in a different time frame. This can be quite small in narrative time as in *Once Upon a Time in the West*, or be a major part of the narrative as in *The English Patient*, and *The Terminator*.

(Parker, 1998, 22-3)

Oddworld, Over Blood (see below, p. 79), *Resident Evil* and *Tomb Raider* all use this basic linear structure, where the essentially linear 'present' adventure is interspersed with prerecorded sequences offering the 'backstory' – the previous history leading up to the present of the beginning of the game.

Parker continues, describing a second screen format, 'episodic structure':

Episodic
A collection of discrete episodes form the narrative. Each episode can be viewed and understood on its own but its real narrative power rests on its being part of a series of episodes which form the narrative. This is the dominant form in television from *EastEnders* to *Heimat* but it is also present in feature films from *Kaos* to *Night on Earth*.

As with the linear narrative, there are two versions of the episodic narrative. The simple episodic narrative, in which each episode is told discretely and follows one after the other. Examples of this would be *The Bill*, *Colombo* or *The Canterbury Tales*. It is possible within one narrative to have episodes which reflect on, or relate to, each other in some way but nonetheless are structured as discrete episodes, e.g. *Rashomon*.

The complex or the multi-stranded narrative, in which a combination of stories are woven into the narrative, some of which are contained within the episode, while the others run across several episodes. Examples include *NYPD Blue*, *Northern Exposure*, *Boys from the Blackstuff*. (Parker, 1998, 22)

While *Tomb Raider*, *Resident Evil* and *Oddworld* represent an episodic structure, in that they each comprised, by 2001, a series of titles, PlayStation games *Broken Sword II, Discworld*, and *Final Fantasy VII* use versions of this structure inside each game. In the search for the story these become more or less convoluted depending on the routes the storyseeker chooses through the narrative. Like Parker's linear structure, this is a common form of narrative in the novel – for example, *Jane Eyre*, Charlotte Brontë (GB, 1848); *Bleak House*, Charles Dickens (GB, 1853); *The Moonstone*, William Wilkie Collins (GB, 1868); *A la Recherche du Temps Perdu*, Marcel Proust (France, 1913-27); *The Age of Innocence*, Edith Wharton (US, 1920); *Mrs Dalloway*, Virginia Woolf (GB, 1925); *The Lady in the Lake*, Raymond Chandler (GB, 1943); *Body of Glass*, Marge Piercy (US, 1991); *Snow Crash*, Stephen Neal (US, 1992); *The Family Tree*, Sheri S Tepper (US, 1997); *Someone to Watch Over Me*, Tricia Sullivan (GB, 1997); *All the World's Parties*, William Gibson, (US, 2000) – a form thoroughly familiar in Western culture. *Jane Eyre, Bleak House, The Moonstone, Swann's Way, The Age of Innocence, Mrs Dalloway* and *The Lady in the Lake* have all been adapted for the screen, which, since the growth of popularity of the 'feature-length' cinema movie in the 1930s, has assimilated many of the functions and story-structures of the novel, and used them as a pattern for new screen stories.

Parker describes his third category of screen formats, the 'associational structure':

Associational
Here the narrative is formed from a series of moments which are linked by common elements and do not rely on chronology or episodic relationhips to produce their meaning or effect. This is the dominant form of advertising, which promotes everything from cars to ecology. It is also evident in animation and short films e.g. *Sunsets*, *The Old Man and the Sea*. However, it has been used on longer narratives, e.g. *Koyaanisqatsi*, *Blue*. (Parker, 1998, 23)

Broken Sword II, *Final Fantasy VII* and *Oddworld* use associational narrative as a secondary structure. In novels, it is the basic form of 'stream of consciousness' and much 'post-modern' fiction – James Joyce, Stevie Smith and Virginia Woolf habitually worked with it, and most 20th-century novels of the drug culture exploit it, from William Burroughs' *The Naked Lunch* (US, 1959) through Ken Kesey's *One Flew Over the Cuckoo's Nest* (US, 1969) and Hunter S Thompson's *Fear and Loathing in Las Vegas* (US, 1967) to Jeff Noon's *Pollen* (GB, 1995), Tricia Sullivan's *Someone to Watch Over Me* (GB, 1997) or Viktor Pelevin's *Clay Machine Gun* (Russia 1996, GB 1999). In film, associational structures predominate in surrealist work such as Buñuel's *Phantom of Liberty* (France, 1974) but are also fundamental in the work of Andrei Tarkovsky, such as *Mirror* (USSR, 1974), and Sergei Paradjanov – *The Colour of Pomegranates* (USSR, 1969). They are an important base for Welles' 'cinema classic' *Citizen Kane* (US, 1941) – though this film also employs all the other structures Parker summarises. We are thoroughly used to associational editing – where the story moves from an element of a scene or place directly to a parallel element in another scene or place (a technique early developed in English prose fiction) – as part of screen storytelling. It is subtly used by Alfred Hitchcock, overused by television melodrama and standard fare in, say, James Cameron's work – for example, *Terminator* (US, 1984), *Alien* (US, 1986), *Abyss* (US, 1989) – as well as the George Lucas' *Star Wars* series (US, 1977-97) and cult movies such as *Forbidden Planet* (Fred McLeod Wilcox, US, 1956) and *2001: A Space Odyssey* (Stanley Kubrick, GB, 1968) – films which were the pabulum of many, if not most, late-20th-century games designers.

The effect of associational narrative is usually to manipulate the audience response into being convincingly subjective and involving – to allow the reader or audience to feel as though the experiences on the page or screen are their own. By disobeying the rules of straightforward linear narrative, the narration obliges readers/perceivers to be active in following (or making) the associations necessary to understand why one sequence follows another, and they therefore seem to participate strongly in the experience and emotions (or mind) of the protagonist/characters, who is/are also trying to make sense of input received. *The X-Files* TV show/films (Chris Carter, US, 1993-, Ten Thirteen Productions/20th Century Television) habitually use this technique, to great effect.

Parker offers a final screen story structure – the 'circular':

Circular
Here the narrative is formed from repeated events. This has been used in one-off narratives such as *Groundhog Day* and the various episodes of *Road Runner*. However, its major contemporary use is in the form of interactive games from *Super Mario* to *Doom*. (Parker, 1998: 23 contd.)

Broken Sword II, *Discworld*, *Final Fantasy VII* and *Resident Evil* include *circular* structure, though falling into it is usually the result of a failure of skill on the part of the player (*not* defeating the monster and therefore having to try a different path) or of a 'dead end' in a branch in the narrative/physical environment (the path does not lead to achieving the quest, the object is not in the place where you are seeking it). Circularity is a fundamental structure in *Excalibur* – the characters with whom its hero, Beth, interacts in her search for King Arthur's vanished sword, as often as not tell her she has to go back and re-explore a section of her route, picking up, on the way, some object she did not know she needed when she passed it before – she may not even have realised it existed.

The necessity of backtracking without much motivation – such as might be provided by identification with the protagonist and the wish to help her in her plight, or reward in terms of solving a mystery which contributes to the understanding of the story, or even reaching a new prerecorded backstory sequence – can make this, and titles like it, a tedious game. Playing it is a bit like playing the boardgame of chance, *Snakes & Ladders,* where players cast dice to move forward a number of squares – if they land on the head of a snake, they slide back down the board and lose ground; if they land at the foot of a ladder, they zoom up it and jump ahead. But *Excalibur* is an excessively prolonged seesaw of accident, without the element of competition against another player which incites players of games of chance to be interested in the outcome. In *Excalibur*, the strongest sensation is simply that the hapless player is the toy of Fortune, entirely and frustratingly at the mercy of an inscrutable Fate.

By contrast, the movie *Groundhog Day* (Harold Ramis, US, 1993), which uses a circular structure very successfully, relies heavily on character exposition and the development of relationships to engage the audience. Although the protagonist (a slick and exploitative media person, Phil) becomes stuck in a time-loop, condemned to live the same day over and over, he is smart enough to realise that he can exploit his advantages, using the experience of each successive visit to the day to manipulate the people he interacts with – particularly Rita, his producer, whom he decides to seduce – to improve his position. His characteristically selfish approach has the interesting dramatic effect of forcing him to get to know Rita's taste (so as to manipulate her) and pretend to be the kind of (nice) guy she might actually be attracted to. Each time Phil makes a tactical error or expresses an opinion Rita disapproves of, he is cunning enough to change his attitude at that point in the interaction next time round. The audience is drawn in by the drama – will Phil really become nice and win his reward, the girl (Rita), and everyone be happy ever after? Or will Phil become a real villain, pretending to be someone he is not, and break Rita's heart? Will Rita see through Phil (in time)? How will it affect her, and their relationship, if Rita discovers Phil's deception just as he is becoming sincere? In terms of story, without this interplay between the characters – and therefore their fates – the circular structure would be more frustrating than intriguing, as it often is in interactive titles. There is, however, no intrinsic reason why *Groundhog Day*'s successful approach should not be exploited by adventure games.

Episode 3.48 of the popular cult TV series *Xena Warrior Princess*, 'Been There, Done That' (Andrew Merrifield, Universal Television Enterprises Inc, US, 1998), uses a circular formula, where there is a logistics problem to be solved (someone has to arrive against apparently impossible physical odds at a specific time, at a specific place, in order to prevent an irrevocable step which will precipitate tragedy). Xena, with Gabrielle and Joxer, her companions, relives the same day until Xena can work out a strategy to outwit Destiny and avert the loss of life. Xena's repetitions of the day's events finally result in success, as from each failure she learns more about the complex balance of cause and effect in the social environment; but this is not just a personal triumph against hard odds – it is the resolution of the plot in traditional storytelling terms. When Xena does succeed, the tale (loosely based on Shakespeare's *Romeo and Juliet*) ends happily – the girl (misled by circumstances) is prevented, at the crucial moment, from taking poison, so that girl and boy are united and their families call off their vendetta, which has been the root cause of the killings Xena has laboured to forestall.

In Tom Tykwer's film *Run Lola Run* (Germany, 1999), Lola has three chances to live through a few crucial hours in her life and her boyfriend's, competing with time to achieve a happy ending. Because the first version of her day ends in shocking bloodshed, the audience is drawn into willing Lola to find a way of dealing with events that will bring about a more traditional movie 'happy ending', in the subsequent versions of her day, identifying with her drive to save her boyfriend from disaster. In addition, Tykwer uses a dazzling panoply of cinematic and animation visual strategies to provide aesthetic variation and changes of rhythm, from shifts in point of view, and the use of different close-ups and subjective camera angles in different tellings of the 'same' incidents, to a highly sophisticated soundtrack.

Repetition in interactive titles rarely if ever shows any of this sophistication and inventiveness in developing plot and character, or using a variety of narrative strategies to hold attention, and they usually fail to grip as screen entertainment. The story and character elements are thoroughly subordinated to the puzzle-solving, run 'n' gun, steering and navigational problems as ways of engaging the player.

It is striking that in 1998, Parker cites *Groundhog Day* as a 'one-off' circular' movie, while by 2001, the 'repeating' structure is a well-understood screen form. This is surely partly attributable to the circular form's familiarity by then from computer and console games, where repetition is a built-in factor, since a player's failure to solve a problem or achieve a goal causes them to 'lose a life' (literally the life of their character), and sends them back to go through the sequence again. In the examples cited, film uses traditional techniques to make something formally engaging out of what in the games world is a frustrating necessity, dictated by lack of skill – very far from an intriguing structural device for narration.

Parker concludes his summary of effective movie structure by noting:

> Each structure can be used as the basis for narrative construction. They can also be used
> in conjunction with each other. However, in working with two structural forms you need
> to be sure which will dominate the narrative and which will play the role of adding
> variety to the dominant form. For example, *Pulp Fiction* is an episodic narrative with
> circular events adding a beginning and end and allowing references to elements of each
> separate episode to be made throughout the narrative. (Parker 1998, 23 contd.)

This is a clear way of distinguishing between genres – where one of the four structures (linear, episodic, circular, associative) predominates, the audience will tend to recognise its features and rules as generic, and so be able to follow the story easily.

The Spatial Organisation of Narrative

Of the four standard narrative formats Parker offers, in fact the popular choice for console games has been *linear*, although flashbacks to a backstory are a frequent substitute, in the form of a prologue, for any real story structure at all (*Space Hulk, Excalibur*). *Episodic* structure is the one most frequently exploited in titles which attempt to create drama through the interaction of a protagonist with characters in the environment she or he traverses (*Discworld, Excalibur, Broken Sword, Final Fantasy VII & VIII, Silent Hill*). This is probably because the potential for the protagonist (player/storyseeker) to react in more than one way to a supporting character's dialogue, and the potential for new information to send the protagonist in alternative directions, tends toward a location-based 'spatial' story layout, where each storyspace (location) contains an episode, which must be completed before the player can proceed to find a new episode (the game *Zelda*, like *Super Mario*, uses this format).

Although this spatial layout is superficially like the place-based structure of most films, where episodes happen at different locations which connect to other locations through the action or through an associative link, in film narratives, by the time it reaches the screen, the sequence is fully predetermined. In 'interactive' storyseeking in the RT3D virtual environment, you can be encouraged to recombine locations in optional linear or associational sequences (*Discworld, Broken Sword II, Excalibur, Tomb Raider, Final Fantasy VII*). The environment has the potential to become a storyscape, which the storyseeker must explore in order to find the story, rather than purely a dramatic setting, contributing atmosphere, credibility and style (from naturalism to surrealism) as it usually is in film or television drama. In other words, the environment becomes an active and important ingredient in the storytelling itself.

This active potential of the location is exploited in *Oddworld*, which uses traditional animation techniques and aesthetics extended by digital technology to make Abe's environment constantly inviting and explorable as well as dramatically intriguing, appropriate and effective. Each exploration yields a reward, both in terms of skill and in terms of finding new story elements – immediately in saving a slave or two, in the long term, by bringing Abe closer to achieving his mission (in the later stages of the game his quest) and throughout, revealing prerecorded backstory, and new characters, or new relationships with old characters, bringing a new understanding of the tasks to be fulfilled, and explaining why Abe should be the one fulfilling them. The *form* of the narrative and its *plot* are thus very close together. Players, whether primarily story people or primarily games people, are both stimulated and satisfied by it.

Final Fantasy VII & VIII have many of the same satisfactions as *Oddworld*, but the combat sequences are abstracted from the actual parameters of the story – set in a culture where it is recognized that achievement depends on ascending through a stepped series of more and more difficult learning processes and tests of that learning, where physical dexterity is strongly linked with spiritual and mental progress. This culture is epitomised in martial arts, a frequent basis for Manga video as well as the Hong Kong and Taiwan 'Kung Fu' movies. The fairy-tale embodiments of these arts in the combat sequences of *Final Fantasy VII* connect with the story elements, not through unity of place, time or action, but as a continuing series of stages in the development of the player/protagonist, who is deemed ready for the next phase of the adventure when each combat, with its complex and changing strategic and skills demands, has been successfully negotiated. The skills-based relationship between player and protagonist developed here is also to be found in *Tekken II*, which has virtually no story elements, though it has strong differential characterisation in terms of power, skill and maturity (none in terms of life experience and attitude, emotional development, or relationships with others, except through combat).

Tekken II depends on a real identification of the player(s) with the skills of the fighters, hence their personas, to create any sense of involvement.

In 1998, Foursome Co produced a linear 2D video animation feature, *Tekken* (the movie), (Hunihisha Sugishima, Japan, 1997/8) with Sony Music Entertainment Japan, based on the Namco fighting game published for PlayStation. The video cassette jacket claims that (RD Vision, 1998) 'the awesome rendering power of state-of-the-art computers merges with the stunning graphic style and dynamics of anime in an adventure that will rip you right out of your living room... into the most incredible martial arts battle ever created! Each fighter has a name, and each has a story. Professional assassins, champions of justice, meet with one common goal: to prove their TEKKEN.' The movie places two of the *Tekken* characters, as children, in a traditional story world, and shows how they turn into heroes through a series of life-experiences which develop their spiritual and physical strengths. The movie provides the continuity of fictive emotional identification with a story hero – which the game does not. Despite Espen Aarseth's claim, in his book *Cybertext,* that '...in the adventure game: the user assumes the role of the main character, and, therefore, will not come to see this person as an other, or as a person at all, but rather as a remote controlled extension of herself' (Aarseth, 1997: 113), the success of and demand for movies based on games shows how gamers who in the games world are proving their own 'tekken' through their control of the game's cast of fighters without involvement in a storyworld, also have a desire to fill out their knowledge of their favourite characters' lives and backgrounds; to find an understanding of who they are, and of how they think and feel, through the traditional means of engaging screen storytelling.

Namco and Sony took the decision to provide these two aspects of adventure storygame in different packages – the active interaction in the console game, the storyworld in the linear video, which aims to 'rip you right out of your living room' by capturing your imagination, not your manual dexterity. Each format has an appeal of its own, but there is a wide area of overlap between. This kind of multipublishing of material grows easier and easier as digital technology facilitates producing and storing all the components in compatible digital formats, which can be translated directly into numerous media – video, game, TV, DVD, d-cinema, e-cinema and graphic novel, for example.

Final Fantasy VII, also a Japanese production, incorporates the story element in the game, taking the process of involvement with character into the storyscape, providing a kind of identification both of and with the protagonist(s), as players try to work out for themselves what is happening to the Spirits, while contributing actively to helping Cloud Strife save the planet, against odds which make the outcome uncertain. *In Final*

Figure 5. Tekken, II/III (Namco/SCEE 1995, 1996, 1998).

Fantasy VIII, with Squall, not only do you discover more and more about 'Garden's' plan to change the earth as you complete your missions – you also go through shifts in your relationship to Seifer and your team-mates, as their characters are revealed through their actions and responses under combat and other conditions. These discoveries are fleshed out and given some emotional affect through the rich animated prerecorded FMV scenes between levels.

The multilevel involvement created by alternating animated participatory story with evolutionary combats and sensuously animated, prerecorded episodes is afforded neither by traditional screen narration, nor by pure skills games. In *Final Fantasy VII,* both the finding of the story and the personal satisfaction of the player/storyseeker depend on combat skills acquired throughout the game.

The combats are not one-to-one fights – the player/storyseeker has to learn the skills of a team of players and deploy them appropriately against the various monsters encountered. Part of the process is discovering the monster's own strengths and weaknesses and preferred forms of attack – its characteristics – before the team gets destroyed, and responding strategically and with agility (dexterity), calling on supernatural aid where appropriate. *Final Fantasy VIII,* where you control a member of a mercenary team who has a developing relationship with a team-mate, and experiences a number of the traditional episodes of a dramatic hero's life between fighting missions and combats, incorporates more elements of dramatic, cinematic narrative than its predecessor – more dialogue, more central characters, more development in the relationships between them – and also a higher degree of 2D- and 3D-like action, which brings it closer to the look expected in games at the beginning of the 21st century, when problems of storage space and processing power were rapidly being overcome.

In both *Final Fantasy VII* and *VIII,* the *form* of the narrative and its *plot* are very close together, and players, whether primarily story people or primarily games people, become intrigued and involved by both. Like *Oddworld: Abe's Oddysee,* these titles combine effectively appropriate traditional elements of screen and animation storytelling with the skills-based and active storyseeking features enabled by digital interactive environments. In *Final Fantasy VII,* the focus is not on RT3D – it uses detailed and sophisticated traditional 2D animation techniques to create a rich and evocative visual storytelling style, which appeals to those who appreciate good animation, and enables fast and complex multiplayer combats but disappoints those who come to the console seeking full 3D experience of the sort to be found in the *Tekken* games world. The *Final Fantasy* games are feeling their way toward a form which marries animation, graphic novel and cinematic styles in a real-time 3D environment, and at the same time experimenting with plots that match the form. The *Final Fantasy* series does this explicitly, insofar as the serial numbers do not refer to a repeated environment (as in the *Discworld* series), a repeated motif (as in the *Resident Evil* series), a repeated situation (as in the *Tekken* series) or the same protagonist (as in the *Tomb Raider* series) – or, like *Oddworld,* repeat environment, motif, situation and character while refining and varying in-game interaction, puzzles, adversaries and artwork. The *Final Fantasy* numbered titles refer to the genre itself: the evolving and particular blend of epic hero-led drama and participatory graphic novel and animation storytelling with quasi non-diagetic (in other words, outside the story) combat.

In *The Art and Science of Screenwriting,* Parker explains concisely the operative relationship between *form* and *plot,* two of the traditional screen storytelling elements normal in film and very relevant to emerging image-based storyforms:

Figure 6. Final Fantasy VIII (Squaresoft/Squaresoft, 1999).

Form is the dramatic shape of the narrative while plot is the way the story and thematic elements are dramatically revealed within this dramatic shape. (Parker, 1998, p. 21)

.Active questions – which hold the whole narrative together – form the basis of framing plots. The following are examples of this type of active question:

- *The Romance* – Will the protagonists fall in love and at what cost?
- *The Thriller* – Will the protagonist/s survive the threat of death?
- *The Investigation*— Will the missing elements of a puzzle be found?
- *The Journey* – Will the protagonist/s complete their journey and why is it important?
- *The Revenge* – Will the debt be repaid and to whom?

- *The Contest* – Who will ultimately win and when?
- *The Disaster* – Who will survive?

These large active questions work to hold the whole narrative together. They provide a framework within which all the various stories can be told. However, for a narrative actually to work, active questions are raised and answered from moment to moment, from scene to scene, from sequence to sequence throughout the narrative.

The key purpose of the plot as a whole though is to work at the emotional level in terms of engaging the audience in the narrative's development. (Parker, 1998, 26-27)

Leaving aside for a moment the issue of emotional engagement, *Final Fantasy VI/VIII, Oddworld: Abe's Oddysee/Abe's Exoddus*, *Tomb Raider (I thru IV + Chronicles)* and *Resident Evil (+ II, III, IV)* all, to a greater or lesser extent, draw on *all* these traditional plot frameworks – with the notable exception of the Romance, in the sense that the players or storyseekers themselves are engaged throughout the adventure in posing a number of the active questions Parker formulates, and trying to find the answers. All four titles rank high in the consistent bestseller list, and an important ingredient in their success may well be their deployment of tried-and-tested plot devices, but in a mode which requires the storyseeker to be the active questioner exploring the 'plot' embedded in the storyscape of the gameworld. In this environment, the questions have to be asked, and answered, through exploring the narrative landscape, and the answers supply not only information about the story but also gradually define the genre in which the story is realized.

Of the games investigated here, only *Broken Sword II* and *Over Blood* actually call on the Romance tradition for structural support. Although *Final Fantasy VIII* includes some romantic moments, such as the 'ball-scene' – which could have been modelled on the grand ball in Disney's *Beauty & the Beast* (Gary Trousdale, Kirk Wise, US, 1991), and has some of that scene's aesthetic and sensual impact – these are incidental to the characters' passage through the storyworld, providing punctuation and emotional colouring, rather than being integral to the dramatic development of the story.

Broken Sword II deploys its Romance element in the most perfunctory way, although at first glance it may seem to be a formal kingpin.

Broken Sword II – save the kidnapped girl!

The player takes control of George Stobart, who searches for his girlfriend Nico – kidnapped by evil Dr Oubier and his henchmen, who are searching a Mayan landscape for an antique artefact (which Nico has in fact taken back to France). Characters are presented in a simulation of 2D animated film style, visually inspired by the classic *Tintin* series, and within the same field of story reference (Conan Doyle's 'Professor Challenger' again). Created as a comic strip in 1929 by Georges Rémi, whose commercial signature was 'Hergé' and who died in 1990, *Tintin* sold in the UK and the US in comic-strip-album form from 1958 onward, and was adapted for TV and film animation worldwide. The influence of Hergé's clearcut drawn style and subtle coloration on 2D animated adventure has been huge, and *Broken Sword II* is a tribute to the tradition.

Figure 7. Broken Sword II (Revolution Software/SCEE 1997).

However, the game tells its story in a navigable environment, using a range of camera angles, shots and setups – though these lack the variety and continuity cutting-strategy of traditional animated film, live-action film or TV adventure, when staging narrative dialogue. George can have (spoken) conversations with the inhabitants of the exotic landscape, which give him help in his mission, only if the player selects icons to cue the prerecorded dialogues. The result lacks narrative flow, and is very frustrating if the icon you activate produces irrelevant or uninteresting speeches, which it has a high chance of doing. Nico herself is scarcely a character, and the relationship between her and George is scarcely a matter of suspense or an arena for development (as it is in the relationship between Phil and Rita in *Groundhog Day* (Harold Ramis, US, 1993), or between Lola and Manni in *Run Lola Run* (Tom Tykwer, Germany, 1999). Their relationship is merely a defining aspect for George's quest – ostensibly for the kidnapped woman – of which the lost treasure provides the more dynamic focus.

In *Over Blood -discover who you are, where you are, and why you are awakening from cryogenic sleep* – the romance may at first glance appear to be more central. The player guides Raz (seen from behind, full figure, but able to survey his surroundings if the player deploys direction and tilt buttons on the joypad) from the moment he wakes from cryogenic sleep as he explores a *2001*-like environment (*2001: A Space Odyssey*, Stanley Kubrick, GB, 1968) to discover what he can about himself and his mission.

There is clearly some inspiration both in opening structure and film style from Franklin J Schaffer's *Planet of the Apes* (US, 1967) as well as *2001*. Raz finds a robot,

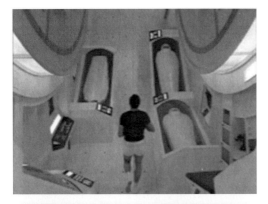

I have to warm this place up...

Figure 8. 2001: A Space Odyssey, Stanley Kubrick, GB, 1968)(top); Over Blood (Electronic Arts/Electronic Arts 1997).

which becomes his companion and helper, and the player can change protagonist and play the robot at will.

As Raz – who, it transpires, has no memory of why he is here or who he is (the robot has some) – explores the environment and manages to avoid death by hazard (from trap to temperature-change to attackers), he discovers that his former wife is held captive somewhere in this environment, though he has great difficulty in communicating with her. Her presence and his are both shrouded in mystery, which is only finally explained when Raz discovers – through long prerecorded animated video sequences – that he is the subject/victim of a complex experiment. He is a full clone of the scientist, Raz(1), who is hoping to produce the perfect human fighter. Raz1 has cloned several versions of himself, minus memories, to use as 'laboratory mice', and these are suspended in cryogenic sleep here in the sealed biogenic research facility waiting their turn for experimental testing. Raz2 (the protagonist), who is proving a skilful combat machine, seems likely to have a degenerative viral problem. Raz1 (the now mad scientist) lost his wife in an earthquake (which also woke Raz2 prematurely). However, Raz1 cloned his beloved and gave the clone the original memories of his dead wife. Now Raz2 has fallen in love (very peremptorily – not really in the game, but by assumption in the interludes) with Wife2. After the testing of Raz2 through forcing him to solve the puzzles of his environment and of his identity with only the aid of Pipo the robot, the player and the character are rewarded by the discovery that love is true.

At the very end of the final video sequence, when Raz1, out of jealousy, tries to destroy Raz2, Wife2, abhorring the violent Raz1, (who has turned his talents to perpetrating aggression) cleaves to Raz2, whom (presumably) she loves for himself. It is Raz1 who crumbles away through the mysterious degenerative virus Raz2 has been taught to fear.

Although Romance is used as a plot frame, the robot is by far the most engaging character in this protracted saga. This is because it has animated reactions of joy, anxiety, sorrow and anger, as well as the final pathos of being blown up in its attempt to help Raz2, the human white mouse trying to solve the maze puzzle. Raz2 and Wife2 are so primitively animated as human beings that they utterly fail to engage on the performance level. Pipo, on the other hand, comes from a long line of lovable sci-fi robot helpers, from Robbie in *Forbidden Planet* (Fred McLeod Wilcox, US, 1956) to the highly user-friendly R2D2 and C3PO in *Star Wars* (George Lucas, US, 1977-97).

Animation, Staging for the Camera, and Storyboarding

The art of the 2D animator has long refined the magic of giving life to *things*, to objects made of metal or other hard substances rather than flesh and blood, and there is an established tradition of imparting emotion to such objects through gesture and posture. John Lasseter's *Luxo Junior* (US, 1987) is a shining example of how successfully computer animation can carry forward the effective dramatic methods of its hand-drawn predecessors. Imbuing objects such as a desk-lamp (Luxo) or a robot, which have no 'real-life' living referent, with character, through expressive movement, is nearly always much more convincing than trying to make cartoon characters look like real people, who have a formidably complex range of ways to express emotion. No one really knows how dinosaurs moved, so it is easier, on the whole, to create a convincing 3D digital dinosaur from scratch than a convincing 3D computer-generated digital human – we expect humans to move like humans, and find them coarse and unbelievable if they do not.

Characters are revealed, in screen drama of every kind, through the mise en scène – staging of the action for the camera – whether the camera be virtual or actual. In *Over Blood*, there are three basic camera positions – tracking Raz2 or Pipo from behind close-up, mostly full-figure or extreme close-up; Raz2's Point Of View (POV) of an obstacle (such as the Pit); and reverse angle shooting, looking back at Raz2 who is face-on to the camera (for example, across the Pit). However, normal continuity shooting/editing strategies are not usually applied – there is no close-up of Raz2's face before the cut to his POV, for example, and the camera is not motivated by Raz2 or Pipo's glance, as it might easily be, and would certainly be in cinematic or televisual language.

Although the love story in *Over Blood* appears, in synopsis, central to the plot, in fact it is not really a part of the interactive experience *per se* – it forms a staged backstory which is played out in prerecorded computer generated animation between levels. This animation is unlike traditional animation, apparently aiming for a 3D effect and some naturalism, but automated, without traditional graphic aesthetics, characterisation or mise en scène. The design of the environment and characters harks back to *2001: A Space Odyssey* (Stanley Kubrick, GB, 1968) and *Planet of the Apes* (Franklin J Schaffer, US, 1967), but without the visual maturity and carefully structured camera POVs. Characterisation and dialogue are somewhere between graphic novel and generic science-fiction novel (rather than '50s B-movie) style, and the delivery is melodramatic and at times embarrassingly histrionic. Although the plot is complex, the dialogue-script, casting, direction and performance show no signs of the sophistication

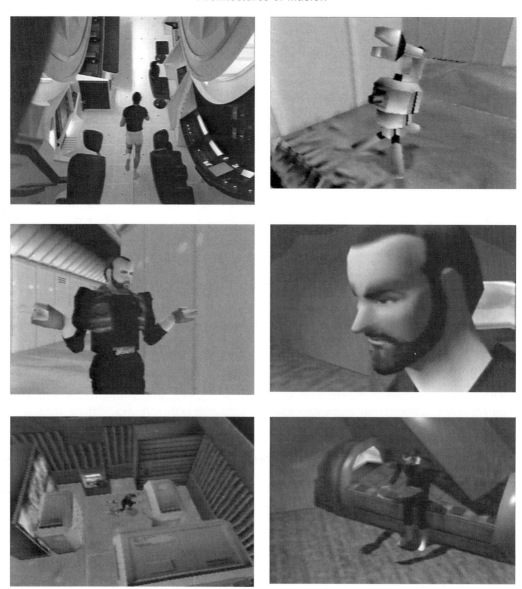

Figure 9 2001, a Space Odyssey (Stanley Kubrick, GB 1968)(top left); Over Blood (Electronic Arts/Electronic Arts 1997).

of radio, TV or cinema drama. The sequences draw on graphic novel and film storyboard techniques for presenting action, but do not deploy the traditional arts of film or television mise en scène, or use the (virtual) camera consistently, to create a smooth 'continuity' style of narration.

The effect is that in *Over Blood*, although the story is told, it fails to grip in the way live-action film or classic narrative animation does – for example, in features such as John Lasseter's *Toy Story* (US, 1995) and *Toy Story Two* (US, 1999), Disney Studios' *Aladdin* (Ron Clements, John Musker, US, 1992), 20th Century Fox's *Anastasia* (Don Bluth, Gary Goldman, US, 1997), Disney's *Mulan* (Tony Bancroft, Barry Cook, US, 1998) or Miyazaki's *My Neighbour Totoro* (Japan, 1987) and *The Princess Mononoke* (Japan, 1996). These, like Disney's classic *Snow White and the Seven Dwarfs* (Walt Disney, David Hand, US, 1937*)*, *Dumbo* (Walt Disney, Ben Sharpsteen, US, 1941) and *Bambi* (Walt Disney, David Hand, US, 1942*)*, use strategies familiar from classic film narration. They also use other devices, which until the 20th–century were only possible in cel animation, but have since entered live-action, digitally processed film – such as *Jurassic Park* (Stephen Spielberg, US, 1993), *The Mask* (Charles Russell, US, 1996), *The Fifth Element* (Luc Besson, France, 1997), *Judge Dredd* (Danny Cannon, US, 1997), *Titanic* (James Cameron, US, 1998), *Kundun* (Martin Scorsese, US, 1998) and *The Matrix* (Wachowski Brothers, US, 1999).

At the end of the first century of cinema, with the arrival of digital effects and image manipulation, the borderline between the entirely constructed, make-believe world of cartoon animation and the reality-based world of traditional, live-action shooting began to blur. The expectation as well as the potential of what moving-image narrative drama can deliver extended rapidly from that point on, affecting small-screen products (including console games) as well as big-screen ones.

Unlike *Oddworld* and *Final Fantasy*, *Over Blood* does not bring the form of the narrative and its plot together, and it fails – though it contains a complex story (mainly in the prerecorded FMV sequences) – to deploy the sophisticated, audiovisual techniques a storyseeker nurtured on screen narrative is familiar with and expects. Its interest and impact are substantially diminished by the lack of these devices, and this may partly explain its lack of commercial success. In many ways, the whole plot might make a very watchable movie – but without the devices of effective screen narration, including careful characterization and performance as well as fluent mise en scène, the complexity of the story in the end only interferes with the pace, and hinders the speed, of the game.

Tradition and Innovation – Narration

Stephen D Katz, like Philip Parker approaching screen arts and sciences from the point of view of a practitioner and tutor, summarises what he sees as the most central of the traditional techniques of screen storytelling in his book *Film Directing Shot by Shot* (US, 1991). He emphasises, in particular, the importance of shot flow and composition:

> Shot flow is the name given to the kinetic effect of a sequence of shots... often comprised of complex rhythmic and dynamic continuity relationships that... merge into a single unified structure. But no matter how intricate the relationships between shots, there are two essential ingredients that are fundamental to our understanding of visualisation: shot size and camera angle. There are also many other compositional elements familiar to artists from photography and painting that contribute to a sequence, but camera angle and shot size are the dominant physical changes that determine shot flow. (Katz, 1991,159)

The reliance of *Over Blood* on storyboarding techniques as an element in its final presentation has already been mentioned. A storyboard normally represents shots in a sequence which will eventually create flow; but the flow itself comes from the kinetic process of structuring the narration – staging the action and selecting the camera angles and movements and editing for continuity – not just determining the sequence of shots. However, it is in general more common for console-game, prerecorded animated sequences to offer something that reads like a storyboard than something that reads as a completed kinetic screen narrative. This is as true of the early *Tomb Raider* prerecorded sequences as the *Over Blood* ones, though by *Tomb Raider IV*, somewhat more cinematic language is employed. The choice of medium – highly computerized 3D animation which, though it moves, seems to be deployed rather amateurishly, not as a skilled narrative animator (say Miyazaki or Lasseter) would deploy it – may be partly responsible.

There is rarely a match between the graphic style of the prerecorded sequences and the graphics of the game itself – *Oddworld – Abe's Oddysee* is a notable and successful exception. Lara Croft is a far more sympathetic character inside her games world, with her motion-capture-based movement and her normal human voice (more skilfully characterised in *Tomb Raider I* than subsequently), than is the very different-looking, plasticized, computer-aided animated insect-featured Lara in the story interludes. There, she is characterised in an exaggerated 'cyberbabe' style somewhere between Dark Horse Comics and Manga.

The mismatch between the prerecorded sequences and the games themselves, both in animation quality and mise en scène, doubtless owes much to the way the games are produced, incorporating the requirement for prototype characters to pitch the concept before the product is made. However, storyboarding techniques used as a substitute for, rather than a sketch to prepare, continuity visual narration, when coupled with inconsistent physical characterisation, detract seriously from the titles' capacity to involve storyseekers at the level of dramatic screen narration. In particular, the crudity of the representation of humans, especially their facial expressions – compared, say, with the sophistication of the animation and mise en scène in *Anastasia* (Don Bluth,, Gary Goldman, 20th Century Fox, US, 1998) or *Toy Story*'s careful characterisation (John Lasseter, US, 1995/1999) – militates against the use of the close-up in its traditional role; a crucial one in engaging the storyseeker's emotions in the story.

On the importance of the face on the screen, Katz remarks:

> Television has greatly increased the use of the close-up. To compensate for the small size of the screen, the close-up is used to bring us into closer contact with the action. For dialogue sequences the shoulder-and-head shot has become the predominant framing. (Katz, 1991, 123)

When we are watching the small screen – as we most often are when we play a console game – we expect close-ups. We need them to help us identify, and identify with, the characters. The lack of them in console games works against the storyseeker's entering an emotional engagement with the protagonist.

Figure 10. Anastasia (Don Bluth, Gary Goldman, US, 1997).

The close-up has long been a great screen resource: one the theatre did not and does not share, and that can be used very powerfully to intensify emotion. Silent film, which, like console games, relies on visuals and action rather than dialogue to engage audiences, was a great exponent of the close-up – for example, *Broken Blossoms* (DW Griffith, US, 1919), *Nosferatu* (FW Murnau, Germany, 1922), *The Navigator* (Buster Keaton, US, 1924), *The Passion of Joan of Arc* (Carl Dreyer, France, 1926), *Sunrise* (FW Murnau, US, 1927) and *The Crowd* (King Vidor, US, 1928). Katz amplifies:

> In film the eyes have it. Jean-Luc Godard once said that the most natural cut is the cut on the look. The powerful suggestiveness of this gesture helps explain film's love-affair with winks, glances, stares, tears, squints, glares and the whole range of language that the eyes command.
>
> The eyes are perhaps the most expressive feature of the human face, communicating silently what the mouth must do largely with words and sounds. A look can tell us that an object out of frame is of interest, and it can tell us in which direction the object is located. In the same way that the focal length of the lens and the angle of the camera can place the viewer in a definite relationship with the subjects on the screen, the eye-line of a subject clearly determines spatial relations in the scene space.
>
> The close-up can bring us into a more intimate relationship with the subjects on the screen than we would normally have with anyone but our closest friends or family. (Katz, 1991, 123)

Although Western 2D animation and Manga video, which comes out of the tradition of graphic novels (and, further back, from the Japanese narrative, expressive or portrait woodcut), both rely heavily on the close-up, in the active, playable sections of console games it is almost never used. If it does occur (as it can sometimes do in passing in *Tomb Raider*, for example), it is so much a product of the impetus of the animated figure carrying out her movements and so little an element in staging, characterization or camera narration, that its effect is not to increase emotional engagement. The facial animation is so crude that it cannot invite the kind of intimacy Katz describes (above). In addition, following traditional cinematographic convention since the 1950s in photographing a female character (see, for example, *There's No Business Like Show Business* (Walter Lang, US, 1954, ph. Leon Shamroy), *The Seven Year Itch* (Billy Wilder, US, 1955, ph. Milton Krasner), *Tie Me Up Tie Me Down* (Pedro Almodóvar, Spain, 1989, ph. José Luís Alcaine), *Erin Brockovich* (Steven Soderbergh, US, 2000, ph. Ed Lachman), and traditional comic books and graphic novels featuring sexual human females or superfemales (Marvel Comics through Manga/Anime to Titan Books' *Aliens: Female War* (US, 1997), the point of focus in *Tomb Raider* is usually the female breast, that universal token of desire.

By contrast, *Resident Evil II* does recognise the power of the close-up, as it does of many of the devices of traditional screen language, deploying them as a formal part of the virtual shooting strategy. Staging action with edit points in mind and editing for continuity of action are two of these devices.

Of course, where the action is performed by animated (sometimes motion-captured and animated) figures in a computer-generated 3D 'set' or environment, the action is not 'staged' in the conventional sense. Lara Croft in *Tomb Raider* does not, for example, interact with other members of a cast, except in prerecorded dialogue sequences which are unalterable, or chases when they act like Lara's other (monstrous) opponents in the tombs. In *Tomb Raider II*, which moves towards naturalism, Lara kills humans and takes their weapons, but the action of taking them is extremely stylized, not staged naturalistically and rendered through continuity shooting and editing. Lara – who carries a pack to accommodate necessaries – has a choreographed move, in which she drops to her knees and reaches for the object, which then magically appears on a non-diagetic (outside the story) screen menu in a list of her accoutrements. When she stands up, it is assumed within the storyworld that the object is now in Lara's pack, and she can take it out by reaching for it, at the player's command, when it will appear in her hand. Where Lara does interact with human protagonists (for example, her rival Pierre and Jacqueline Natla, her 'employer'), it is either to try to shoot them (with the active help of the player, she kills Pierre) or through an uninterruptible, prerecorded dialogue sequence (FMV sequence) inside the game.

In *Resident Evil* the protagonist does have brief dialogue interactions with other characters, and though in *Resident Evil I* these are as stilted and uncinematic as the pre-recorded dialogues in *Over Blood* – largely because they rely more on storyboarding storytelling than on kinetic narration and animation techniques – in *Resident Evil II* the synthetic actors are 'directed' like real live-action actors; as are the claymation figures in the work of Nick Park (*The Wrong Trousers*, GB, 1993 and *Chicken Run*, (with Peter Lord)

Figure 11. Indiana Jones and the Last Crusade (Steven Spielberg, US, 1989); Tomb Raider (Core Design/Eidos Interactive 1996-2000(bottom 2 images)).

GB, 2000) and the 2D animated characters in *Anastasia* (Don Bluth, Gary Goldman, US, 1998) or the 3D digitally animated characters in *Toy Story* (John Lasseter, US, 1995/1999). The action is 'staged' (mise en scène) like traditional film action, with edit points facilitating continuity picture editing. *Metal Gear Solid* also uses the virtual camera to create the effect of cinematic mise en scène, in a semblance of continuity editing.

Katz explains this approach:

Edit points are 'placed' in the shot or at least anticipated by the director in the staging of action. There are three ways in which an edit can be made to preserve the continuity of action when two or more views of a subject are being combined. Suppose we have a shot of a boy running across the front lawn of his home and jumping over a hedge onto the sidewalk... The first shot runs the entire length of the action. Now we decide to cut to a new angle somewhere into the first shot. Here are the three options: 1) We can cut to the new shot at the point where the boy reaches the hedge and begins to jump; 2) We can cut to the new shot while the boy is in midjump; 3) we can cut to the new shot after he lands on the ground.

These are all acceptable edit points, but the common practice in the continuity style would locate the cut somewhere into the action rather than before or after the boy has left the ground. This tends to hide the cut and make the transition to a new shot invisible. The exact point of the cut is dependent on the subject and the editor's sense of movement.

Cutting on the action is found in virtually all types of sequences whether the subject of the shot is lifting a drink to his or her lips or merely turning his head or moving his eyes. Film-makers mindful of this essential editing strategy will stage action so that it will overlap an anticipated edit point between camera angles. (Katz, 1991, 154-5)

Katz is describing the film director's palette of strategies for creating a narration which will convince and hold an audience familiar with the screen language of the 20th century – a language which crosses over from live action to animation and *vice versa*, and which audiences familiar with it read so fluently that they easily forget that it has a rhetorical structure at all. However, as Katz emphasises, in fact, deploying that language is a complex combination of a number of processes: staging (for the camera); recording (image and sound); and presentation (ordering, through the editing process, during which sound and picture can be manipulated):

The visual challenge of staging is essentially a spatial problem – the ability to predict in three-dimensional space what will work on a two-dimensional screen. The spatial effect of a filmed sequence is particularly difficult to visualise because it is comprised of so many different fluid elements, such as the changing composition of the filmed image when the camera or subject is in motion. (Katz, 1991, 173)

This process of fluidity, which took a century to perfect, is very different from either the capture of poses and joining them together in an illusion of continuous movement of 2D animation, or the static 'strip' cartoon storyteller's art of captured moments in the characters' drama, given emphasis by exaggerated spatial arrangements within the frame and variety of graphic style. These animation and graphic-novel devices have, however, often been incorporated into late-20th-century storyboarding, and they seem to have found their way from there directly into console-games narration, where they are often used in an unmediated form, as a substitute for mise en scène rather than a schematic diagram or type of notation for the dynamic process of continuity staging, shooting and editing.

Figure 12. Metal Gear Solid (Konami/Konami 1999).

The direct use of storyboarding setups on the screen is not confined to interactive titles, however. Big-screen linear movies, which rely heavily on digital special effects, are always heavily storyboarded so that the final image can be assembled from disparate parts of the frame. This frame-by-frame approach can produce sequences which, even on the big screen, work more like graphic novels than traditional continuity-shot movies. Examples of this style would be *Johnny Mnemonic* (Robert Longo, US, 1998) or *The Matrix* (Wachowski Brothers, US, 1999). Both these films draw on the conventions of interactive console games, staging their action in sets which resemble the enclosed environments created in the 3D navigable worlds of the 1990s, where open skies and daylight sequences posed problems for the computer in the real-time handling of light sources. Highly storyboarded, digital effects-heavy films also use the murky colour-scales favoured by RT3D, which facilitate handling light in a synthetic imaging environment. *The Matrix* goes further, using shots and set-ups based on RT3D virtual camera movements to portray, in live action, using real actors, a world which, in the story, is one great virtual domain.

3. Big Screen/Small Screen –
– Cross-Fertilization between Film & Interactive Games

The Matrix (Wachowski Brothers, US, 1999) is in a number of ways a hybrid, a cross between the traditional cinema film and a game title. It has a conventional cast of characters and follows the hero pattern of the standard epic movie, but substitutes adrenaline-driven action and three-dimensional screen experience for depth of characterisation, character development and emotional engagement. By 2000, as noted earlier in examples such as *Tekken*, *Run Lola Run* and *Xena: Warrior Princess*, there was already a reciprocal flow between the small screen of the console (and computer) game and the big screen. Movies based on strip cartoons or comic books or graphic novels were not new – Roger Vadim's *Barbarella* (US, 1968), Warren Beatty's *Dick Tracy* (US, 1990), Tim Burton's *Batman* (US, 1989), and Robert Iscove's *Flash* (US, 1995) all transmute extant 2D paper characters into moving images, using live actors and real sets plus special effects. However, each finds its own style of narration – *Barbarella* exploits the new film emulsions, cameras and sound possibilities of the 1960s to achieve a lush, fantasy atmosphere, using continuity shooting and gorgeous, sensuous sets designed by Garbuglia to give the effects maximum impact as part of the story – for example, Jane Fonda's famous weightless striptease and the illusions-sequence of the Great Tyrant's Dream Bed, inside its transparent bubble. *Dick Tracy* lovingly reproduces colour from 1950s print media and uses prosthetic make-up to create the caricatured villains Tracy fights, borrowing traditional comic-book framing. *Flash* uses 1950s-toned sets and non-naturalistic lighting to create a timeless, placeless comic-book setting in which contemporary 1990s characters are rendered with the skills of 1980s movie-making. *Batman* exploits the fact that digital effects give a new range of shooting strategies to the live-action film-maker, many borrowed from traditional 2D animation.

Judge Dredd (Danny Cannon, US, 1996) makes the leap to presenting a film looking very like a console game, using the spatial possibilities of digital camera strategies and effects to offer what amounts to a grand shoot-'em-up/beat-'em-up on the big screen, but one where the audience watches rather than participates actively as the characters swoop on skybikes in evasive action through a 3D rendering of canyons of big-city apartment-blocks, spurting fire and brimstone.

The Fifth Element (Luc Besson, France, 1997) builds on some of the features of framing, setup and camera strategy developed in these earlier movies – also seen in Francis Ford Coppola's *Bram Stoker's Dracula* (US, 1992) – to generate a moving-image narration where some of the devices of strip cartoon are substituted for continuity

Figure 13. Dick Tracy (Warren Beatty, US. 1990).

shooting and filmic shot-flow. Besson achieves a synthesis where the spatiality of the digitally-created sets and action can be utilized to the full, and the live action matched to the effects sequences without major aesthetic dislocation. To do this, he uses a sophisticated and coherent strategy based on extensions of both comic book/storyboard and traditional live-action shooting and editing techniques, unlike the more haphazard hybrids which tend to predominate in the console games world. Besson juxtaposes close-ups and extreme close-ups, lit and shot so as to emphasize the physicality and humanity of his characters, with dizzying chases through digital cityscape; and constructs his action sequences to maximise their subjective viewpoints. These features of Besson's style are particularly striking in the sequence where Lilou, the perfect 'Fifth Element', is cloned back to life and escapes from captivity in Korben Dallas' sky-taxi.

It seems likely that the early 21st century will see a phase in developing camera and editing strategies which mediate between traditional shooting styles and fully digital image creation, capture, mise en scène, and editing – an amplification and refinement of Besson's version of moving image narration. Ang Lee's highly successful *Crouching Tiger, Hidden Dragon* (US, China, HK, Taiwan, 2000), building on earlier Kung Fu cult movies such as *Touch of Zen* (*Xianu*) (King Hu, Taiwan, 1972) and *Challenge of the Masters* (*Luacai yu huangfeihon*) (Liu Jialiang, Hong Kong, 1976) – themselves an inspiration for interactive beat-'em-ups – incorporates many of the features of martial-arts based console games. The moves in the console game *Tenchu: Stealth Assassins* and the rooftop settings are very much akin to those favoured in *Crouching Tiger*. Unlike Danny Cannon, however, who, in *Judge Dredd* (US, 1996), imported games and special effects features without balancing them with the traditional plot, structure and continuity of movies, Ang Lee builds his movie on character, using a traditional episodic epic structure in the framework of romance and melodrama, and underscoring the whole with moral lessons about courage, passion, loyalty, maturity, discipline, respect, the use and abuse of martial arts, and philosophy. He also uses a full range of effective big-screen shooting strategies, with particular and highly-sensitive emphasis on the expressive character of place and landscape, made possible by the use of locations in China and Taiwan.

In 2001, Simon West, director of *Tomb Raider* – the movie (GB, 2001), said in an interview (*Total Film*, 2001, 48): 'My task was to do something fresh and new in this genre 'cos it's so well known'. He is presumably referring to the five blockbusting PlayStation *Tomb Raider* titles issued between 1996 and 2001. Also perhaps to the movies-based-on-a-game, such as *Super Mario Bros* (Annabel Jankel/Rocky Morton, US, 1993*), Street Fighter* (Steven E de Souza, US, 1994, starring Jean-Claude van Damme) or *Mortal Kombat* (Paul Anderson, US, 1995, starring Christopher Lambert)— none of which made a great impact in the cinema. In addition, West had to take into account digital special-effects action films such as Besson's *Fifth Element*, Lee's *Crouching Tiger* and the Wachowskis' *The Matrix*, as well as John Milius' *Conan the Barbarian* (US, 1982) and Spielberg's 'Indiana Jones' films – *Raiders of the Lost Ark* (US, 1981*), Indiana Jones and the Temple of Doom (*US, 1984), *Indiana Jones and the Last Crusade* (US, 1989), continuing through the 1990s and into the 2000s as the Young Indiana Jones 'historical'

TV/video series; all with their roots in the Professor Challenger tradition, which clearly inspired much of the environment-design as well as the adventure/quest format of the original *Tomb Raider* games. West claims that he was actually referring to David Lean's *Doctor Zhivago* (US, 1965) and *Lawrence of Arabia* (GB, 1962), both movies which use the big screen to transport audiences into a vast and rich exotic world, a 'different' time and place. However, his final combination of quest-plot with a cool, highly active glamour star and a host of special effects is not very reminiscent of Lean's mature treatment of drama, passion and landscape.

Sporting, as it does, a cool British action heroine and a good deal of explosive contemporary action, *Tomb Raider,* the movie, has perhaps more in common with the Bond films than with the Indiana Jones series, despite the archaeological motif; but it fails to come together with the panache of Bonds at their best – because, finally, it lacks their stylistic confidence and their wit. Calculating the special-effects moves, and perhaps the commercials' predilection for 30-second bursts of moodily-lit, dialogue-free condensed action featuring products, types and action rather than individuals, seem to weigh too heavily on the direction and script to allow the convincing creation of character, mood, dramatic tension or continuous action – the ghost of the storyboard haunts the movie.

Tomb Raider star Angelina Jolie sports long hair, facial bone structure and exaggeratedly-pouty lips modelled as closely as possible on those of the plastically, computer-animated Lara Croft, and wears costumes which emphasise a pneumatic bust rising from a slender but resilient frame, familiar from the FMVs in the games. Before starting filming, Jolie went through a three-month intensive training session to enable her to perfect Lara's physical presence.

In Lara's case, a human actor and the screen storytellers are actually making a virtual character real, and they evoke the visual conventions of the pre-existing games rather than those of big-screen cinema. Jolie is photographed using sophisticated digital effects techniques, which allow her to appear to accomplish the astonishing athletic feats of the original virtual Lara. The camera strategy uses dizzying angles, fast swings and tricks of perspective to simulate, using live actors on the big screen, the effects of the player-operated virtual camerawork and FMV animations in the game. In dialogue scenes and plot-moving sequences, *Tomb Raider* the movie tends to favour graphic-novel framing and cutting rather than traditional cinematic dramatic continuity. Sometimes Lara, medium-close-up and in profile, closer to the audience than the action, appears almost aware of us, almost to be speaking for our benefit. This was a technique Vadim used very successfully in *Barbarella* (US, 1968), where Jane Fonda several times speaks directly to the audience, in strip-cartoon-style commentary on the action of the film, pointing up the ironies and formal jokes the movie continually makes.

It is noteworthy that the *Tomb Raider* games of the 1990s differ radically from Spielberg's Indiana Jones movie convention of the 1980s in one major respect – Lara is a self-actuated, intelligent, well-educated and trained, highly qualified and very, very competent female action hero. She is thus not unlike Indi himself, but most unlike, say, the diamond-lusting, ludicrous and incapable nightclub singer Willy

Scott (Kate Capshaw) who provides the female foil for Indi and his brave and capable boy-sidekick Shorty, in *Indiana Jones and the Temple of Doom* – screaming her way through the animal-infested jungle in high heels, or shrinkingly negotiating a creepy-crawly-infested secret tunnel in bare feet and satin pyjamas. In motivation, temperament and above all ethics, Lara is equally unlike the snaky blonde Nazi female Alison Doody plays in *Indiana Jones and the Last Crusade*, who, though physically courageous and athletic, uses her sexuality to come between Indi and his dad, while extracting the information she needs to betray them, and then finally, propelled by pure greed, transgresses the holy laws of the Grail she seeks. In the games, Lara's sexuality, cyberbabe that she is, is for the player alone. And unlike Besson's perfect being, 1990s Lilou, in *The Fifth Element*, played by supermodel Milla Jovovich, Lara in the games does not lose heart at the crucial moment and require a kiss from a hero (such as Bruce Willis in the *Fifth Element)* before she can save the world – though she does conclude the *Tomb Raider* movie with a gesture which simultaneously saves hunky Alex West, her rival intrepid tomb-raider (and evidently sometimes playmate), and recovers her dead father's watchcase (which holds the portrait of Lara's mother – also dead).

Trinity (played by Carrie Anne Moss) in *The Matrix* is surely modelled, to some extent, on the Lara of the *Tomb Raider* games and comes close to her confident, expert style. Both use their intelligence, learning and wit as well as their physical stamina, agility and prowess with weapons, to deal with puzzles and physical ordeals quite as testing and much more athletic than anything Professor Challenger ever faced, and both rescue their male peers from danger.

Lara in the *Tomb Raider* movie does not take on the quasi-mystical status of Lee's female protagonists in *Crouching Tiger* – such powers are left to a venerable Cambodian-style, saffron-robed monk. But, like Xena, Warrior Princess in the TV series, movie Lara has all the martial arts skills she needs to achieve her goals. Partial inheritor though she may be of the talents of Milius' expert, lithe, female companion-in-deeds to *Conan the Barbarian*, movie Lara, unlike her barbaric predecessor, is not called upon to sacrifice herself in order to save her man. Maybe it's the year 2001-style Uzis that give Lara just that edge she needs to retain her self-preservation, self-reliance and self-esteem. How different from the resourceful spacer Barbarella in 1968, whose mission was to locate and eradicate the 'Positronic Ray', which threatens, by reintroducing the concept of weapons, to bring back to a pacified universe the outdated phenomenon of war.

The move from game to cinematic convention has some interesting fundamental effects on Lara Croft and her story. Adrian Smith, Operations Director of Core Design, the company that originated Lara, says:

> Lara was clearly the right character at precisely the right time. Featuring a lead woman shook up the die-hard male gameplayers and also caused *Tomb Raider* to cross over into the female market. I also think she got caught up in the whole Girl Power vibe that was prevalent at the time thanks to the Spice Girls. But I don't think it's just one single thing that has made Lara one of the most instantly recognisable figures of the past decade.

People seem to relate to Lara's positive attitude and aspire to be like her. They also love the mystery that surrounds her action-packed lifestyle – where she's really coming from and the whole mystique about her background. I do think the *Tomb Raider* series opened up the possibilities of what people now expect from a computer game. They wanted an escapist experience like the movie-going one, and they got it in spades. Because we always visualised *Tomb Raider* in cinematic terms, licensing a movie version of the game seemed exactly right as the next logical step in her format progression. Never in our wildest dreams could we have predicted the nuclear explosion we were creating with Lara Croft. (Jones, 2001, pp. 16-17)

In fact, *Tomb Raider* the movie performed comparatively disappointingly at the box office, despite stunning exotic sets and locations presented with panache to evoke the designs in the games in 'real' (cinematic) reality, plus a committed cast of actors, plenty of action, and a story which explains where Lara 'is really coming from'. The mystery behind Lara's action-packed life is revealed: she is motivated by her desolation at the loss of her genius father ('Lost but never forgotten' reads his tombstone), and carries out her deeds of daring inspired by, and finally to clear, his memory.

In the movie, Lara's adventure starts with her annual commemoration of her father's death, and it is the foresight of Lord Croft which provides his daughter with the key (literally – a time-warping artefact) to the story. Lord Croft, experienced by Lara in dream/timewarp, guides his beloved daughter through her task of thwarting the 'Illuminati', who want to reunite, for their own dark purposes, the halves of an ancient talisman of power, scattered by wise mages of the distant past to opposite ends of the world (Iceland and Cambodia) and hidden by testing tomb-buried puzzles to prevent its exploitation by the wicked. Lord Croft gives Lara the explanations and advice she needs to prevent the evil leaders of the Illuminati from taking over the world, ably assisted by her household geek, Bryce, and her slightly controlling butler, Hillary. Sample dialogue? 'I'm only trying to turn you into a lady,' says the formally clad butler as he hands his half-naked employer – fresh from a shower (accompanied by low jungle music) behind gauze curtains – a nice white frock and heels; 'And a lady should be modest,' he comments, as she flaunts her nudity at him (but not quite at the audience) – Lara, spurning the frock, replies 'Yes, a lady *should* be modest'. Then, towering over Lara, who is dimly backlit, semi-recumbent, with her feet on her desk (the epitome of non-action), Hillary exhorts: 'Back to work I'm afraid,' as he proffers the files, organizing Lara into her next mission, to which she poutily objects: 'Egypt again. Nothing but sand.' 'I know,' retorts Hillary, looming in close-up above Lara. 'Gets everywhere. In the cracks.'

Apparently in its quest for cinematic shape, this story boldly throws away the mystique surrounding virtual Lara, which Smith considers one of her main attractions. It also transforms her from a capable, self-actuated, ethically driven young woman – an expert archaeologist – to a bereft daughter, who so longs to reverse the effects of time to be with her daddy again that she is prepared to go to the ends of the earth and risk everything – but who has to rely on the care of a domineering butler, the expertise of a male geek, and the knowledge of the all-male Illuminati and their minion Manfred

Powell (who turns out to master them), as well as the help of a monastery of Buddhist monks (male, of course), to accomplish her mission. The only female help Lara receives is from the brief appearances of two exotic young prepubescent girls (one dumb, or speechless), who indicate directives from Lord Croft to do with jasmine flowers. Nor does Lara perform her task alone, as she always does in her games: rival tomb raider Alex West (who, perhaps in the interests of equal opportunities, gets his own solo shower scene to parallel Lara's) – is engaged on the same quest, in the pay of Powell. Lara's solitude and self-reliance, as well as her active personality, self-motivation and drive, are dissipated for the movie, in the interests of softening 'feminine' images, a psychological back-story involving the loss of her white-haired moustachioed father, the suggestion of some love interest, parallel action (Alex West versus Lara Croft), dramatic interaction and cinematic suspense (will Powell and West make it before Lara?).

Not only does this film story reduce Lara from a strong woman in control of her own destiny to the accolyte of her father and the victim of Powell's plotting; the direction itself favours the male protagonists throughout. Lara, who epitomized the games world's successful first-person dramatized persona, for whom indeed new virtual camera angles were invented to enable the player both to see her as a character and experience the environment from her point of view – thus identifying with her dramatically at the same time as controlling her – in the movie does not have her own subjective viewpoint camera.

Instead, Lara is looked at from a predominantly third-person angle, often in wide shots which allow her athletic exploits full range, or from the subjective angles of Lord Croft, Powell or West. In scenes where she interacts with these men, the camera rarely shows her final reaction to a transaction, or follows her from the room; it remains instead with the man she has been speaking with, dwelling on his reaction, telling his story – rather than exploiting the normal cinematic strategies which would tell the story as Lara's, exploring the world with her, showing her reactions and feelings and remaining as much as possible in her cinematic space. When West pursues Lara through the jungle, the 'following camera' familiar from the game is in fact Alex's subjective POV-camera – the audience is invited to identify with West (is that the character or the director?), not with Lara.

Lara's face is rarely even shown in extreme close-up, the traditional cinematic way of inducing empathy with a character; the camera prefers to keep her elastically-upholstered bosom in frame whenever possible. It is through the subjective extreme close-ups of Alex West and his POV shots, not Lara's, that we explore the crucial clues in the Cambodian tomb, where the two are competing to find the first half of the talisman (before the vast phallic battering ram, on which the nimble Lara rides, goes into its destructive action, pricking and puncturing with its needle-sharp point the rotundiform urn whose waters, released, finally reveal the object of their search).

Lara's subjective life and prowess in action are equally undermined by introducing her at the beginning of the film running away from a robotic monster, watched voyeuristically via a computer screen (which turns out also to be the monster's POV) by an unseen observer (Bryce). Although she eventually defeats the monster, much is first made of its huge predatory bipedal form pinning Lara supine to the floor, in best *Jurassic Park* (Steven Spielberg, US, 1993) or *King Kong* (Meriam C Cooper & Ernest B Shoedsack, US, 1933) style. The focal near-escape moment is when Lara spreads her legs wide (naked in their short shorts, and gartered with pistols) to escape the titanic thrust of the monster's vast metallic proboscis, which thumps harmlessly into the concrete at Lara's crotch before she rolls deftly away again. The audience does not experience the action from the hero's point of view (as they do in a typical Indiana Jones movie), except for a few brief moments when the raptor looms above Lara, in the monstrous parody of a lover's embrace. Whoever would have thought of identifying gun-toting, hotpant-sporting, monster-zapping Lara Croft with *King Kong*'s Fay Wray (usually clad only in a flimsy white frock), cowering away from the beast who craves her?

But, despite her scorn of the butler trying to make her into a lady, Lara in the film does turn out to have a penchant for feminine flimsy. For her first real battle of the movie (the monster turns out to be a training device programmed for Lara by Bryce), Lara wears pristine white silky pyjamas (shades of Willy Scott in *Temple of Doom* – though Lara's might perhaps also do duty in a dojo...). On this occasion, Lara is doing her flying-bunjee exercises before retiring for the night when she is attacked, in the intimacy of her own home, by a squad of unusually destructive masked, combat-accoutred treasure hunters. Lara puts in a lot of action (much of it evasive) – asking Bryce to 'be her eyes', and using surveillance cams and voice transmission to follow his directions – before the attackers get away with the precious 'key' to the adventure.

Virtual Lara in her games is always the active heroine, penetrating hostile territory, never the victim of a night attack, clad in her pyjamas. And so the film goes on – Lara vulnerable, asleep in her negligee; Lara in the shower; Lara being told what to do by the fatherly butler; Lara following her father's instructions. In the final scene of the film, Lara Croft is actually wearing a picture hat à la Audrey Hepburn, together with the heels and white strappy frock originally proposed by butler Hillary to 'make her into a lady' – almost indistinguishable from Fay Wray's costume as the ingénue in *King Kong*.

Director Simon West, after reading the final script developed by producers Gordon and Levin, decided to 'change everything... and start from scratch', describing the process as 'a great opportunity to develop Lara's personality and bring her to a wider audience while putting an excitingly fresh spin on the entire fantasy adventure genre' (Jones, 2001, 23).

Developing Lara's personality seems to mean turning her into a good little daddy's girl (for extra emphasis, were any needed, actor Jon Voight, who plays Lord Croft, actually is Angelina Jolie's real-life father), for which purpose she is infantilized, both literally (flashbacks to childhood, looking trustfully up at daddy and learning at his knee) and figuratively (motivated by her desire for reunion with her lost protector). And Lara's traditional screen 'femininity' is established by giving her a number of generic movie scenes of a type more suited to Indiana Jones' female sidekicks than to Indi himself, complete with gauze curtains and jasmine flowers. Alas for Smith's 'lead woman with the positive attitude who shook up the die-hard male gameplayers' in 1996.

West, who remarks, 'I can't honestly say I was a fan of the game as I never have much time to play it' (Jones, 2001, 22), appears, in his attempt to translate game into movie – to give Lara a more rounded character – to have opted for cinematic clichés combined with lavish sets taken from the game, and a wardrobe extended to show Lara's less active sides. The rather gratuitous, if spectacular, bunjee work that features early in the film neither replaces the learning sequences for the player entering the game, nor provides the thrill of directing Lara in action; nor has it any real function in the language of movies – it says little about Lara's character or emotional state and does nothing to forward the plot.

It is hardly surprising if the film fails to deliver either engaging cinema or a convincing evocation of the mysterious, tough, self-actuated Lara Croft, identified with by the millions of gaming fans who have spent hours in her company. 'Tomb Raider II became the fastest selling title in the computer games industry's history and to date the combined *Tomb Raider* series has sold well over 30 million units worldwide and won a host of awards, most notably a BAFTA for outstanding contribution to the industry' (Jones, 2001, 14). Fans clearly love and want the mysterious, enterprising Lara they know from the *Tomb Raider* games – why should they welcome a 'feminized' supermodel version, who is neither proper screen action hero (like Xena) nor game protagonist? Adaptation, like translation, requires a thorough knowledge of both the source and the target medium. There is no intrinsic reason why movie Lara should not have been of the calibre of Ang Lee's *Crouching Tiger* protagonist, had the wit, daring and allure of a Katherine Hepburn or Lauren Bacall character, the commanding presence of a Captain Janaway (from *Star Trek: Voyager*), the self-actuation of a Xena, and the resource and adventurous nature of Barbarella, to bring her nearer to the Lara of the games.

The other big-screen, game-inspired movie released in 2001 was *Final Fantasy – the Spirits Within* (Hironobu Sakaguchi, Japan, 2001), based on the *Final Fantasy* games and produced by Square Co. This film boasts all-digital 3D animation, with characters verging on the lifelike (the kind of resolution anticipated by the PlayStation 2 and Microsoft X-Box consoles) in appearance and movement, the epic drama played out in neorealistic, exotic settings. Aki Ross, beautiful and brilliant scientist, with the guidance of her mentor, Dr Sid, traverses her dreamscape and the Earth (plagued by virus-carrying aliens whose infection can devour your spirit), searching for the eight spirit waves which will save the planet, racing against the alternative solution proposed by General Hein: he intends to annihilate the monsters with a phenomenally powerful space canon that risks destroying the Earth itself along with the plague. Set in 2065, the movie combines an Anime-Manga, science-fiction feel with the game-like structure of collecting ingredients to solve a puzzle.

Final Fantasy – the Spirits Within experiments with the style perfected in the FMVs of the game *Final Fantasy VIII*, essentially extending them to feature length. The slightly plasticy texture of the human characters and Manga-animation qualities of the script (performed with commitment by the actors) is countered by a film score using the piano to create a romantic, people-centred atmosphere. The drama is not quite engaging in the way of a traditional live-action movie, because the plot and characters are a new hybrid between game story and epic-hero story, created with computer animation techniques, which has not yet found its level. The creators are so preoccupied with demonstrating the range of their animation technique (particularly the play of light) that the action of a perfectly acceptable and at times moving cinematic tale is slowed down to snail's pace because shots linger over technical achievements to the detriment of the drama. The mise en scène is an interesting combination of Manga animation and live action. The film does not use songs as an immersive support to its stylisation, as does Bluth and Goldman's 1997 *Anastasia*, which successfully staged human 2D-animated characters, but *Final Fantasy* does extend 3D animation beyond Lasseter's *Toy Story* (US 1995, 1999) and *Bug's Life* (US, 1998) by introducing fully human characters as the main protagonists. It also continues to build the 'Final Fantasy World' popularised through the games, though not by copying it. Predictions that multi-publishing would be the norm by the end of the 20th century seem close to fulfilment, and this appears a potentially fruitful way to view the cross-fertilization of game and movie.

Fictive worlds are created and characters born – the use to which they are put is not limited by the technology, or the genre, or even style or delivery platform in which they originate, but by the imaginations, knowledge and skills of the creative teams making productions, and the economic organization required to develop, produce, market and distribute titles. A creative ethos of multi-publishing is not far from that of the mainly non-literate European Middle Ages, where stories circulated across national boundaries and cultures in many versions and many forms, with many local variants; or to the world of adaptation, where drama for theatre, musical stage, cinema, TV, animation and computer games cross-pollinates with novels. At the beginning of the 21st century, Peter Jackson's *Lord of the Rings* (US/NZ, 2001-2003) trilogy, based on JRR Tolkien's novels – already the inspiration for a multitude of role-playing and computer adventure-games – was a huge international box-office and critical success, and brought in its wake a massive republication of the books which inspired it. Fantasy worlds for fiction are dynamic and expanding, and will generate more and more modes of telling in the digital context.

The development of hybrid styles between game and film, such as those discussed above, is of major importance, as far as structures and rhetoric are concerned, to designers for entertainment consoles, as to others working in the mainly or purely digital production world. Just as digital effects make it possible to use the 'virtual' camera strategies in action movie-making, so as 'virtual' cameras programmed to reproduce traditional cinematic shooting strategies are developed for virtual environments, for those who know what they are doing, it becomes possible to impart to real-time 3D interactive narrative some of the dramatic impact of film and TV rhetoric. As the geometries of digital special effects for the big screen are better and better understood and more and more smoothly integrated into the medium, so a wider range of possibilities become available for imaginative movie as well as RT3D storytelling.

The traditionally continuity-oriented shooting style of James Cameron's *Titanic* (US, 1998), extended and enhanced as it is through sophisticated digital treatment – for example, the long sequence of Jack (Leonardo di Caprio) and his friend celebrating their expedition west by savouring the wind in the bows of the ship – offers one route toward a synthesis of live-action, physical and virtual camera strategies, which is likely to develop in both big and small screen narration for stories not set in a (thoroughly!) fantasy environment.

In *Titanic*, crowds and moving people, for example, in impossible places (like the decks of the sinking liner) are represented by motion-captured and digitally processed 'synthespians' – actors whose original performance is extended by means of digital animation techniques and dropped into whatever part of the film frame they are required to populate. Work continues on refining the methodology, and the FMV animations of *Silent Hill* and *Final Fantasy VIII* show how the combination of motion capture and animation can create highly characterized styles in a totally synthetic-image environment. *Tekken* and *Bust A Groove* (see Appendix) rely entirely upon combining motion capture with characterization and other features taken from animation for the aesthetic appeal and kinetic attraction which gives them their impact.

Nonetheless, the deployment of continuity shooting and editing, whether in live action or animation (as in the widescreen *Anastasia*), is a very powerful convention, widely used to involve the viewer and create the sense of identifying with the characters in a drama, sharing their emotions and their plights; and its effectiveness cannot be emphasised enough. Katz clarifies the film director's repertoire in controlling the image in the frame, point of view and narrative stance:

Figure 14. Silent Hill (Konami/Konami 1999).

Graphic and editorial techniques determine the *level of involvement* the viewer has with the characters on the screen. Point of view, on the other hand, determines who the viewer identifies with. The two concepts are closely related and nearly always work together in any sequence.

Each shot in a film expresses a point of view, and in narrative film the point of view changes often, sometimes with each new shot. For the most part, point of view – what is often called narrative stance – is largely invisible to the audience, though the accumulated effect of the changes profoundly affects the way the audience interprets any scene. (Katz, 1991, 173)

4. Narrative, Narration and Engagement in Adventure-Game Stories

Up to 1998, it was rare to see console games which utilise the power of mise en scène and systematic narration through choice of camera angles to create identifications or a narrative stance, and intensify the dramatic experience for the storyseeker. *Resident Evil II* broke the mould, proving that the conventions by which live-action shooting represents 3D space on a 2D screen, and offers audiences a way to approach not only fundamental narrative and its narration but also approach the characters within the story and how they relate to each other, to objects and to the space itself, can helpfully be used to orient a storyseeker in a storyscape via a games console and a television screen.

Greg Roach of Hyperbole, Director of *The X-Files Adventure* (Fox Interactive/Sony PlayStation, US/GB, 1999), used his experience of experimental live-action interactive movies to create an adventure story game where the storyseeker/player helps Detectives Scully and Mulder solve the mystery that faces them. He worked with the TV *X-Files* actors, cinematographers and designers to create a digitally processed but essentially photorealistic storyscape (originally shot on Digital Beta tape), which the player can explore in a number of ways, using an intelligent cursor – that is, a cursor which changes its shape on the screen as it passes over a 'hot' spot, to indicate what form of interaction the player can pursue at this particular place. The storyseeker can, as an invisible third investigator, interact with the two main protagonists to solve the mystery. Icons (as in *Broken Sword II* or *Discworld*) allow the storyseeker to select dialogue interactions and story pathways. Normal techniques of screen narration and dramatization, such as those described by Parker (1997) and Katz (1991), are employed throughout the narration of *The X-Files Adventure*, adapted to enable storyseekers to follow different paths through the storyscape, but exploiting recognizable conventions of continuity editing and shooting.

The *X-Files Adventure* was a new departure in console narrative games. In it, storyseekers are enabled to enter the world of Scully and Mulder, brought to their own television screens at home whenever they load the discs. The eerie atmosphere developed for the television show translates via the console, with the help of music in the mode of the series, but composed by a seasoned interactive composer, and a soundtrack aware of the range of effects and illusions normally employed in film and television to create suspense and enhance emotional reactions. Within the storyscape, storyseekers are invited to extend the familiar experience of television in a novel way,

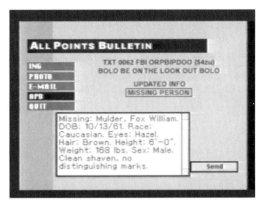

Figure 15. The X-Files Adventure (Fox Interactive/Sony PlayStation, US/GB, 1999).

while gamesplayers are invited to enter the world of screen storytelling through the general conventions of adventure games. The storyworld contains the capacity to 'ramp up' the 'games aspect' or the 'story aspect' of the adventure, according to taste, and allows both storyseekers and gamers to be more or less active or passive as the mood takes them. They can obtain help inside the storyworld if they cannot solve puzzles, and they do not have to replay levels if they fail to solve a mystery – they can move the narrative on through direct control icons – while a default setting will continue the action if the player does nothing. The narration is constructed with awareness of the normal conventions of viewpoint, the use of close-ups, and other screen rhetoric effective in involving the audience in the story and with the characters.

When the title was produced, the software support and digital production technology for interactive video were in their infancy. However, as big-screen movie-making became more digital and games production became more lucrative at the beginning of the 21st century, and as TV broadcasting turned away from the airwaves toward digital communications channels, the means of production for movies, television and games drew suddenly much closer together. The needs of all three converged, and techniques began to emerge which exploit the strengths of all. The problems of picture and sound compression, storage capacity and computer-processing-power, which slow down the *X-Files Adventure* and make it unwieldy because of its use of photo-realistic video, had effectually been solved by the time PlayStation 2 came on to the market in 2001.

With the development of DVD and digital interactive broadcasting technologies as well as Webcasting, there is no reason why experiments in live-action-based interactive storytelling should not continue and be fruitful, incorporating traditional movie strategies to draw the storyseeker into the world of the action. At the same time, virtual camera operation, which enables RT3D presentation to exploit the same features, is being refined. The chemistry between big screen and entertainment console continues, and in order to exploit the resources of the interactive adventure fully, designers need to understand better how screen conventions work.

Katz provides a summary of effective – and transferable – devices for screen narration, stressing the importance of point of view as a strategy to involve an audience in a screen story:

> To better understand how the filmmaker can use the camera to determine point of view, let us begin by looking at the three types of narration used in films, borrowing the terminology used to denote point of view in literature.
>
> **First-Person Point of View**
> First-person narratives are exemplified by the subjective techniques of Hitchcock in which we see events through the eyes of a character – the "I" of the story. Extensive use of the subjective viewpoint has always been awkward in narrative film largely because we are only given the visual point of view of a character and are deprived of seeing his or her reactions through facial or other gestures.
>
> **Third Person Restricted Point of View**
> Third-person restricted, which presents the action as seen by an ideal observer, is the style of narrative most common in Hollywood movies, but rarely is it used as the sole viewpoint. Most of the time it is combined with limited use of omniscient and subjective passages.
>
> **Omniscient Point of View**
> For film to present the omniscient point of view we have to know what the characters are thinking. This requires some type of narration, voice-over or graphics. (Katz, 1991, 267-8)

The first-person point of view is the one that early games and all shoot-'em-ups (for obvious reasons – you need to get a sightline on your target in order to hit it) tend to employ – usually with virtually no variation of shots and the negative results Katz warns of – and emerge in the discussion of *Tomb Raider* and *Over Blood* above. The big-screen movie that uses this device throughout, Robert Montgomery's *The Lady in the Lake* (US, 1947), is most often held up as a curio which tried an experiment and failed. The main character, Raymond Chandler's detective Philip Marlowe, 'is' the camera for virtually the whole film – after a brief prologue, we see him only once, reflected in a mirror. *Time Out*'s review describes the film as 'stubbornly loopy' and goes on:

> Shot entirely with subjective camera, it lets the audience see the world through Marlowe's eyes. Hired to track down someone's hated wife, you stumble on a dead body, and as Audrey Totter offers you her lips, darkness fills the screen: you have closed your eyes. Even novelty items like mysterious puffs of smoke from invisible cigarettes cannot disguise the high irritation factor in what Chandler himself described as 'a cheap Hollywood trick'. (*Time Out Film Guide*, 1998, 473)

The 'irritation factor' is mainly the one identified by Katz – we are deprived of the reactions of the main character to the situation. In fact, the movie tries to provide Marlowe's reactions through his voice-over commentary, read by Montgomery himself – an unsuccessful author, and a stage actor and well-known Hollywood 'leading man' in the 1930s and 1940s, before he turned director after World War II. Personally, I find the idea behind this adaptation appealing, and much of the film successful – because Chandler's first-person narration in the novel *The Lady in the Lake* has a very specific tone and language, expressing a layered personality, which is extremely hard to capture in dialogue and action. Unfortunately, when cut, and in places rewritten, as it is for the film, the narrative voice Chandler creates for Marlowe loses much of its subtlety. In any case, the example of *The Lady in the Lake* demonstrates how strong movie convention is, when it comes to narration – people feel very uncomfortable when it is broken. Narrating is not just a matter of the plot or story, but very much the way that you tell it. An important feature of dramatic mise en scène is that action in itself is not drama: drama is action plus reaction. This fundamental point is one which console games-designers, lacking movie experience or a director's training, rarely seem to grasp.

Action adventure games which have a cast of more than one character most often, in fact, operate from the omniscient (overhead) POV, sacrificing the motivated camera of Hollywood, original variety of shots, and engaging storytelling for easy orientation in 3D environments. Although graphics texts on screen are often resorted to (the lip-synch we rely on to help us interpret screen dialogue is course and unreadable in most console-game RT3D animations, which do not normally incorporate close-ups), the 'Voice Over' recommended by Katz is quite commonly used, to more or less effect. Abe's V/O in *Oddworld:- Abe's Oddysee* works well, because it characterizes Abe and gives the storyseeker access to his thoughts and motives, creating a fictive identification for players. Equally, in *Colony Wars* the player learns about the ethical aspects of the dramatic situation through the reflections and voice of the Commander, to whom we relate as we might to a radio dramatic character – since we do not see him – with the illusion of intimacy and therefore engagement created by a one-to-one vocal communication direct to the listener.

In his summary of effective direction – the skilful deployment of screen rhetoric – Katz sees its primary goal as the engagement of the audience (or storyseeker). He declares (and by 'player' he means not 'gamer', but the actor 'playing' the role with which the audience members identify):

Viewer Involvement and Identification
There are two ways to determine viewer identification: by graphic control or by narrative control. Graphic control elicits our identification with a player using composition and staging. The modified subjective shot... is an example of graphic control determined by how a player is composed in the frame.

Narrative control directs our identification using several strategies, but these are largely dependent on editing. For instance, in a detective story, the plot usually follows the private eye. Scenes begin when the private eye arrives at a location and end when he exits a scene. Even when this kind of story is covered in third-person restricted camera setups in closed framings, the narrative context implies that we are learning of events from the private eye's point of view. (Katz, 1991, 269)

This description is applicable to the mise en scène of *Metal Gear Solid* and *Resident Evil III*. The generation of PlayStation games already born by the end of the 20th century, as exemplified by *Resident Evil II* and *The X-Files Adventure*, was ready to employ the powerful rhetoric of point-of-view reinforced by coherent continuity editing which players recognize unconsciously, if not consciously, from the big and small screens, to give storyseekers a relationship to the action and characters, and effortless entry into the illusion of the game's storyworld.

Toward a New Poetics?

Despite the cross-fertilization between movie and game, measured even against the (very summary) overview of dynamic screen narrational techniques given above, the limitations of the average console game in staging scenes containing several characters militate severely against engaging the storyseeker in drama. *Broken Sword II*'s choice of a classic animation visual style (recalling Hergé's *Tintin*) is not sustained by a corresponding consistent narrative viewpoint or mise en scène – the camera angle is usually high, close-ups and over-the-shoulder viewpoint shots are used sparingly. The result is that long dialogue sequences become boring, even when they are moving the story forward, because in the course of them the storyseeker – accustomed to sophisticated screen language – is not pulled by the camera into the emotional conflicts of the scene, or involved with the characters and their dilemmas, but left suspended at a distance from both. The film-maker's care to use changes in location or movement through a space to hold attention while dialogue takes place, is absent, and the storyseeker's attention easily wanders away from the narrative.

The issue of being obliged to prepare, store and match a vast set of potential edit points, if the player of a console adventure is permitted to navigate a scene freely, has been cited to justify maintaining instead a single master shot for the whole duration of long sequences in navigable computer-supported or generated environments. However, since in console gamestories long dialogue sequences (like those in *Broken Sword II*) normally cannot usefully be interrupted by the player/storyseeker, the issue does not really constitute a problem. A cut-sequence can be inserted just as easily as a single mastershot. There seems to be no good reason for the failure to exploit this valuable screen resource. It appears, rather, that in such console adventures, the rhetoric deployed is simply not informed moving-image dramatic narrative rhetoric, and maybe this is because games have in general tended to be developed by designers who have more experience of comic strips and graphic novels than of fluid movie direction.

The small frames of graphic novels or comic strips also accommodate single faces or scenes between two characters more easily than multiple character dialogue sequences. In *Excalibur*, the characterization of Beth's supporting cast is ambitious, but the static quality of the animation, where figures are fixed in place – in medium long shot or long shot – and can only move their lips in rather poor synch with the sound, repeating a small repertory of gestures, is certainly not improved by the lack of a character-based virtual camera strategy. This lack of engaging screen language is coupled with the poor delivery in spoken words of poorly written speeches also offered as text. Both delivery and staging work against, rather than for, the storyseeker's identification either with Beth – the protagonist – or with the other characters. Suspension of disbelief and submersion in the dramatic action in this hybrid storyform is very hard. The attempt to populate the storyscape and produce dramatic interactions, though in itself attractive, fails primarily because, though Beth's world is animated, *Excalibur* fails to use the traditional conventions of animated narration, many derived from live-action, to compensate for or capitalize on the lack of naturalism inherent in the 3D graphics world, in such a way as to create involvement with the protagonist.

Many of the technical problems to do with storage, speed and processing power, which made it hard to produce refined graphics and incorporate speaking characters into RT3D in 1997, when *Excalibur* was released on PlayStation, had been massively diminished by 2001 and PlayStation 2, and could in principle be overcome using up-to-date technology. However, as it is, it is easy to get bored of this game, because you do not really care about the characters, and in addition – and this problem is not technological but dramaturgical – the dramatic interludes (or encounters with in-game characters) are so unrelated to any story that they fail to engage. There is little motivation for the storyseeker to solve the puzzles within the storyworld – the reward in terms of narrative and drama is too meagre.

In addition, the drama is not really drama – in *Excalibur*, though the vocal and gestural mannerisms of the figures Beth encounters are characterized, their contributions to the story are limited to requiring her to exchange objects or perform tasks seemingly arbitrarily. These do not have the weight of the tasks, say, in a traditional fairy tale, where the protagonist who saves the hedgehog today is likely to find the hedgehog helping them – perhaps in the guise of something else – tomorrow. The tasks and the drama seem hardly to come out of the tradition of storytelling at all – they are merely an extension of the concept of puzzle-solving, a set of obstacles placed in the way of the protagonist to prolong the process of reaching the final goal (finding the lost sword, Excalibur). This structure is closer to that of role-playing games than to the adventure stories which generated them, and which are the material of Bettelheim's study of the enchantment of fairy tale (Bettelheim, 1976, quoted earlier).

The world of King Arthur of Britain and his famous sword 'Excalibur', which inspires Beth's console-game adventure, does very much depend on quests where obstacles prevent heroes from achieving their goals, it is true. However, although a 12th-century story (formally closely related to fairy tale) of questing Arthurian knights seeking a grail, or a girl, or a sword – for example, Chrétien de Troyes' *Perceval* (France, 1188, filmed by Eric Rohmer, France, 1976) – is likely to contain obstacles, often in the form of small tasks to be achieved on the way to the main objective, in such a story each task tests – sometimes very ingeniously and unexpectedly – a specific skill or spiritual accomplishment in the knight. Not until he has acquired all the degrees of accomplishment required to achieve the task can he reach his goal – and the audience/reader of the tale learns something new about the way human beings relate to their moral universe through each test.

A system of sub-quests within a main quest, the achievement of which gains 'experience points' for the player, is common in role-playing-based adventure. However, in console games such as *Excalibur*, such experiences are usually (not always) unrelated to the story matter. They are variables within a computer script, which allows any number of 'If Beth... (opens the door) ...then (the mouse emerges from its hole)' constructions. If Beth picks up the mousetrap, then (a) she can enter the corridor leading to the cell where the prisoner is confined and (b) she loses some energy (say, two points). It is not difficult to reduce the episodic knightly quest to a series of such formulations: 'If Perceval kills the Red Knight, he can leave the Court of Arthur and go to Gornemant's Castle'; 'if Perceval does not kill the Knight, he can go to the Hermit's cave and receive information which will lead him to a second encounter with the Red Knight and a second chance to overcome him'. However, without a plot – or genre – structure to give them significance, such encounters and mini-quests are meaningless and uninteresting from a story point of view. 'If Beth puts the chicken leg on the table, she can open the door' (but she will need the chicken leg later to replenish her energy in order to meet the trials beyond the door) does not have the same story weight as 'If Yvain chooses to save the lion from the attack of the serpent, and wins the fight, he can continue his quest, because he has shown compassion and supported good against evil.'

Mere ingenuity in working out a puzzle (how to tempt a rat from a hole in order to bring it to a man who will then divulge a useful piece of information, for example, in *Excalibur*) leaves no sense of moral achievement in the player/storyseeker, nor any impression that the Universe has given up any of its secrets.

The important element of giving the player/storyseeker a stake in the outcome of the quest is lost in *Excalibur*. It doesn't really matter whether the sword gets found or not. Neither Beth nor the player develops as a result of the quest, and in the course of the action the player finds out very little that was not evident before the game began. This is true of many games that begin with an FMV framework of 'backstory' – nearly all the storytelling is done before the action begins. In movie-making, the 'backstory' is only there for the scriptwriter and film-makers, for reference – it never appears on the screen, only informs the characterization and action in the process of making the film. Much of the fun of following a story is working out how all the elements fit together – if you are told all that before you begin, you have very little incentive to continue.

Oddworld, *Resident Evil*, *The X-Files Adventure*, *Final Fantasy VII* and *VIII* and *Silent Hill* are exceptional in console-game terms in this respect, since they all incorporate some degree of story reward into the gameplay, and *Tomb Raider* – most notably in *Tomb Raider IV: The Final Revelation* – builds story rewards into each episode/level of Lara's adventures. On the other hand, *Excalibur*'s translation of the new insights and understandings acquired by the questing knight-figure at each stage of the journey into a simple collection of objects without which tasks cannot be completed, robs the encounters of real experience value, and fails to provide any solidly rewarding motivation for the storyseeker to go on through the adventure.

Final Fantasy VII, however, through the abstracted concept of acquiring appropriate levels of combat skill to entitle you to face each succeeding hazard and reach each new level of story and storyworld knowledge, does refer to the traditional schema embedded in mediaeval quest tales of the acquisition of spiritual, moral or street-wisdom leading to improvement and reward as the basis for adventure. *Final Fantasy VII* also fields – as do most console games – monsters or brutes as the opponents to be overcome.

The tradition of monstrous opponents in mediaeval stories and more ancient fairy tales can be a powerful ingredient in staging a psychological or spiritual journey through an internal landscape, where the enemy to be slain is a symbolic creature representing the combatant's own fears, or selfishness, or other vice (for example, Chrétien de Troyes' *Yvain, the Knight with the Lion* (France, 1175)). It has been suggested by Joseph Campbell in his book *The Inner Reaches of Outer Space* (US, 1986) that the ubiquitous Alien of the screen since the 1950s (exploited in Tim Burton's film *Mars Attacks* (US, 1996) is the 20th-century manifestation of the parallel mediaeval phenomenon of mortal combat against humanoid monsters rather than fully human beings. At the manifest level of story, it is more morally acceptable to destroy a monster, with all the horror it may represent at the latent level, than it is to kill a human being, and in this respect aliens from outer space fulfil the same function as beastlike creatures from the unexplored wilds in classical and mediaeval adventures. Don Chaffey's film *Jason and the Argonauts* (GB, 1963), inspired by the ancient Greek epic the *Iliad* (attributed to Homer, 8th cent. BC), provides a good demonstration, as do dehumanised or sub-human mortals such as the 19th-century Frankenstein's monster (*Frankenstein*, Mary Shelley, GB, 1818), Dracula (*Dracula*, Bram Stoker, GB, 1869), or Mr Hyde (*The Strange Case of Dr Jekyll and Mr Hyde*, Robert Louis Stevenson, GB, 1886), all of whom have translated effectively from page to screen.

Almost all of the adventure games looked at in detail here share the feature of monstrous opponents – as do most listed in the Appendix, with the exception of *Nuclear Strike*, which offers the IndoChinese as the quasi sub-human 'others' to be destroyed, *Colony Wars*, which, unusually, makes Earth Empire's human beings (us) the oppressive enemy (though the combat is between graphic representations, semi-abstract, of warships in space, not between 'living' characters), and *Tenchu: Stealth Assassins*, where it is made clear that humans who have abandoned ethics, loyalty and honour, no longer count as human.

Nuclear Strike draws on the sound design, imagery and camera narration of war movies such as *Apocalypse Now* (Francis Ford Coppola, US, 1979) and *Full Metal Jacket* (Stanley Kubrick, UK, 1987) rather than on the range of adventure films referred to above in the context of fairy-tale/fantasy/science-fiction adventure/epic games. In the flow of exchange between game and film, the movie *Pearl Harbor* (Michael Bay, US, 2001) picks up its central special effects section (the trajectory of a bomb from release to target) directly from the experience of RT3D VE games design – the impossible camera angles, possible for virtual cameras in virtual environments, are created on the big screen using digital image generation, capture, animation and manipulation. Such visuals have entered the film-maker's vocabulary directly from the realm of gaming.

Pearl Harbor, like *Judge Dredd* before it, relies heavily on simulating the effect of a computer game in the cinema – not exploiting the possibilities of human actors but overwhelming the dramatic cast with high-decibel activity, and reducing the plot, human interaction and dialogue to the barest minimum.

The console game *Colony Wars* refers to science-fiction films such as *Planet of the Apes* (Franklin J Schaffer, US, 1967) and *The Empire Strikes Back* (Irvin Kirshner, US, 1980) but uses computer graphics to transform the action away from realism, while creating a dramatic experience for the player through voice-over identification with a narrative, rather than visual representation of the backstory. This form, with its combination of radio and film narrational techniques with digital graphics, is intriguing and potentially very strong – though it seems to be little exploited in the games-production world, it could be used there effectively to create dramatic adventures in other genres than that of the space attack.

Engagement and Involvement in the Fiction Gameworld

Final Fantasy VII meets the challenge of involving the player in the fiction by staging the narrative sequences of the story using expert traditional 2D animation rhetoric, from characterization through background design and mise en scène to a consistent narrative camera narration strategy, as well as other refined devices of effective screen language. The storyseeker is engaged in the story by the traditional means of screen narrative/drama, but the skills element of the game – the staging of the fully interactive fight-sequences – is in a mode different from the main story both graphically and in terms of interaction. The fight sequences demand involvement through dexterity, speed of reaction, combat thinking and adrenaline drive, not at all through story means. The connection of characters, story and locations with the fight sequences is quite arbitrary – the protagonist, Cloud Strife, simply finds himself in the fight arena whenever a combat is needed to move the level forward, no matter where he was before. His companions materialize to take part in these fights, although they are not with him when he (the lone hero with whom the player identifies) is negotiating the obstacles and solving the mysteries of the planet which lead him into the combats. The player (or players) can take control of any or all of Cloud Strife's companions during the combats, which are with spectacularly supernatural monsters whose fighting properties are hard to fathom and very difficult to overcome. When the fight is won, Cloud Strife can go on with his mission to blow up the reactor and discover what to do about his quondam mentor, Sephiroth.

In *Final Fantasy VII*, then, the rewards for the storyseeker exploit the medium. The computer makes it possible both to deploy animation narrative and narrational ideas, and also to create the digital convention of combat whose significance is personal and symbolic to the player, rather as the medieval knight Yvain's vanquishing of the serpent is meaningful for his inner development. The storyseeker identifies with the protagonist actively through skill and the ability to negotiate the increasingly difficult fights on behalf of Cloud Strife, and is rewarded with access to the next level of convincing storytelling. This form originated in Japan, although it proved popular in the West, but the scale and ambition of the venture, the range of skills and talents required to implement it, have fallen outside the scope of European productions.

Final Fantasy VIII follows, in its use of the visual medium, the development of computer-aided animation, characterized in the West by the rapid move in the Disney Studios computer-supported animation from 'somewhat 3Dish' in *Aladdin* (Ron Clements, John Musker, US, 1992) to predominantly so in *Tarzan* (Chris Buck and Keven Lima, US, 1999). The change in style and emphasis can be clearly appreciated by comparing *Fantasia* (Ben Sharpsteen, Joe Grant, Dick Heumer, US, 1940) with *Fantasia 2000* (Eric Goldberg, Hendel Butoy, Pixote Hunt, James Algar, Francis Glebas, Gaetan Brizzi & Paul Brizzi, Don Hahn, US, 2000). The use of '2½D'effects in big-screen animation echoes the more varied style of the small screen, and the diversity of shots and mise en scène in *Final Fantasy VIII* surpasses that of most other contemporary games, approaching not only the style of Japanese Manga in the action sequences but also that of Disney in the narrative/dramatic sequences. It has, however, its own distinctive aesthetic, exploiting the increased processing power of the entertainment console at the beginning of the third millennium. Its FMV 'look', far from the crude figures of *Over Blood*, offers a refined palette of colours, textures and movement; its graceful lines are far more reminiscent of the

Tenchu Stealth Assassins

Figure 16. Final Fantasy VIII (Squaresoft/Squaresoft 1999).

fluent tradition of Japanese calligraphy and woodcuts than of the rather grotesque planes of Lara Croft's inhuman plastic curves or those of the more sophisticated FMV characters in *Silent Hill*.

Potentials

It is clear that at the beginning of the second century of cinema history, interactive console games are only beginning to exploit the potential of screen language to tell their own kinds of stories. They succeed well when, like *Tomb Raider*, they employ the strategy of engaging the storyseeker with the protagonist, not through the usual screen narrative devices but by identifying the manual dexterity and adrenaline drive of the player and their problem-solving skills absolutely, through physical action, with the prowess and success of the story protagonist, Lara. If the player does nothing, Lara will die. Only through the player's direct steering of Lara can the protagonist even move forward through the storyscape. This is a very powerful form of empathic identification with the character, her misfortunes and successes. The building of a game through 'levels' of difficulty also serves to bind a player to the character, as player skill improves with commitment and effort, and allows the character to tackle more and more challenging physical feats at greater and greater speed, in direct proportion to the energy and concentration invested by the player. This is the method by which physical skills games and actual sports, such as tennis, darts, skating or dance, absorb their proponents. In the adventure game, the drive to acquire and improve new skills is identified with progress through the storyworld, and this is a very strong device for engagement.

Adventure games also succeed in gripping when, as in *Oddworld*, they use the arts and sciences of characterisation, mise en scène and camera narration developed by skilled animators to portray characters and to create atmospheric locations.

Of the examples examined here, *Oddworld: Abe's Oddysee* is the one which seems to combine most effectively the power of fairy tale with traditional screen language and narration – though the use of coloration, line and movement in the story sequences of *Final Fantasy VIII* perhaps comes closer to achieving the sensual engagement associated with memorable imaginative fantasy. *Oddworld* also has the closest match between intra-level narrative (in FMV – full motion video) and game/story narration, in style of animation and consistency of rhetoric. The use of Abe's own voice-over, telling his story in flashback, creates a real sense of identification with Abe as a character. The fact that his words are in verse gives the whole the stylized cadence of traditional epic nursery tales – as typified, perhaps, by Browning's *Pied Piper of Hamelin* (*Dramatic Lyrics*, GB, 1842). As a result, although the automaton-like little Mudokan slaves in *Oddworld: Abe's Oddysee* have a limited range of reactions, they are still charming and satisfying as characters, both because stylization is the aesthetic of the whole and because their range, though small, is the right dramatic range to engage players emotionally.

Oddworld: Abe's Exoddus goes further in this direction. Here, the Mudokan slaves express a wider range of emotions through their action and speech, and Abe (steered by you) has to produce appropriate responses to these – begging the slaves to move them on, hugging to comfort them, or slapping them to pull them out of the slough of despond – in order to induce them to act to help save themselves. As a dramaturgical approach, *Oddworld*'s technique has considerable promise, within the framework of an appropriate story and supported by expert artwork and strong scripting – though the focus on Abe's ability to fart and then transform his organic gases into useful explosives in *Oddworld: Abe's Exoddus* keeps the style definitely comic.

Abe's limited but effective social exchanges with his fellow Mudokans in *Oddworld* contrast with the much more complex dialogue elements in *Broken Sword II* and *Excalibur*, where the actual speech is not of itself expressive, dramatic, or fully character-based, but primarily expository; and is staged in such a way that the screen narration does not create drama. Complexity is not the same as dramatic effect. In good (screen) drama as well as in novels, information may be embedded in dialogue, but it is usually carefully wrapped in characterization or expressed as indirect reference. *Final Fantasy VII* and *VIII* approach these strategies, but the balance they find between information, characterization, expressive dialogue, pace and formal fluency is still somewhat uncomfortable, and in any case finally closer to graphic novel storytelling than cinematic narrative.

It helps in *Oddworld: Abe's Oddysee* that the Mudokans' attention-span is short, so the storyseeker is drawn in to identify with Abe, whose agility and problem-solving skills she or he controls, when Abe tries to get the slaves both to follow him in the first place and then to remain active in the face of danger – the Mudokans have to be constantly nudged, or they fall back into apathy and automatism. There is real pleasure to be had when, at Abe's (verbal) invitation to, 'Follow me!' a worker replies, in lacklustre tones, 'OK!' and matches the words with the action; and more satisfaction still if you can succeed in keeping the Mudokan following you (Abe) in order to get it out of danger. It is genuinely engaging in *Abe's Exoddus* to try to find the appropriate emotional cue to persuade a tortured Mudokan to take heart and act for freedom, because in order to do so you have to bring your own powers of empathy into play, in however limited a fashion. Similarly, in *Abe's Oddysee*, when you are getting frustrated by Abe's obligation to release slaves without the help of weapons, it is very satisfying to take over a guard and wreak havoc on the side of good.

As Bettelheim emphasizes, removing the dark side from stories makes them unsatisfying and unconvincing because everyone knows that life is not always sunny. Allowing the protagonist to control the evil is a very reassuring and empowering tactic, especially when s/he (Abe/the storyseeker) did not invent the evil, and does not become permanently degraded by temporarily borrowing the violent means of the predator to reverse the balance for a moment in order to achieve escape from a vicious world. The real moral nature of the storyseeker is engaged in ethical decision-making on Abe's behalf, as it is in classic drama from the *Orestaeia* of Aeschylus (525-456) through Shakespeare's *Hamlet* (1603) and on to Disney's *Dumbo* (Walt Disney and Ben Sharpsteen, US, 1941) , Powell and Pressburger's *Matter of Life and Death* (GB 1946) via Stanley Kubrick's *2001: A Space Odyssey* (UK 1968) to Miyazaki's *Princess Mononoke* (Japan 1996) or Cocks/Cameron/Bigelow's *Strange Days* (US 1996) and Ang Lee's *Crouching Tiger, Hidden Dragon* (US, China, HK, Taiwan, 2000).

Oddworld is pioneering in that it combines elements of expert screen storytelling (through 2D animation) with skills-based action gameplaying, and does so seamlessly. It also uses irony, referring to the Great Epics of our culture with clear intent to contrast them with Abe's humble adventures in the meat-packing factory, releasing the game from the obligation of taking itself too seriously, or asking too much of the player in terms of fictive engagement. It is not surprising that the game achieved best-seller status, and this type of structure may be a fruitful direction for future development in the medium of interactive adventure storytelling.

Final Fantasy's sophisticated use of combat experience to test the readiness of the player/hero to continue to more complex levels of moral action and narrative, combined with its use of graphic novel, animation, cinematic and dramatic storyforms, offers a great deal of potential at a high level of technical sophistication.

Combined with *Colony Wars*' impressive use of radio techniques, *Oddworld*'s engagement of the player in active dialogue with the characters, and *Tomb Raider* (the game)'s smooth fictionalization of the main character and identification with her through physical prowess and dependence on the player, make another powerful nexus for engagement in the games world. *Resident Evil* and *Metal Gear Solid* show that it is possible to use some of the strategies of traditional screen language effectively in the RT3D environment. *Silent Hill* demonstrates that the medium can also be used in a very sophisticated way to engage the storyseeker through subjective viewpoint in navigating the storyworld.

All these features are technically available, and if they were combined with the fundamental structural approaches and mise en scène outlined in Section 3 above, they could no doubt generate moving and powerful story experiences in adventure-game form, which would combine some of the strengths of traditional screen narrative with the power of interactive engagement specific to the computer as medium.

5. Storyscapes, Storyseekers and Storymakers – Dramatic Narrative in Navigable, Expressive Space

Identification, the Interactor and the Underlying System

Despite the rapid evolution and inventiveness of console adventure games, there are aspects of the potential of interactive digital storyseeking and dramatic storymaking that the titles reviewed here have not touched.

Brenda Laurel in her study, *Computers as Theatre* (US, 1991), looked at the relationship between traditional theatrical modes of thinking and the emerging computer culture. Although Laurel's book is pioneering and stimulating, its chief strength is also its major weakness: it begins from Aristotle's *Poetics* (4th century BC) and proceeds to classify various aspects of human computer interaction in terms derived from his categories and theorization of drama and poetics. Inevitably, the classification system is as limiting as it is liberating.

Subsequent studies, such as Allucquère Rosanne Stone's *War of Desire and Technology at the close of the mechanical age* (US, 1996), Sherry Turkle's *Life on the Screen* (US, 1996), William J Mitchell's *City of Bits* (US, 1996), and Donna J Haraway's

Modest_Witness@Second_Millenium.FemaleMan(c)_Meets_OncoMouse (US, 1997), focused on the crisis of identity precipitated by the computer as communicator, creative tool and creative medium. In so doing, they opened up the discussion of a new relationship between drama and audience/participator as well as drama and author(s).

Aristotle viewed drama as essentially a medium of imitation, which he asserts is fundamental to human nature – arguing from the de facto position that all art is imitation (mimesis). During the performance, the audience colludes with the actors in sharing the identity of the characters through an act of imagination or projection. The actors imitate the actions of the dramatis personae, whose identities they assume – though, note, in the ancient Greek context, not naturalistically but with masks, music, choreographed movement and stylized action – and the audience projects itself into that drama. The group of 1990s writers cited above are all fascinated by the fact that the relationship between a 'user' and a computer increasingly allows the process of assuming a new identity or a number of identities to happen not through imitation and projection but through direct participation – a kind of role-playing where the animated figures or avatars in a virtual world have no life until the 'user' or player breathes it into them.

In a shared space or Multi-User Domain (MUD) or in the simplest e-mail exchange, the sender of a digital message can adopt the persona of anyone they care to choose or invent or impersonate; and there is nothing about the nature of an e-mail address itself, or the off-the-peg or self-generated avatar a visitor in a shared space might use, that can act as a reliable indicator of that person's identity, as it would be recognized by their day-to-day friends, family and acquaintance. In online communities, although users may choose an avatar which resembles in some way their outward or visible characteristics or classifiable social position, they may equally choose one with diametrically opposed connotations, or one which presents a wished-for or distorted persona. Digital identity provides precious little clue to real-world status, class, culture, background, age, gender or location. It offers the storyseeker the possibility of becoming an actor and assuming the identity of a character, rather than, as a member of the audience, projecting into the actor's assumption/portrayal of a dramatic persona. Janet H Murray in her book, *Hamlet on the Holodeck: the Future of Narrative in Cyberspace* (US, 1997), habitually uses the term 'interactor' to designate the 'user' in an interactive digital narrative/dramatic context.

Allucquère Rosanne Stone finds the way digitality opens up the potential of multiple identities extremely exciting. It would be possible from her work to suggest that Freud's contention that art is the symptom of neurosis (*positively interpreted: and those who produce and enjoy it are vicarious beneficiaries of a form of therapy*) could perhaps be reviewed in the light of virtual characters. Human beings, instead of attempting – often with a lack of success which sometimes leads to their classification as insane – to conform to the single identity and single cultural position most societies allow them, might, with the help of the Net, 'avatars' and role-playing games, easily adopt all the identities they need in order to remain fulfilled and balanced people.

In the 21st century, in the West, most compulsive readers, theatre- and film-goers, TV-watchers and graphic-novel readers who project into the characters they follow are not labelled 'mad' but left to enjoy their 'therapy' in peace, identifying with the characters in their fictional dramas in the safe arena of the shared space of art. The ability to take on different identities, as an 'interactor', very directly, in the digital domain, may function safely as dramatic/narrative/lyric performance has always functioned, to precipitate *catharsis* or release – but of an unusually complete and socially acceptable kind. Acting out anger in the digital realm by zapping virtual monsters may be preferable to acting it out on the streets, just as reading Ian Fleming's James Bond books (from *Casino Royale* GB, 1951 to *Goldfinger* GB, 1964) or watching James Bond movies (from Terence Young's *Dr No* GB, 1962 onward), may be preferable to trying to act out the fantasies they embody. The Bond movies use sumptuous design and photography coupled with wit and style, in the scripting and directing as well as the acting, to locate the action firmly in the realms of fantasy. Early RT3D work with graphic environments rarely attains anything like this combination, but with the exponential increase in computing power and the consequent improvement in quality, there is no reason why new work, benefiting from earlier examples, should not – provided the crucial role of the set/production designer in creating expressive narrative space is fully recognized.

Watching films which provide spectator action/violence fests – such as Danny Cannon's *Judge Dredd* (US, 1995) and Tim Burton's *Mars Attacks* (US, 1996), based on the paranoia of the 1950s (cold war) and 1960s (overpopulation and urban horror), inspired by American comic books but with an eye to the interactive mayhem shoot 'em-up game – probably makes for less effective catharsis than playing a well-designed console game yourself. Bursting those Martian skulls full of green goo or splatting those cannibalistic, extra-urban lowlife cultists using your own rapid reflexes and joy-controlled deadly aim; zooming your skybike between the obstacles while firing on your attackers, without having to project into a character on the screen to enjoy the effect, offers more *inst. grat.* Especially as characterization and identification are evidently not the priority of the film-makers in these movies, which scarcely exploit dramatic live-action film rhetoric to involve audiences. Flying with the heroes of Ang Lee's *Crouching Tiger, Hidden Dragon* (US, China, HK, Taiwan, 2000) and soaring with them through hypernatural feats of strength and grace offers emotional release through the melodrama of the story, and inspirational and moral precepts through the development of its female protagonist; but playing *Tekken III* enables you to do something very close to performing those martial arts feats yourself.

Stone, in *The War of Desire and Technology*, addresses the topic of violence – cathartic or otherwise – in the storyworld (referred to by Bettelheim [1976] in the context of the fairy tale) as she looks at the question of hierarchies of power, freedom and control raised by digitality:

> *"Will virtual systems mean the end of gender binarism? Will virtual systems create a level playing field for everyone, regardless of ethnicity, color, gender, age, education, financial status, or the ability to load and fire semiautomatic weapons?"*

That, in fine, is why understanding how a few crazies at keyboards wind up influencing the social behavior of thousands of game players is an urgent undertaking. Is the answer, then, to outlaw violence and sexism in games? Almost certainly not. The Band-Aid approach of prohibition has a lousy and ineffectual history. For example, in the United States, since the Comics Code, which prohibits extreme violence in comic books, became the de facto industry standard in the late 1950s, violence among young persons has increased several *hundred* percent. If there is, in fact, some way to remold society closer to the heart's desire, it shows no visible signs of having anything to do with curing bad behavior by not looking at all those dangerous images. It's not the images, and it's not the technologies either. Neither, simply by itself, is going to "save" society. In fact, the idea that technology in and of itself is going to change the world for the better, as the myths surrounding VR would have it, is merely pernicious.

From time to time we have thought we found our Holy Grail in one or another of its manifestations... most recently, perhaps, computers. The metaphor of salvation that runs in a continual shining thread throughout our trafficking with all these technologies continues unbroken into VR. So it's important to consider how we make meaning, and the battles we fight over who gets to own the meanings of our technologies. Salvation is a particularly situated cluster of meanings in Western culture. It's androcentric; it's original-ly Caucasian in its world view; it's a central theme of particular national and political hegemonies. When we start talking about virtual technologies in terms of salvation we are simply retelling the old stories of technology as Holy Grail, as a hardware object, something condensed and made visible through the tellings and retellings of the cultural myths particular to us. These myths are extremely powerful, because they carry in veiled form the entire cultural force and imagined *progressus* of our Western societies. But, as the knights who searched for the Grail found out the hard way, if it's salvation that you simply must have, you will never find it in a physical object. (Stone, 1996,168-9)

Stone here warns that we should be careful not to misidentify the real power of digital technology. Ideology manifests in complex ways. Her thoughts resonate with those of Janet Murray:

Political assumptions behind the [game] are hidden from the player... The basic competitive premise... is not emphasised as an interpretive choice... In an interactive medium the interpretive framework is embedded in the rules by which the system works and in the way in which participation is shaped. But the encyclopedic capacity of the computer can distract us from asking why things work the way they do and why we are being asked to play one role rather than another. As these systems take on more narrative content, the interpretive nature of these structures will be more and more important. We do not yet have much practice in identifying the underlying values of a multiform story. We will have to learn to notice the patterns displayed over multiple plays of a simulation in the same way that we now notice the worldview behind a single-plot story. (Murray, 1997, 89)

Murray is here warning, like Stone, that there has scarcely yet been time to apply a political or deconstructive eyeglass to the emerging and very powerful cultural poetics of interactivity and narrative/drama in the digital domain. She also notes that, 'The earliest vision of hypertext reflects the classic American quest – a charting of the wilderness, an imposition of order over chaos, and the mastery of vast resources for concrete, practical purposes' (Murray, 1997, 91).

As suggested earlier, in art, and particularly in console games, the quest (or mission) motif touched on by both Stone and Murray – with all its cultural resonances – is very powerful. *Indiana Jones and the Last Crusade, The Lord of the Rings, Star Wars* – all works which are a fertile inspiration and source of characters, plots and images for console games of the 1990s – draw on the 'quest' archetype. As Bettelheim pointed out (p.55 above), the lone hero in the fairy tale (who inhabits the epic story as well as the adventure tale) symbolizes and absorbs our need to find, as individuals, the confidence to go out into the unknown world and deal with all the challenges and surprises, pleasant or unpleasant, it may contain. The other side of the coin, Murray (1997) and Stone (1996) imply, may be a hidden – perhaps not particularly well hidden – tendency toward patterns of control, hierarchy and exploitation, in the very structure of storygames based on conquest scenarios. Where these require interactors to take on the role of lone hero turned conqueror, and provide little or none of the traditional mediation through narrative stance which might contextualize, ironize or moralize the position, the player may have less choice than the reader, or audience of representational fiction, in identifying with storyworld personas – and perhaps internalizing their values. Perhaps players may find the reflexes of defence, attack, and achieving the goal despite the obstacles, 'hardwired' into their physical beings through repeated practice, rather than sublimated through projection and imaginative effort.

Finally, it seems to me, the onus is on the authors and producers to take responsibility or not for the wider ramifications of a story, a play, a film, television programme or interactive title. Some of the titles examined here implicitly contain an ethical stance in their premises. Abe in *Oddworld* has to save fellow slaves without the aid of a weapon – unless he appropriates the persona of a (wicked) guard and can utilize its weapon for freedom, or uses his cunning method of converting his own farts into explosives. The *Lost Vikings* (see Appendix) cannot proceed without each other's skills in combat – the player has to deploy them as a team, all helping each other, to get them back to where they belong. In *Final Fantasy VII* Cloud Strife is out to destroy corporate power gone mad, and restore the balance of nature – and the player has to work through a co-ordinated team of helpers, though Cloud Strife fulfils the role of the lone adventurer.

Tomb Raider sets up a female protagonist who is refined, artistic and educated as well as wealthy, strong and physically fearless, requiring the storyseeker to familiarize themselves with Lara's natural surroundings and her character while they learn her powers of movement and how to operate her. The video intro (FMV) explicitly tells us that Lara's adventures are undertaken 'for the sport', not to achieve power or status. In the adventure game Lara shoots only in self-defence – but, nonetheless, the game, especially in *Tomb Raider II* and *III* (though *IV* offers the possibility that Lara is conscious of her own responsibility for the unrolling of events) is not very closely interwoven with the video interludes telling the story, and can easily be played without reference to those interludes.

Jedi Masters retains none of the archetypal storypattern or moral dimension of the film *Return of the Jedi* (US, 1983) and *Nuclear Strike* explicitly demands that players identify with the American (voiced) attackers against the Indo-Chinese, their (our) legitimate victims.

Tenchu: Stealth Assassins builds missions (familiar from overtly military games like *Colony Wars* and *Nuclear Srtike*) into the martial arts world offered in *Tekken* only as a zone for single combat. *Tenchu*, like *Metal Gear Solid*, requires that you complete your mission by stealth – that you are fast and inventive at avoiding attack, escaping from danger, outwitting your assailants, and using speed and agility to convert your opponents' brute force into their downfall. This development away from destructive violence toward martial arts parallels the progress in the cinema from the James Bond action movies of the 1960s through the Indiana Jones/Conan the Barbarian' epic adventures of the 1980s and the science- and cyber-fiction of the 1990s, such as *The Fifth Element* and *The Matrix*, toward Ang Lee's *Crouching Tiger, Hidden Dragon* martial-arts movie of the early 21st century.

Bust a Groove uses similar choreographed motion-capture-based animation to *Tekken*, but does so to create a game where rather than fighting with your partner, you dance with them. However, you dance in competition and you can learn moves that will slow down the contestant who is dancing against/with you as well as routines that will gain you points.

Apart from *The X-Files Adventure,* the 3D *Resident Evil II* and *III*, and to a certain extent *Metal Gear Solid,* come closest to traditional filmic narration in terms of technique and mediating the way storyseekers experience content. There is no doubt that the zombies in *Resident Evil*, who attack ruthlessly, need to die (they are by definition dead already and only tormented by their living death, so, though technically human, they are clearly monstrous opponents) and the player role is one of helper, searching for team mates or relatives in need of rescue. The story of the 'T' virus is more closely integrated into the fabric of the narrative in *Resident Evil* than the 'G' virus in *Resident Evil II*, and it is interesting that *Resident Evil III* does attempt to enrich the basic formula by adding a revenge motif – your character is, so to speak, hoist with his own petard. *Resident Evil II* exploits the possibilities of a circular storyform and the capabilities of the computer by asking the storyseeker to inhabit both the female and the male adventurer – if you play Part One as Claire, you are inducted into Part Two as Leon, and vice versa. The adventure is essentially the same, with the same monsters and events, whichever character you play – though, interestingly, the language of the dialogues has active, effective, quick-witted Claire called 'love' by the characters who address Leon as 'mate'. Does calling someone 'love' imply that she is 'other'? Of lower status than you? Does calling someone 'mate' imply equality? Narrative stance includes more than merely the camera's point of view.

It is striking that on the big screen, the active female protagonist has battled her way determinedly from the leading role(s) in the Franco-Italian *Barbarella*, where sexuality and sensuality are emphasized but women are self-actuated and free, in 1968; through the supporting cast in America's *Conan the Barbarian* in 1985, where shared experience and interests plus physical tenderness between the physically strong create a partnership; via France's 1997 Lilou, the 'Fifth Element', invincible according to the plotline, but who, through Besson's narrative stance, is portrayed as finally vulnerable and needy of Willis' Korben (the tough guy with the soft heart); to cool and effective British *Tomb Raider* Lara Croft, who lands in and sorts out her own adventures, as interpreted by Angelina Jolie in 2001.

Like movies, the games looked at above involve a protagonist, played by the interactor, who is fictionalized, presented visibly as a character; and some of the conventions of screen narrative and narration are quite naturally incorporated into the play. Bone-bare shoot-'em-ups, such as *Alien Trilogy*, represent the subjective position of the interactor with a hand (triggering a gun) alone (also the practice of online shared shoot-'em-ups like *Half-Life, Unreal Tournament, Quake* and *Doom*). Despite *Alien Trilogy*'s claim that the protagonist is Ellen Ripley from the (very carefully structured) *Alien* films – *Alien* (Ridley Scott, GB, 1969), *Aliens* (James Cameron, US, 1986),and *Alien 3* (Peter Fincher, US 1992) – she never in fact appears and the story is not a story but a jumping off place for the unreasoning destruction of generic Aliens by the players themselves.

In general, while the rhetoric of 'interactive' narration is in the process of developing, there often seems little consistency in narrative stance or attitude towards the action embedded in console gamestories. In film, Tim Burton's *Mars Attacks* (US, 1996), a sort of antithesis of Kubrick's *Dr Strangelove* (GB, 1963), offers an illustration of what happens when insecurity and paranoia blossom into imperialist violence, racism and hatred-driven mayhem. Unmediated by a clear stance in the narration, satirizing indiscriminately every aspect both of contemporary culture and its own film genre and stars, *Mars Attacks* provides the audience with the alternatives only of standing clear, or projecting into and sharing the general paranoia (regarding it as sanity) – or hoping, with the fairy-tale 'third son' hero (the one who can do nothing right until at the final crunch his values turn out, almost by accident, to save the day), that everything will be okay if we defend ourselves with yuck music and perhaps try living in tepees so as to balance overtech. The lack of interpretation or a consistent narrational stance – in contrast to Kubrick's carefully controlled anti-paranoia rhapsody, *Dr Strangelove*, which addresses the same theme of trigger-happy militarism and the need for attack-based defensive strategy – arguably makes *Mars Attacks* a presentation of violence that can quite easily be read as a celebration or affirmation rather than a meditation upon its subject.

While Bigelow's *Strange Days* contains both implicit and explicit reflections on the nature of the violence and victimization it portrays, and on the ethics of an entertainment industry which lives by drawing audiences into violent and sadistic fantasies, Paul Verhoven's *Starship Troopers* (US, 1997), another 1990s film which, like Danny Cannon's *Judge Dredd*, exploits the idiom of shoot-'em-up games on the big screen, is open to the same criticism as *Mars Attacks* – the perpetuation of paranoia and the celebration of beligerence, racism and power-driven violence – for the same reasons. Lack of narrational stance, or its presence, is not a necessary concomitant of any particular medium. Deploying it is the responsibility of the people creating and producing work in that medium.

Narration and narrative strategies such as contextualizing stance are, however, not the only considerations in understanding how screen arts and sciences achieve their effects. Christopher Vogler, in *The Writer's Journey: Mythic Structure for Storytellers and Screenwriters* (US, Micheal Wiese Productions, Studio City, 1992), borrowing freely from Joseph Campbell's *The Hero with a Thousand Faces* (US, 1973) and Vladimir Propp's *Morphology of the Folktale* (US/GB 1968, trans. Laurence Scott), claims that 'all stories consist of a few common structural elements found universally in myths, fairy tales, dreams, and movies' (Weise, 1992, 3). His words express a popular general approach embraced and developed by Spielberg, Lucas and Stone/Milius in particular, in the 1970s and 1980s, which still informed the films of the 1990s, many of which were mined for 'look', incident, backstory and characters by the creators of early console games. However, console games, even when they refer directly – like *Alien Trilogy* and *Jedi Masters* – to films with archetypal stories, by no means automatically incorporate the essence of those stories any more than their narrative stance. An understanding of how moving-image storytelling conventions work is a crucial tool in structuring RT3D dramatic adventures which reach beyond the surface mechanics of film-like sequences, and which deliver their violence and mayhem as part of, rather than all of, a story package.

In the end, no medium is in itself evil or good. Moral and ethical choices lie with authors, directors, producers and consumers, just as they always have with the tellers of tales and not with computers or cameras.

Creativity and Computers

The computer's ability to empower us to actively take the part of the 'Hero with a Thousand Faces' of the archetypal fairy-tale-like narratives beloved of console entertainment is extremely alluring. But can we – and should we – find ways of combining traditional arts and crafts (not only those of screen narrative, but of other kinds of storytelling and drama as well) with the fertile potential of this protean medium, able to adopt and adapt other media, as well as provide unique contributions of its own?

The potential for making such a powerful combination, or convergence, looks glorious in theory, but actually exploiting it requires us to review carefully our ways of thinking about narrative structures, exploration and control. The traditional possibiities of *linear, episodic, associational* and *circular* narrative (as outlined by Parks, 1998), for example, can surely provide solid groundwork for interactive storymaking; but they need re-exploration and re-deployment if they are to respond to the constraints as well as the freedoms of computational storytelling.

'Branching' story structures such as the one used in Peter Howitt's movie, *Sliding Doors* (GB/US, 1997) – where the main character steps through sliding doors into an alternative version of her reality, and the movie switches between events in both – or, to some extent in *The X-Files Adventure*, where different choices open (slightly) different paths through the story, have proved problematic in actual practice in the interactive environment. The immense amount of footage/data required to make all the possible alternatives work craves too much work (and money) to create, too much space to store, and too much processing power to handle smoothly; while the clumsiness of interacting with a mouse or joypad and a series of non-diagetic devices like icons and screen menus at critical points in the narrative flow make the whole experience too mechanical and distant to really engage storyseekers with the story.

At the beginning of the third millennium, storyworlds where characters may be shaped, as 'autonymous' or 'semi-autonymous', 'artificially intelligent' agents, to react to story possibilities in ways close to dramatic improvisation; or where they develop according to behaviour rules partly or wholly determined by players (as in simulation games like *The Sims*), rather than playing dramatic roles within a fully composed play or story, absorb the attention of many console entertainment designers, and may develop along the lines of television soap. Stephen Poole in his ardent and provocative book, *Trigger Happy* (GB, 2000), claims that because the nature of interactive gaming is to engage the interactor in a continuous present, it lacks the vital ability of other forms of narrative (such as the cinematic) to combine the 'synchronic' and 'diachronic' elements ('present time' and 'other time') of plot, and will therefore never be a proper story medium (Poole, 2000, 106). He concludes that, 'Videogames can only continue to thrive and evolve as long as they concentrate on what they do best: build us ever more realistic constructions of ever more aesthetically wondrous worlds' (Poole, 2000, 255) – apparently dismissing altogether the potential attractions of a non-realistic construction and a different kind of narrative experience.

Indeed, the *associational* form of narrative, though it has already been exploited in hypertext fiction, has scarcely yet been approached in moving-image-based interactive media, and certainly not in the popular arena of console games – though *Final Fantasy VII* and *VIII* begin to touch on its potential. Nonetheless, this would seem an ideally flexible type of narrative in the context of the computer, and one which needs to be explored in the interactive environment with something of the spatio-temporal and rhetorical inventiveness, both visual and dramatic, of Tom Tykwer's 1999 movie, *Run Lola Run*, Andrei Tarkovsky's 1974 *Mirror,* or Stanley Kubrick's 1968 *2001: A Space Odyssey*. Cyberspace is navigable in every dimension, and plots which merely confine themselves to the continuity of following the recovery of an amnesiac's memory or travelling through continuous spatial environments solving puzzles or collecting objects, exploit only a tiny range of the possible spectrum.

George P Landow in his book, *Hypertext – the Convergence of Contemporary Critical Theory and Technology* (US, 1997), outlines an optimistic and inspiring attitude to the potential of non-linear types of narrative (he uses *hypertext* and *hypermedia* interchangeably, so 'textuality' refers to moving-image based work as much as to print media):

> In *S/Z*, Roland Barthes describes an ideal textuality that precisely matches that which in computing has come to be called hypertext – text composed of blocks of words (or images) linked electronically by multiple paths, chains, or trails in an open-ended, perpetually unfinished textuality described by the terms *link, node, network, web* and

path: "In this ideal text," says Barthes, "the networks [*réseaux*] are many and interact, without any one of them being able to surpass the rest; this text is a galaxy of signifiers, not a structure of signifieds; it has no beginning; it is reversible; we gain access to it by several entrances, none of which can be authoritatively declared to be the main one; the codes it mobilizes extend *as far as the eye can reach*, they are indeterminable...; the systems of meaning can take over this absolutely plural text, but their number is never closed, based as it is on the infinity of language" (emphasis in original; 5-6 [English translation]; 11-12 [French]. (Landow 1997, 3)

Artistically speaking, this line of inquiry is inspiring for moving-image stoytellers. It also represents a view of the potential of shared space and networked participation in an artistic event, which excited and stimulated many in the late 1990s. However, here as elsewhere, the human mind has reached further than technology. The software to author and support sophisticated distributed interpersonal interactions in storyscapes and moving-image narration requires a lot of work before it is perfected. In order for it to develop effectively, it will be necessary for storymakers to work very closely with software designers. If the creation of digital adventure story games is left largely with software designers, the pure problem-solving element that drives so much of their work is likely to predominate, as it does in *Excalibur*, to the detriment of dramatic and narrative qualities. The constraints imposed by the state of the art in staging character-based action in RT3D environments, instead of being analysed and overcome, will *de facto* determine the parameters of the storytelling and drama. There is no intrinsic need to limit the potential of navigable dramatic narrative in the moving-image environment in this way, and the commercial imperatives have been challenged by work like *Final Fantasy VIII* as well as *The X-Files Adventure*.

Janet Murray sees the special properties of the computer as great potential enablers of fiction:

> When we stop thinking of the computer as a multimedia telephone link, we can identify its four principal properties, which separately and collectively make it a powerful vehicle for literary creation. Digital environments are procedural, participatory, spatial and encyclopedic. (Murray, 1997, 71)

She goes on to amplify:

> The new digital medium is intrinsically procedural... To be a computer scientist is to think in terms of algorithms and heuristics, that is, to be constantly identifying the exact or general rules of behavior that describe any process, from running a payroll to flying an airplane... The computer can be a compelling medium for storytelling if we can write rules for it which are recognizable as an interpretation of the world. The challenge for the future is how to make such rule writing as available to writers as musical notation is to composers. (Murray, 1997, 71)

The appeal, to this way of thinking, of the Vladimir Propp – Joseph Campbell –

Christopher Vogler analysis of archetypal story and character structures, is obvious; and it is not surprising that console-game stories tend to look to embody such pattern behaviours and structures, finding their easiest inspiration in those films and other fictive media which already exploit formulaic story-building. However, many genres, from film noir (flirted with in *Discworld Noir*) to the backstage musical, remain to be explored in console story games, and genre can be much stronger and more interesting than formulaic plot as a framework within which to build creatively. Murray makes a dubious assumption in equating 'the world' with 'the storyworld' – another echo of Aristotle's 'mimesis' theory. As successful animation-based interactive dramatic fiction shows, the storyworld a computer can generate is, in a myriad of exhilarating ways, more flexible, exciting and imaginative than the world of real reality we all inhabit, and this is one of its great powers. The 'non-reality' offered by the cinematic and TV genres of film noir or space opera seem ripe for experiment with computer creativity.

Considering the potential of computer-supported narrativity, Murray looks at a second narrative property of the computer – its capacity to enable active participation:

> A second core property of the computer [is] its participatory organization. Procedural environments are appealing to us not just because they exhibit rule-generated behavior but because we can induce the behavior. They are responsive to our input. Just as the primary representational property of the computer is the codified rendering of responsive behaviors. This is what is most often meant when we say that computers are *interactive*. We mean they create an environment that is both procedural and participatory... (p. 79) The first step in making an enticing narrative world is to script the interactor... [provide] an appropriate repertoire of actions that players could be expected to know before they enter the program... By using literary and gaming conventions to constrain the players' behaviors to a dramatically appropriate but limited set of commands... designers could focus their inventive powers on making the virtual world as responsive as possible to every possible combination of these commands. But if the key to compelling storytelling in a participatory medium lies in scripting the interactor, the challenge for the future is to invent scripts that are formulaic enough to be easily grasped and responded to but flexible enough to capture a wider range of human behavior than treasure hunting and troll slaughter. (Murray, 1997, 74)

Of course, the epitome of human behaviour-based drama is television soap, many of whose narrations tend to work with a naturalism which is not a part of the world of fairy tale and rarely of the world of fantasy. The skills of professional soap-writers have not yet been seriously directed to the creation of console games, though some of them have been integrated in some of the aspects of the *Sims* phenomenon. The 'rules' of soap are much clearer than the 'rules' of many other genres, and the structures of TV soap quite naturally fall into hypertext patterns. However, soap audiences tend not to be predominantly the adolescent male generally favoured by console games marketing. But as Murray points out (Murray, 1997, 85), Web fan culture burgeoned rapidly round such US TV series as *Babylon 5* (J Michael Straczynski's space opera, 1993, GB C4 TV 1994), where interactors create new stories for characters in the series and, as an aid to memory, keep a hypertext 'bible' – not unlike fanzine encyclopaedias – on the model of a traditional soap 'bible', containing all the character and story information pertaining to *dramatis personae* old and new, used by scriptwriters for reference. Soap would seem to lend itself to computer fiction in structure, but not yet in characterization, dramatic mise en scène, and setting. It is a clear 'next step' for interactive digital broadcasting, and entertainment consoles are closer to TV in many respects, such as their domestic 'sit back' alignment, than to computers or cinemas.

Even the potential of the serialized comic book, which might provide models for digital soap, has not been fully exploited – PlayStation's *Marvel Comic Heroes* game only offers (not very sophisticated) combats between well-known characters, not real stories. Nothing as ambitious – and successful in terms of adapting the comic book for the contemporary screen- as Roger Vadim's film *Barbarella* (France/Italy, 1968), Robert Iscove's *Flash* (US, 1996) or even Warren Beatty's *Dick Tracy* (US, 1990) has been attempted for interactive multiplayer console games, though there is no intrinsic reason why it should not be. The move *Final Fantasy VIII* makes toward graphic-novel convention indicates that the medium is potentially capable of handling sophisticated material though generic parameters. The emphasis, however, in games creation, has been on role-playing models, a quite different genre. Nonetheless, soap seems a very fruitful potential sphere for hybrid multiplayer interaction, where video, live broadcast and virtual environments could easily combine within the established stylistic framework.

Murray's remaining two core properties of the computer (and digital environments) as creative tool and medium, are that they are *spatial* and *encyclopaedic*:

> The new digital environments are characterised by their power to represent navigable space. Linear media such as books and films can portray space, either by verbal description or image, but only digital environments can present space that we can move through... The challenge for the future is to invent an increasingly graceful choreography of navigation to lure the interactor through ever more expressive narrative landscapes. (Murray, 1997, 79)

> Computers are the most capacious medium ever invented, promising infinite resources... (p. 84) The encyclopedic capacity of the computer and the encyclopedic expectation it arouses make it a compelling medium for narrative art. The capacity to represent enormous quantities of information in digital form translates into an artist's potential to offer a wealth of detail, to represent the world with both scope and particularity... It offers writers the opportunity to tell stories from multiple vantage points and to offer intersecting stories that form a dense and wide-spreading web. (Murray, 1997, 83)

In the context of console games, the capacity for spatial navigation is fundamental to the *Tomb Raider* concept – though in *Tomb Raider II* and *III*, the detail of landscape seems to have monopolized much of the game's design attention, at the expense of story/drama orientation, and this is a danger in structuring console storygames when environment is regarded primarily as a challenge to the world-imitating powers of software rather than expressive storyscape. RT3D makes spatially organized narrative a reality, and this is a genuinely exciting creative area to explore.

The capacity of the computer to store and retrieve information referred to by Murray is exploited in *Colony Wars*, which has a type of modified branching narrative structure wherein the player, a member of the rebel Colonies' battle starfleet, wages war against an Earth which has become the controlling centre of an Empire, whose power has spread 'like a sickness' through the galaxy, treating colony planets merely as an exploitable source of mineral wealth to replace the necessities now exhausted at home.

The revolution against the Earth is led by an invisible 'Father', represented in the game only by a Voice – which speaks directly to the player – who co-ordinates missions directed against the Earth's aggression, or defence assignments to protect the innocent colonists. The 'Father' can in our own mind stand for any figure of power we trust or commit to, though the mystery of his concealed identity gives room for the doubt everyone sometimes feels of any such powerful and trusted figure. The graphics in this game are purely computer-generated, with virtually no attempt to simulate cel animation or human modelling (which also means that they occupy relatively little storage space and require relatively little processing power to work effectively). The colours are pure and vivid; the lines elegant and dynamic, with a coherent and vibrant aesthetic which provides a perpetual ballet of movement and light on the screen. This is an environment you can find nowhere but in the digital realm – it does not imitate, it makes new electronic representations of spacecraft, stars, planets, space.

In *Colony Wars*, human speech (the Commander) provides commentary on the War, both moral and practical, orienting the player culturally and spatially, while the missions are guided by a computer with a (female) human voice. The objective is to keep fighting bravely, whether or not you think you can ever win – to take part in the common struggle for freedom from oppression, to 'be' human, rejecting the Earth's assumption that colonists (you) are inferior. And the result of each mission (your prowess) actually determines the course of the War. In general, if you fail in an aggressive mission, you are assigned to defensive action until you succeed again. The War can end in a number of ways, after the completion of a range of missions. *Colony Wars* is structured much like traditional *Snakes and Ladders*, a board game which can be played over and over again because its sequences never quite repeat themselves, but it also contains a moral dimension lacking in *Snakes and Ladders*, and a system where the effort of the player really counts to change the outcome of the cyberworld's history – a history with a clear relationship both to actual human history, and the powerful mythos of *Star Trek* (Gene Roddenberry, US, Desilu/Paramount/Norway Corporation; NBC TV 1966-, BBC TV 1969-).

In *Colony Wars* the player identifies directly with a specific situation and problem to be solved, has a defined enemy who is not the expected alien, but the wicked forces of human civilisation (easy to identify as whoever is oppressing us at the time of playing), and enters into a direct relationship with the voice (-over) of the Commander and his thoughts about the War and the Father and the individual missions. Instructions for action come from the spoken voice of the computer, reinforced by 'teletyped' text – a 'natural' medium of communication for a computer screen, though not for human beings (as compared, say, with *Excalibur*, where the combination of recorded voice and text is merely anomalous, or *Final Fantasy VII* and *VIII*, where the text boxes make the whole experience more like reading an animated graphic novel than watching a movie).

In *Colony Wars*, what you see is spacecraft fighting spacecraft, not living creatures doing battle. The speed is fast and the skills level high, though if you keep failing, you get slightly easier missions until you are up to speed. The destruction is always reasoned morally, and there are creative missions (for example, repair and building) as well as destructive ones. The game grips because it really exploits the medium in which it exists, taking a strong narrative stance rather than creating a world of violence and mayhem without moral clarity. It empowers the player to fight to overcome oppression, and to affect the course of the history that is made on the screen. The enigma of who the Father really is, is built into the progress of the War, commented on by the voice of the Commander – not, as so often, played out in prerecorded dramatic sequences involving characters that are badly realized and do not engage the player. As Stone and Murray remark (above, p. 115), ideology is built into the game system itself, as much as into the story content.

Storyscapes, Story Seekers and Story Makers

In the last five years of the 20th century, the Sony PlayStation began to explore the extension of the dramatic storyworld with which listeners, readers, cinema goers and television viewers were already familiar, an exploration then just being made possible by interactive digital technology. Narrative cinema and television continue, like the novel, to dominate their media, and the attraction of dramatic narrative is unlikely to fail in the digital domain – if it can develop a richness, range and effectiveness to rival or exceed its precursors, and which uses to the full the special characteristics of computer interactivity.

Following Landow's way of thinking, interactive narrative may be seen as the ultimate *scriptable* form, to use Barthes' 1970 (*S/Z*) structuralist term – at the opposite end of the scale to the *lisible*. Broadly speaking, the *scriptible*, or writerly, text is one where the readers must be active in puzzling out the meaning, writing it, as it were, for themselves, while the *lisible* or readerly text is one that readers passively consume. The intensely controlled narrative and narration of the typical 19th-century novel (say Charles Dickens' *Great Expectations* (GB, 1861), filmed by David Lean (GB, 1946) and Alfonso Cuarón (US 1997) – considered ultimately *lisible* ('readerly'), can be paralleled in many films created as film, not adapted from novels. A good example of such a parallel is Ingmar Bergman's *Fanny and Alexander* (Sweden, 1982), though *Star Wars* or *Indiana Jones* would certainly fall into the same general category as far as narrative and narrational control by the author(s) is concerned. *Over Blood* attempts to make itself *lisible* by inserting long (inexpert) narrative sequences between the levels of active problem-solving, shoot-'em-up play, but it falls between the stools of consumption and creation because the prepared dishes it offers are not appetizing and the language of its active play fails to exploit moving-image rhetoric to make itself engaging. Why try for the *lisible* – difficult to achieve in interactive narrative – when the *scriptible* is so much more alluring and formally appropriate to the medium?

Although in literary and screen terms the 'post-modern' *scriptable* work still, at the beginning of the 21st century, tends to be regarded as highbrow or not quite mainstream – for example, Milorad Pavic's *Dictionary of the Khazars, a Lexicon Novel in 100,000 words*, trans. Christina Pribicevic-Zoric (US, 1988) – there is in fact no reason why a more associative, more writerly mode of narration might not succeed well in popular computer entertainment. Oliver Stone's *Natural Born Killers* (US, 1996) and Robert Altman's *Short Cuts* (US, 1996) experimented with an associational and writerly approach to film narration (not narrative), and attracted an audience within the mainstream. Popular novels such as Kathleen Ann Goonan's *Queen City Jazz* (US, 1994) or *Crescent City Blues* (US, 2000), Connie Willis' *Bellwether* (GB, 1996) or Viktor Pelevin's *Clay Machine Gun* (USSR, 1998) successfully incorporate the procedural, spatial, encyclopaedic and transformational potentials of digital domain fiction into prose narration and narrative on the page.

By the beginning of the 21st century, console games had already created a group of storyseekers who actively desired to be writerly in the creation of their own stories, at least by 'becoming' the heroes of their own adventures. Many people are growing interested in interactive digital broadcasting and DVD-enabled set-top boxes, a natural platform for interactive fiction, not only for gameplaying, but for more dramatic forms of entertainment – simply because they continue to fulfil the traditional role of the domestic TV set.

This does not necessarily mean that such storyseekers have to be endowed with the hard-won skills or talents and sensibility of a professional writer or storyteller, or that they need, themselves, to internalize the conventions of screen and/or other narrative forms and narrational techniques. It does, however, mean that in addition to utilizing the procedural, participatory, spatial and encyclopedic properties of the computer both as authoring tool and medium, authors who wish to explore 'interactive' narrative drama need to deploy a wide range of appropriate compositional skills. These include the *narrative* (structural, plotting, suspense), *narrational* (telling, mise en scène, narrative stance), *dramatic* (characterization, meaningful interaction) and *generic* – such as fairy tale, quest, film noir, soap, melodrama, character-based drama, and romance. The word 'interactive' is placed in inverted commas because most 20th-century so-called 'interactive' games might more properly be described as *participative*, or non-linear, insofar as, rather as in the experience of some kinds of mixed-media installation, although players of console games can choose perspectives or alternative routes, they can rarely if ever radically affect the precomposed architectures of the stories in which they engage. This does not alter the fact that the medium of 'interactive' console entertainment and its followers and derivatives remains a potentially very powerful one, which by the beginning of the 21st century had only begun to be explored. Of course games will develop and focus as games; but there is plenty of room for new dramatic media content forms alongside them, which use similar technologies.

It says much that the words *lisible* (readerly) and *scriptible* (writerly) themselves embody the terminology of the written text, even though, when they were first employed in the 1970s, they were already beginning to be used to describe kinds of language systems which transcend the written. At the beginning of the 21st century, statistics suggest that many children – as well as young and not-so-young adults – spend much more time with their games consoles than they spend with written texts.

Scriptible, as stories go, could be seen simply to mean, in the context of interactive digital technology, 'a piece of imaginative fiction where storyseekers or interactors do much of the active work of constructing meaning – decompressing the information – themselves, starting from the package supplied by an author or authors'. The storyseekers in sophisticated fiction of this type, by adopting and physically controlling a questing, learning, character(s), have to find a story for themselves in the storyworld environment. They have to 'play' the collaborative, illusory game with the dramatists/narrators/characters, in order to experience the tale. Yet surprisingly little of the richness of the narrative and dramatic potential available to console storyseekers (different genres, different styles, different storyforms, interplay between characters) has been embedded in storyscapes. Although the fairy-tale function of console adventure games as suggested by Bettelheim helps make the patterns analysed here powerful, there is plenty of room to go beyond the narrow scope of a single hero pitted against the monsters.

Many of the ingredients necessary for a much richer approach to interactive narrative drama exist on the entertainment console platform. There is no real reason why we should not at once combine the choreographed movement of the fighters in *Tekken II* and *III* – where the joy of combat can be very fierce if you are in control of a winning character, and its challenge very stimulating if you are struggling to beat a skilled opponent – or the varied dance routines of *Bust A Groove*, with the imaginative 'sets'/locations of *Tomb Raider*, the characterization of Lara Croft and Abe, the mystery and narrational skills of *Resident Evil*, the complex story viewpoint/identification and intrigue of *Silent Hill*, and the in-game interaction and animation expertise of *Oddworld and Final Fantasy VII* and *VIII*, to provide multilayered narrative with expert, informed narration, opening up the possibilities of active storyseeking within a thoroughly satisfying storyscape. The *Tenchu* and *Silent Hill* series approached this by the early 21st century.

In order to engage an audience, and sustain their involvement, using dramatic and storytelling devices as well as skills deployment (dexterity), it seems that it will be necessary to educate new creative generations to appreciate how narrative structures and characterization and screen narration work, in addition to understanding puzzle-solving and skills acquisition as a means of inviting the storyseeker into the storyscape, and incorporating procedural and in particular spatial constructions as an organic part of their fictive rhetoric. The PlayStation game *Jedi Masters,* which has some impressive scenic graphics, had the potential to work in this way – but in fact it only creates combats between *Star Wars* (*Return of the Jedi*) characters, with no consistent drama, story, characterization or motivation behind them to engage players beyond the level of the instant adrenaline reaction. Although *Jedi Power Battles*, which is set within a clearer storyframe, works to fictionalize your character more clearly and enables team play, the story as such is still not woven into the game as an intrinsic part of its design.

Designers need to learn to exploit the spatial possibilities of storyscape not just as a passive backdrop to action, but as an active, explorable story-generating environment – enabling drama of a kind only possible in navigable narrative.

Judging by the popularity of the console games looked at here, the active protagonist approach to storyseeking – and finding – is one which already had great appeal and a willing and eager participator group of enthusiasts by the end of the 20th century. These will not remain adolescents forever. Peter Pan stayed in Neverland, but Wendy grew up – and continued to tell the wonderful stories which author JM Barrie suggests are the original stuff of which Neverland is made.

Play and Players

Although the conflation of story and game is a form that only began to blossom at the turn of the 20th century in digital media, the idea is certainly not new. The English word 'play' used for a theatrical performance since Shakespeare's time (following from the mediaeval 'Christmas games', the enactments of popular seasonal drama) contains the important recognition that theatrical performance or staged action requires both the actors and the audience to take part in the game – to 'play'. Indeed, the word 'player' is still synonymous both with 'actor' or 'performer' in a drama, and with 'gamer', the active player in a game. In drama, the audience has to be complicit with the cast and the performance – without their willing participation in the illusion of theatre, there would be no imaginative experience. The audience has to accept dramatic and narrative conventions for what they are, and enter into the make-believe, become players, very much as children do when they play at being Luke Skywalker or Xena, Warrior Princess, or Lara Croft, and as listeners have always done in the context of folk and fairy tales.

Over its 100-year history, the screen has adopted a number of conventions from both epic and dramatic storytelling modes, and with the development of the computer, the powers of these conventions are available to playwrights in the digital domain. Just as the word 'play' in a dramatic context reminds us that all drama is essentially interactive, the word 'playwright', used meaning someone who creates the dramatic experience, does not denote *writing* scripts but *making* plays (as in 'wheelwright' or 'to wreak havoc' or 'vengeance', or 'wrought iron' – *wreak, wrought, -wright*). Film and television directors are as much dramatists as screenwriters are, when they make the film or the programme – that is, they create a narration appropriate to the narrative.

In the world of computer-aided production, of synthetic imaging and 3D computer graphics and animation, of digitally generated sound and digitally captured images, 'playwrights' have a medium, an arena for creative performance, worthy of the skills of dramatic poet, composer, choreographer, director and performer Aeschylus (Greece, 525-456 BC) plus producer, writer, director and actor William Shakespeare (GB, 1564-1616); with elements of the Olympic athlete, the martial-arts adept and the detective thrown in – not to speak of a Jean Cocteau (France, 1889-1963), a Fritz Lang (Germany, 1890-1976), a Cedric Gibbons (US, 1893-1960), a Van Nest Polglase (US, 1989-1968), a Hermes Pan (1905-1990), a Walt Disney (US, 1901-1966) and a John Lasseter to choreograph spectacle, and design storyworlds and characters. The digital storyscape offers an astonishing range and freedom for innovative and expressive art, and it craves creative teams as strong and knowledgeable as any that have made great entertainment in other media.

In conclusion, it seems that we do not have to completely redefine our standards of excellence or our aesthetic and structural criteria in order to create new dramatic narratives and develop the protean medium provided by the computer. We do, however, need to ensure that we apply critical perspectives and dramaturgical yardsticks that are relevant. The knowledge and technology to make high-quality interactive narrative/drama exists, but we need to bring together the traditional skills of dramatic and epic narrative characterization and structuring, of moving image/sound narration, and movie-production design, with the techniques of computer-aided and generated 3D animation, virtual architecture and graphic environments, if we want to optimize that potential and build on it.

As Alan Kay wrote in 1984: 'The computer... is a medium that... has degrees of freedom for representation and expression never before encountered and as yet barely investigated.' Computer console games began, as the 20th century drew to a close, to explore and exploit this new medium for a responsive market. As console platforms, interactive digital domestic broadcasting and e- and d-cinema draw closer and closer together, it is up to the new 'playwrights' of the 21st century to start building really ambitious edifices on the foundation they laid.

Lev Monovich, in his book, *The Language of New Media*, puts cinematic conceptual thinking right at the centre of the digital universe, emphasising the importance of cinematic language not only to storymaking but to the whole process of computer-enhanced creativity:

> Element by element, cinema is being poured into the computer: first, one-point linear perspective: next, the mobile camera and rectangular window; next, cinematography and editing conventions; and, of course, digital personas based on acting conventions borrowed from cinema, to be followed by make-up, set-designs, and the narrative structures themselves. Rather than being merely one cultural language among others, cinema is now becoming *the* cultural interface, a toolbox for all cultural communication, overtaking the printed word.
>
> Cinema, the major cultural form of the twentieth century, has found a new life as the toolbox of the computer user. Cinematic means of perception, of connecting space and time, of representing human memory, thinking, and emotion have become a way of work and a way of life for millions in the computer age. Cinema's aesthetic strategies have become the basic organizational principles of computer software. The window into a fictional world of cinematic narrative has become a window into a datascape. In short, what was cinema, is now the human computer interface. (Manovich, 2001, 86)

The second millennium ended with the spectacular rise of PlayStation's Lara Croft as a games hero, and the third began with her incarnation as a movie character. Her adventures, both the thrills and the spills – like the parallel events of the *Final Fantasy* and *Resident Evil* stories – perhaps serve, in the context of a wider understanding of the rhetorics of spatially organised narrative, to illuminate a way ahead for the following generation of hybridized technologies and media content forms. These will build fictive and information universes whose moving-image constituents – gameworld, inforworld, storyworld – are connected, through a shared reference to cinematic discourse, by generic, cultural and electronic links. In 1997, Janet Murray proposed: 'The computer looks more and more each day like a movie camera of the 1890s: a truly revolutionary invention humankind is just on the verge of putting to use as a spellbinding storyteller'. (Murray, 1997, 2) The 21st century opened with a tentative exploration of digital storytelling in 3D and 2D moving-image environments in ther console game which even in infancy demonstrated the chemistry between cinematic language and electronic potential. Where these are developed together, they will hopefully create an exhilarating and rewarding fusion of tradition and innovation: a new media content form for the third millennium.

Appendix

Alien Trilogy – shoot the aliens!
Bust A Groove – compete as a hip-hop, disco, techno or house dance-star!
Dark Forces – destroy the attackers and discover the truth!
Discworld – solve the puzzles and explore a zany world!
Discworld Noir – find out what has happened to the missing lover of the *femme fatale* in the dark and
    dangerous city of Ankh Morpork by questioning its unsavoury wisecracking denizens!
Excalibur – find the Sword of King Arthur.
Jedi Masters – fight hand to hand in the personas of your favourite *Return of the Jedi* characters!
Lost Vikings – get the lost Vikings home from the time-zone they have accidentally got themselves into!
Machine Hunter – shoot the captors and rescue the prisoners!
NHL '98 – play top-league ice-hockey!
Nuclear Strike – learn about military hardware and zap the Indo-Chinese!
Parappa The Rapper – learn to learn with rap, rhythm and bright colours!
Space Hulk – rid the space hulks (abandoned spacecraft drifting in space) of their evil inhabitants and make
    them safe!
Tekken II – become a great martial arts exponent!
Wipeout – drive a superspacecraft against others at superspeeds!

Synopses

Alien Trilogy – shoot the aliens!

The player takes control of Ellen Ripley (based on the character from the 1979 US Dan O'Bannon/Ridley Scott film, *Alien*) who, entirely alone, confronts the aliens inhabiting an abandoned colony on a planet in deep space. Viewpoint: only a hand holding the weapon, close up to the viewer, whose hand it is understood to represent.

Dark Forces – destroy the attackers and discover the truth!

Inspired by the US *Star Wars* films *Star Wars* (George Lucas, 1977); *The Empire Strikes Back* (Irvin Kershner, US, 1980); and *The Return of the Jedi* (Richard Marquand, US 1983), *Dark Forces* is a shoot-'em-up where the player sees a self-representation embodied only by a gun hand, which can also operate switches. The character the player controls is Kyle, a mercenary sympathizer with the Rebellion and an enemy to the Empire, who travels through a variety of planetary environments, mainly futuristic architectural interiors, but including some space exteriors. The objective is to find out what happened to an outpost which has been destroyed, taking on a number of missions toward this end, and under constant attack.

Discworld – solve the puzzles and explore a zany world!

Adapted from the works of novelist Terry Pratchett, the game is set in Discworld, a richly animated mediaeval sword and sorcery-type environment inhabited by lively and funny versions of stock fantasy literature and film characters. Essentially a point-and-click transference from a PC game using a mouse, this adventure allows the player to guide Rincewind, incompetent wizard par excellence, from point to point through the kind of (amiable but frustrating) unsought quest you hope will only happen in other people's nightmares, to collect various items and solve various puzzles which fate thrusts upon him. Rincewind's figure – clad in a long robe and gliding as one does in a long robe – is seen face on, in profile or from behind, depending on the direction he is travelling in on a given set or screen, in the convention of traditional narrative 2D animation. Rincewind can exchange (spoken) dialogue with the many colourful characters he meets in various dramatic modes – using icons, the player can choose from polite through humorous to downright snappish.

Jedi Masters – fight hand to hand in the personas of your favourite Return of the Jedi characters!

Again inspired by the US *Star Wars* films: *Star Wars* (George Lucas, 1977); *The Empire Strikes Back* (Irvin Kershner, US, 1980); and *The Return of the Jedi* (Richard Marquand, US, 1983). You can pick characters to control in personal combat and have them fight aginst each other in your chosen combinations. Each character has a (limited) range of shared fighting skills and a (small) number of special moves. There is no story-related or dramatic reason why the characters should fight each other – many of them are on the same side in the *Star Wars* Trilogy stories.

Lost Vikings – get the lost vikings home from the time-zone they have accidentally got themselves into!

The player controls three comic vikings, Erik, Olaf and Baleog, who must help each other, contributing team fighting skills and actions, to find the magic ingredients the Witch needs to teleport them from level to level through an imaginatively designed and colourful series of environments back home. The vikings need to ask questions and get information from the characters in the landscape, which they do through text and spoken voice. They normally cross the screen from left to right, in profile, in traditional 2D animation style.

Machine Hunter – shoot the captors and rescue the prisoners!

A shoot-'em-up and rescue-the-hostages game where the player receives information and instructions from a voice-over narrator (no text). The game is played fast (there are lots of attacking creatures, which have a certain degree of autonymous and therefore unpredictable life) in a non-naturalistic neon environment, which draws on the graphics style of computer wireframe representations of layers and dimensions, and features transformations. If sufficiently skilful, the player's character can take on the identity, characteristics and powers of the monsters s/he overcomes and use them to help save the very hostages the monsters are holding captive. The action is viewed dizzily from above, the virtual camera following the tiny, stylized, pink-overalled character who is directed by the player using the direction buttons on the joypad.

NHL '98 – play top-league ice-hockey!

An ice-hockey simulation in which the player can play either side or two players can play both, controlling whichever ice-hockey players are within reach of the puck at any given moment. The teams – the figures are about the size of a team in a broadcast game – are rendered in quasi-realistic motion-captured animation, and are viewed from numerous camera angles in imitation of normal TV sports coverage. Each character has his own idiosyncracies, and there is a continuous voice-over commentary which adds detail to the information about the team-members just as does broadcast commentary. This commentary gives great immediacy and verisimilitude to the game – it is not unnaturally repetitive, and comments on the action as it unfolds through the intervention of the player(s). The fact that the game is played on skates makes the swift, gliding motion of the figures natural and appropriate.

Nuclear Strike – learn about military hardware and zap the Indo-Chinese!

A military strategy helicopter strike game in which the player takes the role of a helicopter commander as part of the STRIKE team. General le Monde has stolen a nuclear warhead and is threatening to use it for terrorist purposes. He must be pursued (through Indo-China), his plans predicted, and his project stopped – and he is a cunning, highly skilled strategist and opponent. The player undertakes missions which cause death, destruction and mayhem with a range of accurately described superweapons, while avoiding being brought down by the natives. Voice-over exchanges and instructions borrow heavily from the conventions of Vietnam war movies (in particular the soundtrack of *Apocalypse Now*, Francis Ford Copploa, US, 1979) as do the virtual camera angles, which are predominantly wideshots centred on the helicopter seen from above, following its trajectory.

Parappa The Rapper – learn to learn with rap, rhythm and bright colours!

The player controls Parappa, a 2D flat cartoon character who has to learn skills to complete learning tasks. His skills depend on the player's ability to synchronize movement-control button-pushing with musical and visual cues (rather than attackers or explorations). The voice of the rapping commentator both instructs the player and Parappa, and comments on the nature of the tasks to be completed, which range from martial arts skills through driving a car and running a market stall to cooking. Prerecorded animated interludes connect Parappa's need to learn skills with his wish to impress a female flower-character and to nobly outperform a showily-driving bully who ogles her in the fast-food servery where Parappa and his fellow animated flora and fauna young teens hang out. All the characters are in the tradition of Japanese cute, talking animal animation, though Parappa's deliberate 2D look is consistent and effective: he presents as would an animated sheet of paper, with no depth but with the ability to rotate as might a sheet of paper.

Space Hulk – rid the space hulks (abandoned spacecraft drifting in space) of their evil inhabitants and make them safe!

The player takes control of a space marine Terminator (or pair, or a squad of Terminators) from the elite 100 members of the Blood Angels – space marines who, in the next millennium, patrol the galaxy to keep all safe. The Terminators, clad in bulky, anonymous space suits, gravity-walk their unwieldy way into the screen, through the corridors of the stripped ships, avoiding or deactivating traps, attacking the evil Genestealers or being attacked by them; all the time receiving orders, instructions, encouragement and clarification from the electronically transmitted voice of the other squad members. The Terminators are seen from behind , and their rolling progress is convincingly like that of film spacenauts since the first footage of walking on the moon. The interiors and grey, pipe-lined corridors of the hulks recall Captain Nemo's *Nautilus* (20,000 *Leagues Under the Sea*, Richard Fleischer, US, 1954) combined with an amalgam of the ships in *Alien* (Ridley Scott, US, 1979) and *Aliens* (James Cameron, US, 1986). Prerecorded video-clips between levels, much more reminiscent in design of Marvel Comics superheroes and Dan Dare of the *Eagle*, show the brotherhood of the Blood Angels – who, in another incarnation, might have gathered in Klingsor's halls (*Parsifal*, Richard Wagner, 1882) – congratulating the successful and urging the elite on to higher achievements.

Tekken II – be a great martial arts exponent!

The player can control any of 23 characters – mainly 1990s human male and female, but with a few bear/lion/samurai warriors, each with a different build, different fighting technique, different personality – in combat with any of the others; or two players can use characters to fight each other. The player needs manual dexterity, fine hand-eye co-ordination and excellent timing to learn and deploy the capabilities of the fighters. Each combat is played out in a different setting; since all the fight moves are part of a martial-arts sequence, they are choreographed exactly, and although the player has complete freedom to control how the fighter works, the moves themselves unroll smoothly and with no hiatus, giving the player a satisfying sense of power and skill. The game rewards diligent play by introducing new characters and new moves. The virtual camera generally shows the two combatants in a medium long two-shot against a fixed background; but when there is a roll, throw, or speedy turn and jump, the 'camera' follows to keep both combatants in shot, and the background responds as a panorama, so there is no sense of being trapped in an unnaturally static world. The characters utter fighting cries of different kinds – there are sound effects for throws and falls, and a barker keeps the score and announces the wins. Each winning throw is played back in slow motion from a different angle, while the victor makes a characteristic demonstration of triumph. A prerecorded video sequence (optional at the beginning of the game) in the style of Manga combat video introduces each character in a setting (bike-riding, urban walking, training dojo).

Wipeout – drive a superspacecraft against others at superspeeds!

A competitive racing spacecraft game where graphic environment and music generation are as important as the racing to engage the player.

Architecture and the Screen from Photography to Synthetic Imaging
Capturing and Building Space, Time and Motion

François Penz

Architectural animation is a rapidly growing field and a growing number of practices in the UK use moving images at some stage of the project. The vast majority of these projects are Computer Aided Design or 'CAD' animations, produced with the then ubiquitous CAD tools packages. By the beginning of the 21st century, 95 per cent of architectural practices use CAD for 2D or 3D work, and most CAD packages include an animation module. However, most of the animation models they produce 'automatically' are unwieldy, with badly designed 'virtual' camera strategies that encourage or oblige designers, and therefore users, to whiz smoothly but dizzyingly along spline paths which represent no known or recognizable point of view.

However, there is, in fact, a long and fascinating symbiotic relationship between architecture and the moving image, which provides a great resource upon which the many architects aspiring to the use of moving images in their work could and, I believe should, draw.

1. Background
Early Photography
The history of the relationship between cinema and architecture can in fact be said to start in 1895, with the birth of the cinema. However, it is appropriate to consider some interesting examples of photography in the 19th century, and its attempts to capture the spirit of place and of motion, as a background and prelude to the year 1895, when moving pictures proper took over the project.

One of the earliest known photographs of the city of Paris is of the Rue du Boulevard du Temple (Figure 1). This picture needed several minutes of exposure for the image to become 'fixed' on the copper plate, thus excluding all subjects in movement – anything which did not remain stationary for long enough to be captured. The man having his shoes shined, on the left of the photograph, is an exception – sufficient of his body remained still to imprint an image. The empty streets in this photo prompted Walter Benjamin (considering similar photographs by Atget) to comment '...he photographed them like the scenes of crimes' (Arendt, 1973).

The photograph is taken from Daguerre's studio window, in a spontaneous gesture to show the world around us as it is – not unlike the agenda, 120 years later, of the French New Wave film-makers, who embraced location shooting for its freshness and actuality.

Figure1. Rue du Boulevard du Temple, Paris (Daguerre, 1839) (Centre Nationale de la Photographie, 1989).

Following the invention of the 'daguerreotype', Daguerre's method of using light to engrave a copper plate, came the advent of the 'glass negative', which allows the capture of the human figure in movement -in Figure 2 it depicts the study of small electrical (or 'galvanic') impulses as a stimulus to emotional reactions in a patient. The photograph perfectly captures the instant, and while the patient is in focus, the photographer, Duchenne, himself turns his head toward the lens, and this movement registers as a slight blur. It is the precursor of scientific photography. This is one of many stills of the same patient reacting to different electrical impulses, which could easily now be conceived as the basis of an animation.

Nadar's 1886 photograph of Chevreul (Figure 3) encapsulates the first recorded attempt at a 'live' interview. Nadar photographed the celebrated French chemist, and simultaneously recorded the sound of their conversation. Later, the pictures were published, and the images matched with the commentary.

Extraordinary as it may sound in the 21st century, in the latter part of the 19th century, a huge amount of effort went into solving the following problem: whether or not a horse galloping ever has all four hooves off the ground at the same time.

Until the 1870s, this remained an unsolved problem, and the artistic convention in painting represented the horse at full stretch in the position of the flying gallop. In his seminal and well-publicized 1878 work, *Animals and Human Locations*, Muybridge

Figure 2. Mechanism of the Human Physiognomy (Duchenne, 1862).

Figure 3. Interview with Chevreul (Felix Nadar, 1886).

showed for the first time that, indeed, a horse lifts all four feet off the ground at once. However, more importantly for the history of capturing motion on film, this pursuit of the understanding of animal locomotion triggered an intriguing and fruitful collaboration between Marey and Muybridge, whose outcome was to have immense repercussions for the advance of the cinema, and our general understanding of the history of art

Muybridge's way of working with sequential still frames led him to invent the 'zoopraxiscope', the earliest type of film projector, while Marey's invention of the photographic rifle stops just short of the movie camera. But what makes their work so fascinating and relevant are the similarities and differences between their approaches. They were exact contemporaries, each working on opposite sides of the Atlantic, on the same issues. But the great distinction between them is their training and background, which defined their aims and methods. Marey (the lesser known of the two) was a French scientist, a physiologist by training, interested in measuring movement in the human body (pulse, heartrate, and so on). Muybridge was an English photographer, working in California. He was an artist who became interested in animal motion after reading Marey's work *La Machine Animale* (mechanical animal) in 1873.

Muybridge and Marey met briefly in Paris in 1881. Marey was at the time a well-respected scientist, carrying out his experiments at the physiological centre in Paris, while Muybridge's work was in part financed by Governor Leland Stanford of

Figure 4. Horse in Motion (Marey and Muybridge, 1878?).

California, who later founded Stanford University. In his drive to understand animal motion, Marey's work was spurred by the spectacle of the recent Franco-Prussian debacle. His task was to improve the physique of the French soldiers, by carefully studying athletes' movements – which explains why there are no studies of women in Marey's work. There are plenty of such studies in the *Animals and Human Locomotions* books by Muybridge, who came out of the artists' tradition of 'still life' drawing. Marey is very much part of the history of the social control of the body, in the 'Foucaultesque' sense; and, of course, while Marey was busy developing his photographic gun in the early 1880s, none other than the Lumière brothers were his suppliers of the essential photographic plates.

Early Cinema

For the purpose of this study, three areas are worth highlighting in the context of early cinema:

- Early city films
- Issues of narrativity and fiction
- Issues of perspective and depth

Early Documentaries

From 1895 onward, a large number of documentary-like films were produced, and film historians agree that before 1906, documentary was the dominant genre (Gunning, 1990). By 1900, the Lumière brothers alone had an extraordinary catalogue of more than 2,000 short 'documentary' (that is, location-shot) films.

An analysis of their catalogue shows that they covered most cities in the world, sending a small army of camera-operators to travel far and wide (Figure 5). Those were the days of cinema as a fairground attraction, when street scenes in a city were shot in the morning, and shown in that city itself in the afternoon, often with a live voice-over commentary. Although some of the reels from this catalogue must remain in existence, they are very seldom shown. What certainly do remain, and are widely available, are some of the narrative fiction films of the early cinema.

Early Fiction Films

Perhaps the most celebrated early film with a narrative plot is *The Waterer Watered* (Spring, 1895), by Louis Lumière. Here there is clearly a little dramatic story, starting in equilibrium (the Waterer at work), followed by the disruption of the equilibrium (the Boy stops the water), a dramatic recognition of the disruption (the Waterer glares angrily at the Boy), and a response to the disruption (the Waterer is watered); after which the action is resolved (the Waterer thrashes the Boy) into a return to a new equilibrium (the Waterer waters on, relieved of the presence of the disruptive Boy). This was one of the very first motion pictures ever, and is a tribute to Louis Lumière's sense of mise en scène (staging for the camera). Storytelling came very early to the screen, which is not surprising, since moving images are a time-based medium.

Tom Gunning, on the other hand, is keen to moderate the assumption that the history of early cinema coincides with the history of narrative film (Gunning, 1990). He considers that an important aspect of early cinema is its function as a 'cinema of attractions' with an '...ability to show something. Contrasted to the voyeuristic aspect of narrative cinema... this is an exhibitionist cinema'. To him, cinema born out of fairground attraction, where the comedians smirk at the camera, is not narrative cinema. He describes it as part of a cinema of tricks and special effects. Early cineast Georges Méliès (1861-1938) himself explains: 'As for the scenario, the "fable" or "tale", I only consider it at the end... since I use it merely as a pretext for the 'stage effects', the 'tricks' or for a nicely arranged tableau' (Gunning, 1990).

Before 1906, cinema has already acquired several facets, combining traditional elements from the theatre and literature (storytelling) with some of the elements of the fairground attraction, as well as an important component of documentary –

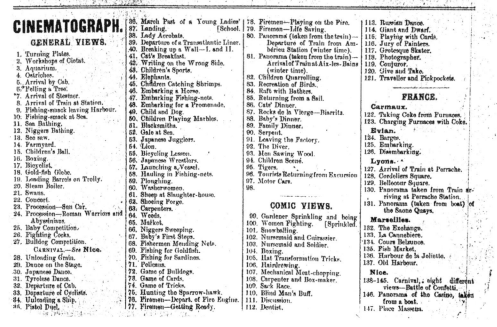

Figure 5. The Lumière Brothers, English Catalogue.

representing the world around us. Clearly, these early forays into moving-image work are an important background to considering the experiments made at a later stage by the avant-garde cineasts who attempted to use moving images in a non-storytelling mode – rather, as Leger proclaimed, as a cinema to '...make images seen' (Gunning, 1990).

Issues of Perspective and Framing

Much has been said about the relationship between Renaissance perspective, photography and cinema, in particular by Stephen Heath in his seminal article, 'Narrative Space' (Heath, 1976). A similar analysis is proposed by Richard DeCordova, who makes the following observation on the *Sortie d'Usine* (Crowd Leaving the Lumière Factory) (1895):

The cyclists, for example, having been masked by the crowd, appear – such an appearance had been impossible in both painting and photography. Masking was the predominant means of the representation of depth in pre-Renaissance painting and an element the system of Renaissance perspective engaged. (DeCordova, 1978)

Looking at a picture of the scene from *Sortie d'usine* (Figure 6), we can see that the camera is placed directly in front of the factory gate, thus offering an elevation-view of the building. The sense of depth and perspective is mainly provided by the people who pass on either side of the camera. This 'elevation view' is a form of tableau, which draws both from contemporary theatre and from classical painting. Some sense of a frontal tableau informs *L'arroseur Arosé* (The Waterer watered) (Louis Lumière, 1895), which establishes the issue of framing in a particularly interesting way: the scene starts with the Waterer on the left, with the water going off-screen to the left, while the Boy appears from the right; and while the Waterer chases the Boy, the frame is temporarily empty of people, until the Waterer brings back the Boy to the centre of the frame.

This alternating relationship between off-screen and on-screen action is a characteristic of the cinema, and hard to conceive of in photography and painting. While we have been considering here a fixed camera set-up (the only kind possible for early cameras, which could not themselves move or cope with changes in focal length), through editing, or more simply through panning or tracking the camera, further perspective depths can be revealed (parallax effect) within the frame; these are akin to those movements of our own heads and eyes that help us to reveal and understand better the spaces around us (spatial relationships) and orient within them.

As cinema became more and more sophisticated, its grammar grew more complex, but also more conventional; and by 1915, with DW Griffith's US movie, *Birth of a Nation* which chronicles Griffith's version of the early days of the US, the language of the screen is pretty well established. This pre-1915 period is often revisited by scholars and film-makers alike, who find in the work of Georges Méliès and the Lumière brothers a constant source of inspiration.

The Avant-Garde Movement

From 1900 onward, a number of art movements emerged and actively engaged with revolutionizing the way art was conceived and described. However, no other movement of that period was more radical than the Futurists. Their spokesperson, Marinetti, published its manifesto in Paris in the newspaper *Le Figaro* on 20 February 1909, proclaiming: 'We declare that the splendour of the world has been enriched by a new beauty: the beauty of speed...'

Futurism as a movement glorified machinery, speed and all the attributes of the modern world they informed, including violence and wars, which bring about rapid change. The Futurist movement was started in Paris by a group of Italian artists, among them Boccione, Bala and Marinetti. Besides those of painting and sculpture, it took many forms, which all had in common the encapsulation of movement. This search for speed and interest in movement stems from the teaching of the philosopher Henry Bergson (1859-1941), whose public lectures had been attended by great numbers

Figure 6. Sortie d'Usine (Louis Lumière, France, 1895).

at the beginning of the 20th century. Bergson published an influential book, *L'évolution creatrice* (*Creative Evolution*) (1907) where he proposes a 'vitalist' philosophy, whereby he contends that the movement around us propagates itself in the spectator, who in turn enters into a state of 'vibration' with his environment. This has been seen as the prime motivation behind some of the work of the painter Delaunay (1885-1841), particularly his series on the *Fenêtres (Windows)* (Figure 7) where the colours meet within each other, achieving the Bergsonian concept of 'pure duration' – where time/space collapse into one, in a world where the spectator's primitive consciousness is in perfect harmony with the outside world.

It is not clear that Delaunay had direct contact with Bergson, but he was certainly influenced by the futurist movement, who in turn directly referred to Bergson's theories. One often refers to a spirit of 'zeitgeist' – flavour of the time' – when considering the widespread interest that artists have shown at the beginning of the 20th century in working with speed and movement, and the Dada movement was not immune to that spirit.

Dada and Surrealist Cinema

The Dada movement was founded by Tristan Tzara in 1915, and was characterized by an anarchic revolt against traditional values. Unlike the Futurist movement, which glorified war, it was founded in part as a reaction against World War I. Among its members was Marcel Duchamp, who started to experiment with optics and movement

Figure 7 Fenêtres (Windows) by Delaunay (1885-1841)

(Figure 8) in his seminal work, *Nude Descending a Staircase* (1913). Duchamp's radical approach led him to experiment with cinema – he produced *Anémic Cinéma* (1926) in collaboration with Man Ray (1890-1976). It is a piece of 'art in movement' where 'moving disks with geometrical spirals regularly alternate in a slow rhythm with disks containing spirally printed poems' (Kuenzli, 1987).

This mixture of art and words in random motion was typical of the Dada movement, which was experimenting with the accidental and chance as a way of disrupting logic and order.

Perhaps the most intriguing of the Dada experiments with film is the piece produced by Eggeling and Richter in 1923. Viking Eggeling, who was Swedish, had been linked to the Dada movement since 1916. He was a painter who was attempting to integrate the time-space continuum into painting and who wanted to see cinema develop as an art, away from fictional narrative forms, as part of an attempt to 'liberate painting'. His resulting work, in collaboration with Hans Richter, was *Diagonal Symphony* (Germany, 1921), which consists of a series of graphical forms (not unlike a painting by Paul Klee), painted on a continuous paper roll, where abstract forms organized around a diagonal axis are captured on film. *Diagonal Symphony* is perhaps the first, and may be the only, attempt on film to combine so many art forms in a single oeuvre. Eggerling was very influenced by the idea of musical counterpoint, and his work was also much inspired by musical analogies and metaphors.

Surrealist Cinema

By contrast with the Dadaists, the Surrealist movement (launched in 1924) was not interested in 'art films'. It is a movement positivist in spirit (as opposed to the Dadaists, whose tendency was towards nihilism), which claimed to have the ability to engage with popular culture, such as the cinema. The work of Louis Feuillade, *Fantomas* (1913), is held in great esteem by Breton, while Fernand Léger's experimentation with *Ballet Mecanique* (1924) was seen as pretentious. Perhaps because of their lack of interest in popular forms, there are not many Surrealist films – film was from its early days recognized as a popular medium. The most famous of Surrealist movies is *Un Chien Andalou* by Salvador Dali and Luis Buñuel (1929), which combines the three elements insisted upon by the Surrealists: it has a narrative, and it portrays characters in a realistic order, which is disrupted by abrupt, terrifying images emanating from the subconscious.

City Symphonies

In the 1920s, tthe 'city symphonie' genre became widespread but three films stand out as representative of this period:

* *Rien que les Heures* (Alberto Cavalcanti, France, 1926)
* *Berlin, Symphonie of a Great City* (Walter Ruttman, Germany, 1927)
* *Man with a Movie Camera* (Dziga Vertov, USSR, 1929)

These three works created a new genre, which in its form – montage – was to prove critical to the history of cinema, and essential to any understanding of the relationship between cinema and the architecture of the city. Leading to the development of these movies in the 1920s were a number of influences.

The Lumière brothers (and others) had been documenting cities across the world from the beginning of motion pictures. In the early days of photography, portraits, group portraits, and in fact city portraits, were very popular, and the opportunity to portray the city in movement proved an instant attraction and challenge. Documenting urban reality was also a powerful incentive to use film, at a time when cities were growing faster than ever before. The city of the 1910s and 1920s is quintessentially 'modern' and film-makers were keen to work with this symbol of modernity. Cities are perpetually on the move, things happen fast, and the idea of capturing the speed of it all embodied the ideal of the Futurist movement. Shortly after the Futurist manifesto was launched, Louis Feuillade had created, with *Fantomas* (1913), an extremely popular 'city mystery', which was held in great esteem by the Surrealists and has since also been seen as an important influence on the French New Wave in cinema. However, the real feel, the spirit of the time – the zeitgeist – which surrounded the making of the 'city symphonies' on film is perhaps best epitomized by the work of Walter Benjamin and James Joyce.

Walter Benjamin wrote elegantly on the concept of the *flâneur*, the 'stroller who appreciates his surroundings', and *flânerie*

Figure 8. Nude Descending a Staircase (Duchamp, 1913).

was an art he perfected when he settled in Paris in 1933. The idea of strolling, idling, watching and observing is a 19th-century concept, and you need a large city to do full justice to the art. Benjamin's earlier painful experience of walking the streets of Moscow led him to proclaim 'only film commands an optical approach to the essence of the city' (Arendt, 1973). In his celebrated essay, ' The Work of Art in the Age of Mechanical Reproduction' (Arendt, 1973), Benjamin makes frequent references to, and comments on, Russian film-makers – Dziga Vertov in particular.

Dziga Vertov started to work on sound and in 1916, in Petrograd, he created the 'Laboratory of hearing'. Interestingly, he started work on sound as 'montage' in a way which might have been influenced by Luigi Russolo's concerto piece *L'Art des bruits* (*The Art of Noises*), performed for the first time in Milan in 1913; it was a 'futuristic' event, regarded by Noguez (Noguez, 1985) as an auditory 'city symphony' -a precursor to the visual city symphony. Whether Vertov was actually aware of Russolo's work is difficult to establish, but there is no doubt that his own experiments, charted in his *Kino Eye* manifesto of 1919, ' I am an eye. I am a mechanical eye...' (Michelson, 1984) was to be extremely influential on generations to come. While elements of montage can be seen in practice in films of the time, such as Fernand Léger's *Ballet Mécanique* (1924), it was Vertov who became the theoretician and formulator of the montage philosophy, in an attempt to move boldly away from the fictional narrative tradition, which, in his opinion, had no future. However, when considering the zeitgeist, the work of Irish author James Joyce (1882-1941) remains outstanding. Of him Eiseinstein said, 'What Joyce does with literature is quite close to what we are doing with new cinematography, and even closer to what we are going to do' (Hart, 1988). In common with Joyce's novel of *flâneurie*, *Ulysses* (1922), there is, in the city symphonies, a unity of place and time – action takes place from dawn to dusk.

Crucially, all three city symphony films – *Rien que les heures* (Alberto Cavalcanti, 1926)*, Berlin Symphony of a Great City* (Walter Ruttman, 1927) and *Man with a Movie Camera* (Dziga Vertov, 1929) – have further visual features in common: the use of montage by analogies (preferred by Cavalcanti), the rows of smoking chimneys (such as those favoured by Ruttman), the series of crowds (human and animal), and Vertov's focus on series of transportation modes (planes, trains, coaches). However, there are also crucial differences between the works of these three film-makers. Cavalcanti's is a predominantly poetic style, and has a strong narrative in the fictional sense; Ruttman's film starts with the sea (nature) and takes us into the city via the mechanical rhythm of the locomotive; while Vertov follows a cameraman filming the city.

2. Architects' Perspectives on Film

While the previous section focused on early cinema and the avant-garde movement, this section concentrates on the modern movement's involvement with film, in particular that of Mallet-Stevens, Le Corbusier and Richter.

Figure 9 encapsulates the close relationship between architects and film-makers in the 1920s, both groups being photographed in La Sarraz, in 1928 and 1929 respectively.

Furthermore, in 1920, the two groups met at the same time in Brussels, and although no debates had been scheduled between the two movements, the film

Figure 9. Architects and film-makers, photographed in La Sarraz, in 1928 and 1929 respectively.

programme of the Congrès International du Cinéma Indépendent (CICI) (International Congress for Independent Cinema) was part of the Congrès International de l'Architecture Moderne (CIAM) (International Congress for Modern Architecture) activities (Jansen, 1997). But in order to understand the motivation of the modern movement's involvement with cinema, it is necessary to go back to 1923, and Le Corbusier's publication of his manifesto, *Vers une Architecture* (*Toward an architecture*). In this book, Le Corbusier defines the art of building as the unification of the new materials, such as concrete, with methods of production – the machine serving as prototype. He proclaims there that 'the house is a machine for living in' (p. 100).

Le Corbusier's own fascination with the aesthetic of the aeroplane and the motor car links him directly to the Futurists. This feeling for experiencing architecture 'in movement' is perhaps most famously enshrined in his concept of the '*promenade architecturale*' (architectural walk) around his Villa Savoye:

> Arab architecture teaches us a valuable lesson – it's best appreciated on foot. Walking — you have to walk through a building with a changing viewpoint, to see the articulation of the building deployed. It's the opposite to that of Baroque architecture, which is conceived on paper, around a fixed theoretical axis. I prefer the teaching of Arab architecture! (Le Corbusier, 1929)

As Tim Benton points out, '...this, in the end, is the basic argument for film as opposed to photography or drawing as a medium of representation for architecture' (Benton, 1997).

The argument for filming architecture is most obviously taken up by architectural historian and theoritician Sigfried Giedion, who declared: 'Still photography does not capture them clearly. One would have to accompany the eye as it moves: Only film can make the new architecture intelligible' (Giedion, 1929). In this statement, he was specifically referring to Le Corbusier's houses at Pessac in Bordeaux, France. Giedion found the relatively irregular and free-flowing layout of the Pessac houses an appropriate example of his concept of the 'perceptive apparatus' – 'the observer does not allow himself to be influenced by the compositional geometry of the building, but rather lets his gaze constantly change its perspective, in order to obtain insights that are, perhaps unavoidably, unintentional' (Georgiadis, 1989)[1]

Even more radical was Mohaly-Nagy's vision, expressed in his book *Von material zu Architektur* (From Materials to Architecture) (1929). He postulates that 'spatial design is not primarily a question of the building material ...spatial design today means, rather, a weaving together of spatial elements, which are mostly achieved in invisible but clearly discernible relationships of multidimensional movement and in fluctuating energy relationships.' Typically, most of the images illustrating his book are of cars racing, trains in motion, street crossings and other foci of movement. This is hardly surprising from someone who, in 1925, published a script of a film project on the 'dynamic of the big city' in an attempt to capture on film the rapid movement of modern life in the city (Noguez, 1985).

Beyond these theoretical considerations of the use of film in architecture in the 1920s, the real motivation for the promoters of the modern movement to use film was as a means of propaganda. It was clearly a powerful motive, and probably a sensible one. Indeed, after World War I, cinema became a very popular form of entertainment. Jansen points out that 'at the end of the 1920s, Berlin had 180,000 cinema seats, and an equal number of people went to the cinema every day' (Jansen, 1997).

In fact, a large number of educational and *Kultur* films were made, from 1918 onward, and in 1926 a German specialized catalogue of such films listed 6,000 titles (Jansen, 1997). Of course, not all of these were about architecture, and a substantial proportion were shown in commercial cinemas, during trade fairs, or as part of larger international fairs or other such events. Three films stand out as representative of the period: *Die Neue Wohnung* (Hans Richter, 1929), *Architectures d'Aujourd'hui* (Pierre Chenal, 1930) and *Les Mystères du Château du Dé* (Man Ray, 1928). The first two are part of the 'documentary' tradition, although they are executed in very different styles (see Jansen 1997 for a comparative analysis), while Man Ray's film has the poetic quality of a surrealist essay.

Interestingly, Man Ray's film is about a house by Robert Mallet-Stevens, who was himself actively involved in the film industry. For example, together with Fernand Léger, he designed the house used as a set in Marcel L'Herbier's film *L'Inhumaine* (1924); while Robert and Sonia Delaunay were responsible for its interior décor.

Less well known than *Die Neue Wohnung*, *Architectures d'Aujourd'hui* and *Les Mystères du Château du Dé* (Man Ray, 1928), but in the same propagandist mode, is *Die Stadt von Morgen* (The City of the Future) (1929), which is probably the first film on the problems of urban planning. It was co-directed by two German planners, Von Goldbeck and Kotzen, with the help of a group of architects, and aimed at highlighting the unhygienic conditions of urban life, while promoting town and country planning. It was shown widely in Europe and America, and in an article in *Artwork* in 1930, Bassett-Lowke hailed it as a great success: 'the co-operation of those who had a knowledge of cinema and those who were concerned with the didactic purpose has been admirable' (Bassett-Lowke, 1930).

With its mixture of aerial shots of model towns and real footage, *Die Stadt von Morgen* is the ancestor of a long line of urban-planning propaganda films, which stretches forward to late 20th-century examples such as the digital video *North by Northeast* (Peng, 2001).

The bird's-eye view deployed in this and many urban films is a mediation between the planners' view of the world (cartography) and a normal experiential perception of the world, arrived at through the use of perspective. This is an 18th-century concept whereby the local ruler could embrace his 'region' from a high vantage view point (Berque, 1995).

Bassett-Lowke's plea for an educational and propagandist cinema made in 1920 appears to have been heard, as a flourish of such films started to be made in England from the mid-1930s onward, under the leadership of John Grierson and Paul Rotha, who steered the Empire Marketing Board's (EMB) Film Unit. Propaganda was very much on the agenda, with titles such as *Where There is Soap, There is Life*, but the best known of these pre-war housing documentaries is *Housing Problems* (1935), which gave a bleak portrait of life in the slums, while advocating new forms of urbanism. In the post-war period, the need for reconstructing Britain was a powerful spur, and films such as *Land of Promise* (Paul Rotha, 1945) contributed to it. Nicholas Bullock describes this area of film-making in his article 'Imagining the Post-war World' (Bullock, 1997).

While the effectiveness of these films in helping to rebuild Britain at the time may be questioned, it is undeniable that the legacy of Grierson's EMB Unit and its co-propagandists has been quite considerable. Film-makers such as Humphrey Jennings and later the 1950s 'free cinema' film-makers Lindsay Anderson, Tony Richardson and Karel Reisz all learned their trade in the documentary film genre, and this heritage is crucial for the understanding of the British tradition of social realism and urban location in film, including the work of fiction directors such as Ken Loach and Mike Leigh at the turn of the second millennium.

Remaining within the theme of architects working with film, but moving along chronologically, a more recent example is the work of Americans Charles and Ray Eames in the 1940s. Charles (an architect) and Ray (an artist and painter) collaborated for more than 40 years, from 1940 onward, on a wide range of projects, but they are probably best known for their furniture. Charles Eames came to film through photography, combined with his friendship with American film-maker Billy Wilder, with whom he collaborated on *Spirit of St Louis* (US, 1957).

The Eames won international acclaim as independent film-makers with their very first films, *Parade, or Here They Come Down the Street* and *Blacktop*, at the Edinburgh Film Festival in 1954. By 1978, the Eames had made 80 short films, which, in the main, were a 'means of communicating ideas rather than for entertainment or creative expression' (Kirkham, 1995). They made both experimental films and corporate films – for example, having a long-term collaboration with IBM. Their best-known film is probably *Powers of Ten* (1968), where in the space of a few minutes we are taken, on one continuous zoom, from a picnic scene to the farthest point in the galaxy, and then back to the picnic scene and down to the level of an atom travelling at the rate of one to the power of 10 every 10 seconds – hence the title. But perhaps the most interesting of their films is *House* (1955). This is an experiment in fast-cut stills, based on hundreds of photographs of their own house. It is organized as though it were a 'house symphony' rather than a room-by-room exploration, and the images – arranged in broad categories (colour, materials, flowers) – are reminiscent of the montage by analogy, discussed earlier in the context of city symphonies. *House* (1955) is accompanied by an original musical score by American composer Elmer Bernstein, who was himself fascinated by the relationship between music and the visual form.

Perhaps not so well known is the role the Eames played as pioneers of multimedia presentations. Their first such endeavour was shown in Moscow in 1959, *Glimpses of the USA*, the seven-screen presentation of a day in the life of America, from coast to coast (Fig.ure 10). It was composed of a mixture of stills and live-action movie, set to an Elmer Bernstein score. The most elaborate example of their multi-screen work was *Think*, prepared for IBM at the 1964-65 New York World's Fair, where they used 22 separate screens of different shapes, in an attempt to illustrate the relationship between modern data processing, technology and the problem-solving methods used in everyday life. The pioneering work of the Eames brothers has been widely acknowledged, though their approach was not without precedent – they could be seen

Figure 10. Glimpses of the USA (Charles and Ray Eames, 1959).

as reviving the long-forgotten attempt at the use of multi-screens by Abel Gance, with his last tryptic tableau in the film *Napoleon* (France, 1927).

3. Film-makers' Perspectives on Architecture

Film-makers have frequently used cities as expressive narrative landscapes, sometimes reconstructing fragments of cities in the studio. How does their practice relate to contemporary architectural movements?

German Expressionist cinema of the 1920s parallels the early developments in France and Russia outlined above, and studio cities were routinely built until the 1960s, when developments in film and camera technology began to make exterior location shooting cheaper than set-building.

The two authoritative works on German expressionist cinema, *The Haunted Screen* (Eisner, 1969) and *From Caligari to Hitler* (Kracauer, 1947), give a mainly political interpretation of the expressionist movement, as an 'expression of troubled souls'. While this is an entirely defensible thesis, there are a number of aesthetic, artistic and architectural considerations which make this movement highly relevant to the study of architecture and moving image arts and sciences. In part, the aesthetic of the German expressionist movement can be traced back to the expressionist movement in architecture, epitomised by Rudolf Steiner's *Goetheanum* (1913). The work of this movement features Hans Poelzig's water tower in Posen, built in 1908, and he designed the sets for Paul Wegener's *Der Golem* (1920) – he was more famous as an architect than Wegener as a director, and on the movie poster his name appears in the largest letters. Figure 11 shows the clear similarity between Poelzig's 'real' projects and his 'imaginary' ones.

Thomas Elsaesser, in his essay on 'Germany, the Weimar Years' (Elsaesser, 1996) attributes, in part, the attraction of the fantastic sets of German expressionist cinema to the fact that after World War I, realist films set on location did not have the dream-like quality people desired. Perhaps the most famous German expressionist film is *The Cabinet of Dr Caligari* (1920). Directed by Robert Wiene, it was very successful, partly due to the fantastic sets which Walter Reinman, one of the three art directors, describes as 'film painting' as opposed to 'film architecture'. The utopian space created by the designers was seen by some at the time as 'the deranged fantasy of a lunatic' (Neaman, 1996), but given the plot – where indeed most of the characters are deranged and end up inhabitants of an asylum – the set is a brilliant realization of narrative expressive space, where the unsettling décor fully supports the story.

German expressionist cinema was in part born out of expressionism in art, which as a movement is clearly identified with Germany and Switzerland. Neither expressionist architecture nor German expressionist cinema exported their influence far beyond those two countries at the time, but the real legacy of German expressionist cinema can be said to have lived on through the film noir genre, in particular through its sharp, contrasted lighting techniques.

By contrast, if the expressionist movement in art did not flourish, the modern movement did take off in a big way from the 1920s onward. Architects had been keen to promote their new ideas, mainly through propaganda films, but this was a meagre

Figure 11. Poelzig's water-tower design (1908), compared with the stair he designed for Paul Wegener's Der Golem (1920).

effort compared with the heavy artillery the film industry now deployed, riding high on the symbols of modernity and, above all, the modernity of the city of the future. Two examples stand out: Fritz Lang's *Metropolis* (Germany, 1927) and Friedrich W Murnau's *Sunrise* (US, 1927). *Metropolis* is the vision of the German city of the future, a city in part inspired by New York, and also by the work of Mies van der Rohe. The set designers, Kettelhut and Hunte, proposed a vision which prompted Buñuel to remark at the Spanish premiere in 1927, 'Now and forever the architect will replace the set designer. Film will be the faithful translation of the architect's boldest dream!' (Neumann, 1996). This view complements strikingly Sigfried Giedion's remark, 'only film can make the new architecture intelligible' (Jansen, 1997). It is interesting to note that in contrast to *Metropolis*, William Cameron Menzies' *Things to Come* (UK, 1936) adapted for the screen HG Wells' vision of the anti-Metropolis, *The Shape of Things to Come* (GB, 1933), in which the inhabitants do not live in skyscrapers but underground; there they attempt to discover, through watching 'TV screens', the sense of what it was like to have windows, in the past (Figure 12).

In the 1920s, however, the city portrayed in Murnau's *Sunrise* (US, 1927) was an architect's dream, a collage of the symbols of modern architecture which existed in no other single urban complex in the world at the time, but notably deploys the grammar of the emerging modern architecture – curtain walls, horizontal protruding slabs, simple cube shapes – as well as its materials, such as glass and concrete.

Figure 12. Scene from William Cameron Menzies'
Things to Come (UK, 1936).

While in *Sunrise* the set designer, Gliese, was offering a vision of a near future just around the corner, the director of *Just Imagine* (US 1930), David Butler, deploys an architecture which can be traced back to the influence of the Italian Futurist Sant'Elia, and offers a science-fiction approach to future life on earth – a filmic tradition which became continuous from the 1920s, from *Metropolis* to *Blade Runner* (Ridley Scott, US, 1982), *The Fifth Element* (Luc Besson, France, 1997) and *The Matrix* (Wachowski Brothers, US, 1999).

However, there is a notable exception in the 1920s to the use of elaborate sets to portray the modern city of the future. René Clair, in *Paris qui Dort* (*Paris Asleep*) (1924) uses actual shots of Paris as the setting for the futurist tale of a mad scientist who, having invented a special 'ray', is able to paralyse the entire city. Clair paints the portrait of a silent, deserted, immobile Paris, where the Eiffel Tower – the true symbol of modernity – plays an important role, as it houses one of the main protagonists of the film. Clair portrays a mad scientist who utilizes a magic ray on the unsuspecting citizens of Paris. The ray causes its victims to freeze in bizarre and often embarrassing positions.

In this case, René Clair's portrayal of modernity is achieved through the eeriness of a silent and deserted mega-city. René Clair went on to create another vision of the modern world in 1930, with *A nous la liberté*, where the factory sets were designed by Lazare Meerson, who went on to design, or reconstruct, Paris for René Clair in *Sous les toits de Paris*, also shot in 1930. Made entirely in the studio at Boulogne-Billancourt (Figure 13), *Sous les toits de Paris* renders Paris 'as everyone knows it', or rather as they thought they knew it. Through a process of 'mental collage', anyone can picture the little street, the restaurant, the bistro that epitomise the city, all part of the grammar and vocabulary of the mythic entity, 'Paris'. However, all the elements of our mental Paris palette almost certainly do not exist next to one another in the 'real' city, and one location from the mythic Paris, or even two locations, would not amount to the whole of what actually exists. René Clair and Lazare Meerson clearly understood that the ideal 'Paris' consists of a collage of epitomes, and decided to reconstruct their Paris in the studio, including all the necessary ingredients to evoke, in a single shot, that cry of 'Oh! Yes, this is Paris, I could swear I have visited that exact spot... but where is it?' 'Real places never are in any map,' remarked Herman Melville in *Moby Dick* (GB 1851) (Tanner, 1988). Meerson's Paris finally exists only in our collective imagination, not unlike the Dublin of James Joyce's *Ulysses* (France 1922) (McGregor, 2000).

Figure 13. The set of René Clair's Sous les toits de Paris (1930)

4. Location Shooting in City Films

Following the introduction of new technologies, the development of the documentary tradition, and the ideological desire to break away from the anti-naturalism of the studio tradition, meant that some narrative city feature films from the 1940s onward preferred to shoot on location, and a grammar of naturalism, or neo-realism, evolved to express the quintessential city.

Although not a 'city film' in the fictional sense, the documentary *The City* (Ralph Steiner, US, 1939) is an allegory on the urban theories of Lewis Mumford (1895-1990) and aims to portray the wonders of the new towns, away from the miasma of the 'wicked city'. It is in many ways the continuation of utopian urban theories stretching back to Ebenezer Howard's 'Garden City ideal' and Le Corbusier 's modernist vision. In this sense, *The City* is closer to a 'fictional documentary', using the montage language of the city symphonies to construct on the silver screen a 'utopian' world where the 'workers are glad to be alive' as the voice-over commentary proclaims.

Figure 14. Scene from Bicycle Thieves (De Sica, Italy 1948).

However, at this time the reality of the (sub)urban dream is also starting to be shown more and more critically, in films of fiction from the 1940s onward, starting with the Italian Neo-Realist movement.

Rossellini's *Roma Città Apperta* (Rome, Open City) (1946) comes at the start of the Italian neo-realist movement, which aimed to break away from the cultural heritage of fascism and propaganda, depicting life as it was really lived. This commitment to the representation of human reality meant that most neo-realist films were shot on location, using non-actors. This approach is typically represented in De Sica's *Ladri di Biciclette (Bicycle Thieves)* (Italy 1948) with its strongly humanist tone and use of the centre of Rome as a contrast to the emerging world of the high-rise block of flats of the suburbs (Figure 14). 'It would not be an exaggeration to say that *Bicycle Thieves* is the story of a walk through Rome by a father and son,' remarks André Bazin (Bazin, 1958), a view which links the movie's protagonists to the flâneur tradition of Walter Benjamin's essay (Arendt, 1973).

In terms of technology, the neo-realists preferred the long, deep-focus shot, which first attracted attention in 1941 in Welles's *Citizen Kane*, photographed by Gregg Toland.'Deep focus', by allowing the eye to see clearly objects in the background as well as the foreground, feels or even is more akin to our perception of the world than the photographic image which does not allow the human eye to explore beyond the focal length of a shorter lens. As such, the technique better serves a neo-realist aesthetic, where fakery is as far as possible avoided, and allows the audience to perceive the city in a way not available on the screen before.

In many ways, the portrayal of the city by the Italian neo-realists has much in common with the vision of English film-makers such as Lindsay Anderson (*Every Day Except Christmas*, 1957), Tony Richardson (*A Taste of Honey*, GB, 1962) and Karel Reisz (*Saturday Night, Sunday Morning*, GB, 1960). These founders of the British free-cinema movement came from the documentary tradition of Grierson's EMB Film Unit, projecting their own brand of social realism into fiction. This British tradition continues throughout the 20th century, on television (most of the free-cinema directors worked for BBC Television in the 1960s) as well as film, with such work as Michael Winterbottom's *Wonderland* (GB, 1999), portraying London, and Penny Woolcock's TV docusoap *Tina Goes Shopping* (1999).

André Bazin, one of the founders of the journal of film criticism, *Cahiers du Cinema*, and theorist of the French new wave (*la nouvelle vague*), was a great admirer of the neo-realist movement, which greatly influenced the founders of the French new wave – Truffaut, Godard, Chabrol, Rohmer and Rivette, all film critics or theorists turned film-makers of the 1950s, who were reacting in some ways against the classic French cinema of the 1930s and its studio system by 'taking to the streets'. With the aid of cinematographer Raoul Coutard, they started to depict a Paris that had never been shown before. Only the Paris of the impressionist (*Sous les toits de Paris,* René Clair, 1931) had been portrayed, the Paris of surrealist literature, or a kind of picture-postcard rendition of the city. Moving away from the reconstructed collages achievable in studios, the film-makers of the new wave started to use the sites and locations they knew best, the places where they worked and lived – cafés, streets and parks never before shown, started to appear on screen. The city itself became the inspiration for the film, as Godard explained: 'Very often, I start to have an idea about a film by looking at a location... in *Breathless* my characters would have seen the Champs Elysées sixty times a day, so of course it had to be shown' (*Cahiers du Cinéma*, 1962).

Again, in the late 1950s and 1960s important advances in technology made shooting on location easier – the advent of a more portable camera, the Ariflex (made in Germany) in 1936, followed by the French-manufactured Éclair (the 16mm version weighed only 9kg) heralded a more naturalistic approach to exteriors. Faster film stock meant that shooting could take place in darker conditions, so studio lamps were not always essential. The introduction of the portable Nagra sound-recorder meant that sync sound was becoming possible in location shooting, though the cameras still made a great deal of noise. The Steadicam, which was perfected in 1976 by camera operator Garret Brown, enabled camera operators to move fluidly through space without jitters or shakes (Belton, 1997, 488), resulting in the appearance of much more dynamic camera styles – for example, in the sequence of the three main characters on the bridge in Truffaut's *Jules et Jim* (France, 1961).

The camera work for *Jules et Jim* was by Raoul Coutard, mentioned above, who, as a screen artist and scientist, is of the same calibre as the inventive American cinematographer Gregg Toland, who shot Welles' *Citizen Kane*. Coutard is one of the most powerful common threads, which unite the core group of film-makers constituting the new wave cinema of the 1960s. He photographed, in *cinema verité* style, Rouch and Morin's *Chronique d'un Eté* (1961) and he is behind the camera for the tour de force of the one-shot sequence in Rouch's *Gare du Nord* (*Paris vu par...* 1965), seen by many as the chef d'oeuvre of the new wave (Marie, 1985).

Coutard is also responsible for the moody rendition of Godard's *Alphaville* (1965), shot entirely on location in Paris, which transposes the futurist vision of the city films into the environment of neo-realism and the new wave; thus creating a 'real' cityscape composed of contemporary buildings and locations which are used as the setting for a thriller, in which Peter Cheyney's 1940s comic noir G-man, Lemmy Caution, is transported to the future. Godard's ironic use of the realist strategies of contemporary cinema to make a genre movie where real locations represent a completely fantastic (future) environment is typical of his delight in playing with cinematic convention, but shows how far these conventions had already become embedded in the practice of the day.

In fact, perhaps one of the most interesting achievements of the new wave, certainly in urban terms, was to render the city attractive again, to make it a place where people

Figure 15. Belmondo and Seaberg in Breathless (Godard, France. 1959).

live, work, love and die... a place of which Bulle Ogier, the main character in Eric Rohmer's *Ma nuit chez Maud* (France, 1969), proclaims: 'Here the air is polluted, but I breathe again... there [the suburbs] the air is clean, but I feel oppressed – I have to be in the Centre'. The city is rediscovered as a romantic place, and in *Breathless* (1959) (Figure 15), with the aid of Coutard's fluent hand-held camera work, Godard projects a vibrant image of Paris.

And yet there are searching questions – 'Etes-vous heureux?' (Are you happy?) asks Marcelline, in Rouch and Morin's *Chronique d'un été (Chronicle of a Summer)* (France, 1961) of passers-by. This sort of scene encapsulates the existentialist dimension of the new-wave film-makers, setting them apart from the Italian neo-realist movement or the British free cinema

Clearly the portrayal of the city by the new wave in the 1950s and '60s is in sharp contrast with the screen image of the city of the 1920s and '30s, where it most often appears as the 'wicked city'. In Murnau's *Sunrise* (US, 1927) it is a 'city woman' who lures a 'good man' away from his wife and village; in Fritz Lang's *Metropolis* (Germany, 1926), the city is a symbol of oppression; in René Clair's *A nous la Liberté* (France, 1930) the modernist factory (designed by Meerson) is a worker's nightmare; and the city of the film noir is usually inhabited by murderers and gangsters, as in Fritz Lang's *M* (Germany, 1931) or Jules Dassin's *Naked City* (US, 1948) and *Night and the City* (GB US/UK, 1950).

Such films gave an essentially dystopian vision of the city, echoing some of the planning theories of the time. Later on, these urban theories brought us the ubiquitous suburbs, with their high-rises and planned environments, again portrayed and mirrored in fiction films such as Kubrick's *Clockwork Orange* (GB, 1971), a vision of the near future 'narrated expressively' through the newly-built Thamesmead Estate in London, or Kassovitz's view of the Paris suburb of Chanteloup-les-vignes in *La Haine* (France, 1995). Both depict these environments as the location of vice and violence.

However, a more rounded and global view of the city and its surroundings can be found in the oeuvre of Jacques Tati (Penz, 1997), who over a period of 20 years (from

1947 to 1967) was the invaluable chronicler, documentarist and critic of the French built environment, from rural to urban, from farmhouse (*Jour de Fête*, 1947) to high-rise office block (*Playtime*, 1967).

In *Mon Oncle* (1957), Tati contrasts the lively atmosphere of St. Maur, an old quarter of Paris, where Monsieur Hulot, the main character (played by Tati himself) lives, with the sterile 'modernist' environment of his brother-in-law's villa. Through his portrayal of the villa and its inhabitants' way of life there, Tati delivers a vitriolic critique of modern architecture. But probably more valuable is his portrait of St. Maur, which is the archetypal small city-centre with its dense living quarters, market square, cafés, multi-racial and multi-language (the vegetable-stall holder speaks Italian) – all factors which contribute to create the perfect environment for that ultimate flâneur, the amiable and naive 'clown' Monsieur Hulot.

Indeed the art of flânerie really requires a proper city centre; it cannot be carried out in an environment of deserted high-rise flats. In fact one could argue that Tati's mise-en-scène of Hulot, as a flâneur on the silver screen, must clearly have influenced the new-wave directors, who greatly admired Tati's work. Urban flânerie is a quintessentially French 19th-century concept and, according to Michel Marie, Godard, Rivette and Rohmer were all great admirers of 19th-century French literature, rarely seen without a Balzac in their pocket (Marie, 1985).

Consciously or not, city flânerie pervades the work of the new wave. It is Marcelline in *Chronique d'un été* walking through Les Halles, it is Belmondo and Jean Seberg walking down the Champs Elysées in *A bout de souffle* (Breathless*)*, it is everywhere in Rohmer's first feature, *Le signe du lion* (France, 1959), which is one long walk across Paris. Indeed, it is arguably through the eyes of the flâneur on the screen that, from the 1960s onward, the city is gradually rediscovered. In *Every Day Except Christmas* (Lindsay Anderson, GB, 1957) London's Covent Garden Market, converted in the 1970s from a fruit and vegetable market into a period-sensitive general market and restaurant quarter, is portrayed in its older form with great sympathy; and in France, its Parisian equivalent, Les Halles, demolished in 1971 to make way for the Centre Georges Pompidou and a vast underground shopping mall, is preserved in *Chronique d'un été* (Rouch & Morin, 1961). An invisible cinematic thread joins city films after the 1940s, despite the move away from static cameras and studio sets toward ever more portable, mobile and versatile cameras and sound equipment, to the allegorical city symphonies of the 1920s. I would suggest that these examples of existentialist-city-symphony-flâneurie portrayed by Tati, Godard, Rohmer and their fellows, have done their share in bringing about the re-evaluation of life in the city; which parallels and mirrors, in the 1960s and 1970s, the work of architects such as the Smithsons in the UK and sociologists such as Henri Lefèbvre in France. In the second half of the 20th century, the combined vision represented by those ideas and movements converged to depict a city which is worth loving and preserving; and it is not beyond the bounds of possibility that 'city films' have also somehow contributed to the debate on city regeneration, which in the UK culminated in the publication of the Task Force Report 'Towards an Urban Renaissance' (1999) chaired by Richard Rogers.

5. Toward the Digital Representation of Architecture and the City

As was pointed out at the beginning of this review of the relationship between architecture and the moving image, architectural animation is a rapidly growing field, which has much to learn from the rich history of screen practice.

Many architectural animations resort to the techniques of the 'fly-through' in long, continuous takes, often plunging at great speed from eerily-blue skies down to empty streets to finally rise again and penetrate buildings (still at great speed) at the nth floor level. This sort of technique may rate highly as a piece of technical prowess, but it does not make attractive or engaging viewing, particularly in comparison to the long history of sophisticated techniques used in cinema and television.

In addition, it is notoriously difficult to model convincing and engaging people using traditional, skilled animation techniques, in the hands of talented artists; and it is hazardous for architects unskilled at such animation to try to do so 'automatically' using packaged software. Most architects recognize this, and as a result most CAD animations are devoid of human presence and scale. Indeed, the empty rooms, empty buildings and empty streets of architectural animations may remind us of Walter Benjamin's remark (commenting on Atget's photography of Paris at the turn of the century, where the streets were stripped of life due to the long exposure needed) quoted earlier: '...he photographed them like the scenes of crimes' (Arendt, 1973), and such an approach is unlikely to engage potential clients or convey the sense of a real building during the design process. At the turn of the second millennium, when digital movie-making began to take over from traditional filming, CAD animations were in their infancy – not unlike photography at the time of Atget or Daguerre in the 19th century.

However, beyond these inherent difficulties associated with CAD in architectural animation, there is the more significant and fundamental issue of the language of the screen. Architecture is a very visual discipline, which offers tremendous potential for mise-en-scène such as Godard and Coutard refined in the Paris films of the 1960s. Both the design process which helps produce architecture (drawings, physical models, CAD models) and the final product (the building) are highly photogenic in the traditional sense; but when it comes to producing moving-image-based projects, using digital video or 3D walk-through animations, the visual raw material is not enough on its own. And here is the paradox: thanks to more than 100 years of cinema (and television more recently) within western culture, we all feel that we understand the language of the screen – and we do; but those of us who are not trained or experienced movie-makers can rarely 'speak' it. Moreover, although we may not ourselves be capable of fluency in screen language, we are highly trained and sophisticated viewers, our tastes formed by a century of expert and sensitive portrayals of buildings and urban environments. Architects and their clients are naturally extremely critical of sub-standard products.

Learning from Moving-image Culture

By the end of the 20th century, audio-visual rhetoric had been evolving for a hundred years. It is a very structured language, highly codified; and given that architects are clearly embracing moving-image culture and appropriating it for their own work, they need to look closely at three key areas of film language in order to address issues vital to their own concerns:

* Issues of screen language – what vocabulary and grammar are best suited to 'narrate' architecture?
* Issues of expressive space, or emotionally realistic spaces, as opposed to photo-realistic spaces – how do we convey mood and feeling through moving-image presentations?
* Issues of human representation within virtual worlds (CAD animations) – how can we bring simulations to life as vividly as the cinema, TV, and the interactive game do?

Issues of Screen Language

The vast majority of narrative films are made using *continuity editing*, where the viewer does not notice the cuts, since the different scenes are joined apparently seamlessly according to familiar conventions – cutting on the gaze, or on the movement within the frame, for example, are a basic part of the grammar of film language developed over a century of movie-making, and used fluently in the work of the new-wave film-makers, which can easily enough be integrated into architectural animation and videos, provided the makers are aware of them.

The main alternative to the tradition of continuity editing is the montage tradition exemplified by the work of Dziga Vertov (*Man with a Movie Camera*, 1929), where the images are juxtaposed in a jarring manner, but where the different sequences can also be brought together by means of 'montage by analogy'.

This model of editing is the ancestor of MTV, and in addition to its wide exploitation in video art and art movies, it is nowadays used frequently throughout the advertising world, where the aim is to get across a rich series of images carrying a clear message in a very short time. This form of editing has its roots in Vertov's *Kino Eye* manifesto of 1919, where he chants, '...I am eye... I am the mechanical eye...'

A range of examples drawn from courses taught at the Cambridge University Moving Image Studio (CUMIS) may serve to help understand better the important issues of screen language for architectural thinking in a movie-literate world, starting with the moving-image induction course for architecture students.

Continuity Editing – Expressive Space

The Expressive Space workshop, based on an exercise which was developed within the Department of Architecture through experimentation between 1994 and 2000, is part of a week-long introduction to working with moving images. The aim of the exercise is threefold: to engage students' active interest in the relationship between cinema and architecture, familiarize them with the rudiments of screen language, and impart sufficient familiarity with equipment and basic technical skills to handle digital image capture and post production effectively. The object of the exercise is to make a portrait of a building in Cambridge by means of the moving image.

A portrait is more than a representation – it is an evocation of personality. Portrait-makers have always struggled to capture 'soul' or 'spirit' – not merely anatomy. Here the students are asked to create on screen an expressive space, not just render its physical characteristics. The models are the portrayals of urban space to be found in the range of movies discussed earlier. Participants start from trying to understand how the building makes them feel, and then move to how they can convey that feeling to someone else. The participants can use colour, or words such as 'warm, cold, safe, dangerous, engaged, alienated, welcome, unwelcome, helped, hindered' in the storyboarding process, to help determine an optimum structure and shooting strategy (lighting, framing, point of view) as they make their digital video portrait. They are asked to consider carefully their narrative stance – are they using subjective or objective points of view? Whose journey around the building are they following? They are also asked to evaluate the relevance of these questions to the representation/recreation of architectural space in moving images. Are we asking who designed the building? Who made it? Who uses it? Who is exploring it? Who it is intended for? Are these concepts which need words to express them clearly (in subtitles or voice-over commentary), or can the relevant questions be posed and answered in the footage itself?

In short, after analysing a series of scenes from a range of movies, participants are asked to use their own skills and talents, their own feeling for space and place, their own 'eye', to explore continuity shooting and editing (creating an illusion of continuous action, even though they are condensing both time and space from real time) in evoking the building for others – exploring it in a coherent narrative style, using human presence to help create that coherence.

A typical product of this exercise is the portrait of the King's College Library, Cambridge, used by one student group as the setting for a traditional 'horror movie', borrowing many elements from this familiar genre (Figure 16).

The Montage Tradition

The method of using moving images as animated collages is well suited to the early stages of a design project, when there is a need to express concepts at a point where very little may exist in terms of drawings or models. An example of the use of this technique can be found in an exercise for the M.Phil degree in Architecture and the Moving Image, which aims to bring together conceptual ideas for a new building – in

Figure 16. King's College Library, Cambridge (Matthew Dolman, Nicholas Hornig and Gail White, 1999).

Figure 17. Still from an M.Phil moving-image exercise, exploring possibilities for the proposed Microsoft building (Yolande Harris, Helen McGregor and Joanna Walker, Cambridge University Dept. of Architecture 1999).

this case the planned Microsoft building in West Cambridge – and make a moving-image presentation sketch. The group explores a number of themes in a narrative mode, but the way the images are juxtaposed together amounts to an animated conceptual collage. Part of the value of such an exercise is the process itself, which should inform the moving-image-makers as much as the client, and teach budding architects to elicit their thoughts in a novel way (Figure 17).

Continuity Editing and Montage

Although most mainstream film-makers follow the Hollywood tradition of continuity editing, there are a number of examples where the director has chosen to mix some elements of montage with continuity editing. Looking back we can find some of those elements in *Les Mystères du château du Dé* (Man Ray, France, 1929), the surrealist exploration of a house designed by architect Mallet-Stevens. A piece on Trinity College Blue Boar Court (architect Richard McCormack), made by a group of Diploma Students in Architecture from Cambridge University, has some of the poetic, surrealistic quality of Man Ray's work, mixing elements of continuity editing in the depiction of a journey with montage, in particular when cutting in architectural details. Similarly, Ben Piper's piece on Cardiff Bay (Figure 18), part of a BA architectural project, is both an exploration

Figure 18. Cardiff Bay (Ben Piper, Cambridge University Dept. of Architecture 1998).

of the possibilities for the site and a presentation of his concept, combining narrative supported by the soundtrack (his own song) with a mix of collage-like images.

Further Questions

What we can extract from this quick overview of architectural screen language is a series of further questions, when we make a representation, a concept design, or a presentation of a building or urban environment in moving-images – whether video or interactive 3D animation – about whose point of view are we adopting? Is it the client's, the architect's, or the user's? Who is commissioning the piece? Can we appropriately use elements of fiction, such as staging action? Should we aim to make a 'building symphony' or 'urban environment symphony' like traditional 'city symphonies'? Is an architectural movie a documentary? Is there such a thing as objective documentary, or should we consciously include and indicate an ideological slant? Should we use continuity editing or montage, or a mixture? All these questions, which are examined in some detail in the other other sections of this volume, create a matrix of possibilities, a complex decision-tree. There is no simple answer, and every project is likely to be different, just as every building design is unique. But there is no guide like knowledge, and familiarity not only with the products of traditional screen culture but also with the logic, grammar and rhetoric of their functioning and of how they are made is an invaluable asset.

Expressive Locations

In film, the architecture – the setting – contributes fundamentally to the story, to the atmosphere. The sets or locations, the surroundings where the action takes place, are never incidental, but carefully chosen. As part of the language of the screen, they represent narrative expressive space. By contrast, CAD animations tend to be eerily surreal, despite technical advances such as increasingly sophisticated radiosity algorithms designed to replicate convincingly natural lighting.

Cinematic approaches taken more and more in digital work, but incorporating some form of 'expressive space' into CAD animation, which is usually generated using predesigned and specified packages, is a challenging proposition. How to give shiny computer-rendered materials the 'weariness' which the eye might expect? Figure 19 illustrates the beginning of an answer, where the 'virtual set' has been 'collaged' together in Photoshop from real textures.

Figure 19. Piano Man (Toby Penrose, designer Dominic Hyman, NFTS, 1998).

The Body In Space

Visuals like these, lifeless computer animations rather than unpopulated photographs, still evoke Benjamin's 'scenes of crimes'. But at the beginning of the 21st century there were already at least two ways to enliven computer animations comparatively easily, using 'people' based on real human beings. One is to use 'synthetic' characters, created from a mixture of motion capture and traditional animation techniques, which the computer delivers to specification as somewhat manipulable figures that can be made to appear to navigate virtual spaces. These figures, rather unrealistic and unconvincing both in their appearance and in their motion, need to be developed and improved, and made more easily available to practices. Until they have become more sophisticated, they are best used in the background, as shown in Figure 20, which is made using Poser (© Metacreations).

However, without a budget of the size of James Cameron's for *Titanic* (US, 1997), realistic motion capture is beyond the reach of the average architect, and the more affordable solution is the second alternative: traditional blue-screen or chroma-key techniques, where the images of actors are captured in a studio on digital video against a plain blue (or green) screen, then 'matted' into a chosen background – that is to say,

Figure 20. The use of a background synthetic actor, with textures edited in Photoshop, as well as traditional blue-screen techniques and real actors.

Figure 21. Superimposing two pieces of footage using transparency.

processed so that the areas which are blue in the original shots (the background) are replaced digitally with a pre-shot location background.

Using this method (as old as film itself – see p. 136–138 referring to the work of Marey and Maybridge – but comparatively simple using modern electronic image-manipulation techniques), both synthetic and real characters can be mixed together in the same scene to achieve a suggestive, sketched, rather than realistic moving-image sequence (Figure 20).

Overall, working with actors and synthetic characters is extremely time-consuming, requires directing talent and skill as well as a knowledge of mise-en-scène, and requires adequate blue-screen studios and reasonably sophisticated post-production facilities and expertise. It also entails matching scales and perspectives, as professional set designers have always done.

Another, less onerous, technique is to use transparency effects by superimposing two sets of footage on top of each other – one shot on location, with a person actually in frame, and the other a similar shot created inside a CAD animation. Equally, these do not give the effect of intentional realism, but match the work-in-process aesthetic of architectural design. The buildings being presented are not normally 'real' at this stage, but projections, virtual versions of something which will later come into physical existence (Figure 21).

Conclusion
More and more, architectural project design and presentation are calling upon the traditional skills of the movie-maker to narrate architectural space, through 3D animated 'walk-throughs' and Digital Video (DV). Architects need to be aware of the history of architecture in the moving-image media, and to learn the rudiments of screen language, if they are to remain in control of effective moving-image projects, which are increasingly popular as a means of architectural representation. CAD animations desperately need to be narrated, populated, and emotionally expressive in order to match the calibre of the other manifestations of moving-image art, craft and entertainment. Architects need to learn not only from the hundred years of development of audio-visual rhetoric, but also from 21st-century advances in computer animation, digital manipulation, and synthetic imaging.

Notes
1. According to Georgiados, Giedion's 'perceptive apparatus concept' may have been derived from a possible misinterpretation of a quote from the Futurist Umberto Boccioni, 'lo spettatore nel centro del quadro'.

The Creative Treatment of Actuality
Visions and Revisions in Representing Truth

Terence Wright

> I've wrestled with reality for 35 years, and I'm happy, Doctor. I finally won out over it.
>
> James Stewart in *Harvey* (Henry Koster, US, 1950)

1. Theory and Practice

It may be an unfortunate consequence of Western cultural conditioning that we have inherited a distinction between practitioners who *do* and theorists who *think*. This state of affairs can generate mistrust on the part of practitioners who see theorists as being critical of their practice and, in the case of documentary production, at worst, that the theory of film becomes an unnecessary distraction: at best, a necessary evil. Set against this background, this section aims to address some theoretical points of view that might generate a considered and informed approach to the practice of documentary movie-makers.

Mainstream documentary movie can conveniently be examined in two broad categories. On the one hand, it can provide a metaphorical 'peep from behind the curtains' to see the funny things that our neighbours get up to; on the other, it can take 'the family of man' approach, whereby 'once the paint and feathers are stripped away – they are really just like us' (Banks, 1990, 3). These two approaches, in themselves, may not be enough to provide an adequate theory of representation. Nonetheless, whether we like it or not, anyone who picks up a camera with the intention of making a movie will be placing themselves in a historical and theoretical context. It makes little difference whether the movie is intended to be a science-fiction fantasy or a home movie – we can always find historical precedents and extensive arguments for and against whichever camera strategy we wish to adopt. If our endeavours finally prove highly innovative, our work will benefit movie-making in general by extending or revising pre-established practices and theoretical contexts. Even if we consciously decide not to be bound by tradition and choose to ignore those contexts, we may be well-advised to give them at least partial recognition in order to avoid reinventing the wheel and making something totally naïve. Too naïve an approach is as dangerous as risking confining the movie to a conceptual straight-jacket by attempting to cite it within a too exactly plotted historical and theoretical location. Whichever course the movie-maker takes, viewers are most likely to gain an understanding of what is put before them by referring to their previous knowledge of such phenomena, and will themselves locate the movie by referring, consciously or otherwise, to their own conceptions of existing movie genres.

A documentary-maker may decide to tell the audience about something: to educate them about some factual aspect of the world (didactic/instructional) or, more forcefully in this context, to convince the audience to alter or form opinion (expressionist/polemic); or they might want to demonstrate how beautifully, terrifyingly or intriguingly the camera can record the world's events (formalist/reflexive); or they may perhaps simply wish to show things as they are and as they happen (realist/observational). Each of these approaches has a long history and extensive ramifications.

This section focuses, though not exclusively, on ethnographic movies. Although ethnographic movie-making may be considered a sub-category of the broader documentary enterprise, it is one in which the most pertinent documentary issues become highly sensitized. Matters that are easily taken for granted, or questions it may seem unnecessary to ask when making a movie about people in our own culture, become especially relevant in the cross-cultural context. In addition, as this section focuses on British movie-making, it recognizes a close connection between anthropology and British documentary practice. Not only did anthropology have some involvement in the formative years of the British documentary tradition, but 21st-century documentary practice in Britain also continues to reflect and/or react against the legacy of a colonial past.

The False Dichotomy of Fact and Fiction

I inscribe a quadrangle of right angles as large as I wish, which is considered to be an open window through which I paint.

Alberti, 1435 (White, 1957, 122)

And what's a film? It's just a window someone peeps through.

Donn Pennebaker (Levin, 1971, 235)

Pennebaker's answer to his rhetorical question, 'What's a film?', amounts to an extension of a long historical tradition of visual representation. From a different perspective, his remark not only provides an updated version of Alberti's point of view, but is characteristic of mainstream western aesthetics. Further back in history, Aristotle identifies representation with imitation. Not only does he opine that our 'earliest lessons' are learnt through an inherent 'instinct for imitation' but that people 'enjoy seeing likenesses because in doing so they acquire information' (*Poetics*, 4). This theory has had lasting influence and it is usually taken for granted that one of the essential characteristics of the movie camera is that it is able to provide a reasonably accurate record of the action that takes place in front of the lens. In trying to define 'documentary film', the reflex is often to describe it as 'factual' (as television streaming does). From this perspective, the film camera has been considered to have photographed what is out there – real people, places and events. The documentary is seen as offering its audience a representation of reality: a view of the world as it really is.

At face value this would seem to offer a fairly straightforward and uncomplicated account. The film, or videotape, in the camera records the action that takes place in front of the lens. It is processed and projected literally to represent, at another time and another place, a reasonably accurate reproduction of whatever has occurred – just as the photograph in my passport provides a reasonable (even if outdated) likeness for the immigration officer to match it to my physiognomy in person and to accept this as evidence enough for admitting me into the country. After all, what happens when we view documentary footage is very like what happens when the immigration officer looks at passport photos. If we have visited London some time in the past, we would probably be able to recognize Parliament Square on the screen. And when we are shown a newsclip of the Queen presiding over the state opening of parliament, we do not need to ask the colour of her dress. The colour on screen may marginally deviate from 'the real thing' but we can see it for ourselves, as if we were actually there. Other information regarding the appearance of things and, to some extent, the layout of the terrain and other physical features, can immediately be perceived by the viewer. Of course this is the great value of the documentary: it can provide us with a 'real life' view of other parts of the world, other ways of life, the sea-bottom, or even other parts of the solar system; and, to a certain degree, it enables us to satisfy our own curiosity with regard to what appears in front of us, on the screen.

While this seems at first glance quite straightforward, to accept that first glance is to take a naïve view of realism. For example, we do not normally view the world through a screen-shaped opening. Even if we do spend our days looking at the world through a window, the actuality bears little comparison to viewing a movie. When we look at the screen, we are not only aware that the sights before us have been selected and sequenced by someone else, but that the images we see are mediated by technology and, on closer examination, we might find that they conform to forms, styles or patterns of images and sounds we can recognize from other productions. In fact, because the camera is not able to give us anything like the experience of 'being there at the time', movie-makers resort to cinematographic techniques to compensate for some of the medium's inherent limitations as a convincing reproducer of experience.

Defining Documentary

Given the suggestion that the movie has little to do with recording facts, and with some doubt hanging over its capability in representing reality, what do we mean by 'documentary'? In 1929 John Grierson made a film on herring fishermen, *Drifters* (GB, 1929) (Figure 1). Three years earlier, to describe this new type of cinema (in his review of Robert Flaherty's *Moana*, GB, 1926), he coined the term 'documentary' which he derived from the French term 'documentaire', meaning 'travelogue'. Acclaimed for its realistic, outdoor portrayal of everyday subject matter, *Drifters* attracted a number of young film-makers with whom Grierson worked, training them to become the documentary film-makers of the 1930s and '40s and thus established the British documentary movement. This generation included Edgar Anstey, William Coldstream, Arthur Elton, Stuart Legg, Paul Rotha, Harry Watt, Basil Wright and Humphrey Jennings. The type of documentary film-makers that emerged from this group might be

Figure 1. Drifters, John Grierson (GB, 1929).

termed 'poetic' – characterized by a recognizable blend of poetry, painting, popular anthropology and surrealism.

Although Grierson and many of his followers held forthright views on the meaning of the term 'documentary', there is no manifesto as such, or fixed set of criteria, to clearly identify the genre. Consider, for instance, Lindsay Anderson's audacious statement: 'Humphrey Jennings is the only real poet the British cinema has yet produced.' [i] Given that Jennings happens to be one of Britain's most celebrated documentary film-makers, the term 'poet' may seem rather an odd label for the profession. Jennings, in association with Charles Madge (a poet in the conventional sense of the term) and anthropologist Tom Harrison, was involved in the setting up of 'Mass-Observation' – a social documentary project that ran from 1937 to 1943. The aim of the project was to bring anthropology home by creating a meticulously detailed ethnography of British popular culture. Bronislaw Malinowski, who has a substantial claim to be the founding father of British social anthropology (Kuper, 1983, 1), was involved during the early stages. He provided support and academic endorsement in the form of the introduction to the 'mass-observation' publication, *First Year's Work 1937-38 by Mass-Observation*. In addition, some of the mass-observers (like photographer Humphrey Spender) attended Malinowski's anthropology seminars at the London School of Economics in the late 1930s.

Figure 2. Spare Time (Humphrey Jennings, GB. 1939).

Out of Mass-Observation's early years emerged Jennings' acutely observed documentary film *Spare Time* (GB, 1939) (Figure 2). Jennings had joined Grierson's GPO (General Post Office) Film Unit in 1934. However, by 1937 Grierson had left the Unit, because of a disagreement over the nature of documentary. The Unit wanted to make films that dramatized reality, with a strong element of entertainment; whereas Grierson wanted to shape reality as found, for the purposes of instruction and education. To support the documentary drama, not only was a rocking set of the interior of a fishing trawler built in the Blackheath Studios for Harry Watt's film *North Sea* (1938), but when the cutaway shots of waves were found to be less dramatic than the film required, footage was appropriated from Grierson's earlier film, *Drifters,* and edited as stock-shots into the new production. *North Sea* was introduced by a brief prologue in the form of a caption card stating: 'The story of this film and all the names, characters and places mentioned or shown are entirely authentic. It reconstructs, as it actually happened, an incident in the life of deep sea fishermen.'

Although the debate between information and entertainment remains a contemporary issue – focusing on the drama documentary or the docusoap – the controversy over differences of viewpoint in the 1930s were rapidly overtaken by events, with the outbreak of World War II. In 1940, the GPO Film Unit became the Crown Film Unit, and the energies of its documentary film-makers were directed to the war effort. This necessitated a move from 'poetic' observation to the provision of information.

2. High and Low Control

'No honey, no sequence!'

Leslie Woodhead (Woodhead, 1987, 55)

In common with other forms of visual representation, the documentary movie needs to be researched, planned and previsualized. Yet it also needs to adopt a framework flexible enough to respond to the unexpected. In some instances, the unforeseen outcome provides the main substance of the movie – for example, in Michael Rubbo's *Waiting for Fidel* (Canada, 1975), in which, having been promised an exclusive interview with Fidel Castro, the three film-makers made a film about themselves and their time in Cuba waiting for the interview to take place. The film is punctuated with various government officials presenting the crew with a variety of excuses following a chain of broken appointments with their leader. Although the crew never get to meet Castro, the film proves to be a highly amusing compromise solution to the problem, though one which is totally different from the initial enterprise.

To get over the controversial fact/fiction dichotomy, it is possible to substitute a sliding scale from 'low control' to 'high control'. An extreme example of a low-control situation might be filming during a war or conflict. In this case, the film-makers may only be able to respond to an unpredictable chain of events unfolding around the film crew. For example, despite David Turton's long association with the Mursi, a tribe of nomadic cattle-herders of south-west Ethiopia (he made five documentaries about them for Granada TV GB's *Disappearing World* slot), the fourth film of his series, *The Mursi – the Land is Bad*, was made in highly unstable circumstances. The final outcome of events was not at all certain. There was a good chance that the anticipated *Nitha* ceremony might not take place, and the fact that a rival tribe, the Bume, had gained possession of Kalashnikov rifles raised the distinct possibility that the Mursi could have been wiped out. Although the filming took place during a period of uneasy peace, we hear eye-witness accounts of the massacre of 1987 during which 500 Mursi were killed, and see the wounds on some of the survivors. Later on in the film we see the Bume, with their automatic weapons, shouting from their territory on the other side of the river, wanting to know what the film crew are doing – and have they brought bullets?

Moving along the scale, *The Condor and the Bull*, by Peter Getzels and Harriet Gordon (GB, 1990), has more control over its subject matter. As the film documents a particular ceremony, part of the 'Fiestas Patrias' which mark the annual Peruvian Independence Holiday, it is safe to assume that the events the camera records are in a shape already structured by the participants – as is the case with most performances. In fact, in this particular example, a condor is captured, intoxicated and, as part of the celebrations, put into the bullring. After the 'contest' the condor is allowed to fly away. Even the outcome of the combat is prearranged, as the bull symbolizes the power and oppression of the conquistadors, and the condor the free and independent spirit of the indigenous population. The bird must fly free in the end. With some ceremonies, there may be some difficulty in estimating when proceedings are actually under way (or

Figure 3. Memories and Dreams, Melissa Llewellyn-Davies (GB. 1993).

indeed when they have finally terminated), but while the coverage of events can be responded to by the movie-makers, the events themselves are usually structured with a beginning, middle and end, of the kind prevalent in much narrative drama and dominating Western performance since the 5th century BC (as described in Aristotle's *Poetics*).

The degree of control increases still further in a production like Melissa Llewellyn-Davies' film *Memories and Dreams* (GB, 1993) (Figure 3). Footage shot by her 20 years previously provides the framework for the formal interviews Llewellyn-Davies conducts with her subjects. At the beginning of the film, it is her stated intention to find out 'what had happened to the people I knew and whether they were happy with the way their lives had turned out'. Needless to say, the things she chooses to address in the film – memories and dreams – are phenomena that evade the lens of the camera.

However, the material shot 20 years earlier acts as a stimulant for the Massai to talk about their recollections and aspirations. *Memories and Dreams* is a diachronic study, edited with contemporary footage interspersed with earlier material (Figure 4).

Llewellyn-Davies has also adopted a reflective strategy, which in some instances results in the Massai women interviewing the film-maker, and putting her 'on the spot' – moments of 'lost control' which are not edited out of the final piece.

Another factor determining degree of control may in fact be the intended audience. For example, in Leslie Woodhead's account of filming in Africa with David Turton, he seems to be assuming that the Mursi's abortive attempt to find honey would not make 'good television' – even though there is every likelihood that most of the tribe's honey

Figure 4. Memories and Dreams – Llewellyn-Davies uses a vignetting effect to distinguish the 'present day' from the footage shot some 20 years earlier.

expeditions may prove equally unproductive, which would mean that recording the experience could impart a real truth, though it might not provide a piece of entertainment which satisfies the expectations aroused, by fiction, of a quest fulfilled:

> Lost in the wet undergrowth, I wondered distractedly if this was how David Attenborough went about those immaculate wildlife films. After a few hopeless minutes when we were just about to call it off in favour of breakfast, we blundered into a clearing and found the Mursi gazing up at the honey bird which was perching unconcernedly in a tree. Mike started filming as the Mursi looked at the bird and the bird looked down at its assembled pursuers. Chris poked the microphone at the tree to catch the odd quizzical tweet. Nothing happened for a while. Then the Mursi turned and walked away. It seemed the honey bird's mission, like ours, had been abortive. No honey, no sequence, and still no breakfast. We trudged back across the river. (Woodhead, 1987, 55)

In contrast to Turton/Woodhead, another *Disappearing World* director, Mike Grigsby, in his *The Eskimos of Pond Inlet* (GB, 1977), turns non-event into an art-form (Figure 5).

He inserts cutaway shots to a landing aircraft or to a misty mountain into the central narrative, seemingly without reason. In fact, they serve the purpose of supplying, in an understated way, visual information about the environment the Ingulingmuit inhabit. In contrast to many, if not most, documentary movies, *Pond Inlet* is able to achieve its success without a strong central character, or a definite storyline,

Figure 5. Pond Inlet (Mike Grigsby, GB, 1977).

through employing some of the realist approaches and criteria defined and prescribed by film critic André Bazin (1918-1958).

Realism, the Camera and its Historical Roots

> A camera with its shutter open, quite passive, recording, not thinking. (Christopher Isherwood, 1939)

From the early 15th century (the period of Alberti's famous window metaphor) visual representation has been based on the theoretical principles of linear perspective. It was generally considered that perspective had gradually evolved over the preceding centuries, but that it was not until the period of the Renaissance that artists finally achieved the representational goal their predecessors had striven for. From a 21st century viewpoint, it appears more accurate to say that although certain transformations in pictorial representation emerged as a response to the social and technological change of the Renaissance, rather than achieving the pinnacle of pictorial realism, they in effect produced a different rather than a perfect system. The decision to use that particular system in preference to others might depend on preference rather than any intrinsic 'improvement'.

For example, in Raphael's painting *The School of Athens* (Figure 7), produced in the early 16th century, the overall composition of the picture is based on linear perspective, yet the artist chose to use an orthographic projection for the representation of a globe

Figure 6. Pond Inlet (Mike Grigsby, GB,1977)

on the right-hand-side of the painting. Had he adhered strictly to the rules of linear perspective, the globe would have had to be painted as an ellipse, appearing in the shape of a rugby ball.[ii] In general, much of the world's visual imagery – whether it be the sand paintings of the Warlbiri Australian Aborigines, Michelangelo's Sistine chapel decorations (1508-1512), or Duchamp's 1913 *Nude Descending a Staircase* – may be regarded as offering a variety of strategies for transcribing a three-dimensional world on to a flat, two-dimensional surface (Wright, 1998).

The function of visual images is not, as Isherwood's comment heading this section might be taken to suggest, limited to passive reflection. Indeed, in some instances, representational images themselves initiate change. For example, social changes occurred as a result of the widespread media coverage that made a major contribution to ending the Vietnam War; and technological changes took place when 17th-century Dutch systems of map-making enabled exploration of the globe, with concomitant international commercial expansion.

Lens-based Systems of Representation

> There's nothing else – just us – and the cameras – and those wonderful people out there in the dark.
>
> Gloria Swanson in *Sunset Boulevard* (Billy Wilder, US, 1950)

Figure 7. Raphael (Rafaello Sanzio) The School of Athens (1509, Vatican, Rome).

After the Renaissance, in the mainstream of European art, visual representation was founded upon the principles of the camera obscura ('dark chamber'). This forerunner of the modern photographic camera not only provided the practical means of projecting an image of the world on to a two-dimensional surface, but (in the early 17th century) provided theoretical support for producing pictures by this means. In 1604, Johannes Kepler proposed that the functioning of the camera was more or less identical to the functioning of the eye. So not only was the camera obscura seen as a useful instrument, aiding artists in their creation of convincing images, but it came to be assumed that these images were so convincing because they were produced by a process similar to the way human beings naturally see the world. From a 21st century point of view, this eye-camera analogy is unable to provide an adequate account of the active exploratory nature of visual perception (Wright, 1992). However, 230 years after Kepler's observations, in 1839 photography was invented.

The medium was able to provide an 'automatic' means of transcribing that which was seen by the eye in the form of a permanent record, free from distortions which might arise from the artist's transcription of the image in the camera obscura. Some of the commentaries written around the time of photography's invention identify the most notable characteristics of the medium as:

- Perfection in detail
- Essential truthfulness" (Frith, 1859, 71)
- Automatic production of images
- The accidental recording of details that had evaded the eye of the photographer '....the operator himself discovers on examination, perhaps long afterwards, that he had depicted many things he had no notion of at the time' (Talbot, 1844)
- Speed of production (Arago, 1839)

Photography, unlike cinema, did not start out as a fairground attraction. It was assumed to belong to a more respectable lineage: to be the result of the union of art and science. For its first 50 years at least, photography maintained a professional standing 'used alike by art and science, by love, business ...in the folio of the painter and architect, among the papers and patterns of the mill-owner and manufacturer, and on the cold brave breast on the battlefield' (Lady Elizabeth Eastlake [1857], in Newhall, 1981, pp. 81-97). These words bring us back to French film critic André Bazin. Writing in 1959, Bazin upheld the belief that lens-based media are able to provide 'automatically' an objective means of recording:

> Originality in photography as distinct from originality in painting lies in the essentially objective character of photography ...between the originating subject and its reproduction there intervenes only the instrumentality of a nonliving agent. (Bazin, 1967, 13)

Bazin went on to advocate certain criteria he deemed necessary for producing a realist cinema. They included:

- Long takes
- Deep focus
- Eye-level camera angle
- Unobtrusive cutting

It was Bazin's belief that a film which employed these techniques, which suppressed the transformational characteristics of the medium, would be most suited to present the viewer with a relatively direct (or transparent) perception of the subject matter. If the criteria listed above were adopted by the film-maker, it was expected that the viewer would be most likely to perceive the film as if it were the direct perception of an unmediated scene. We can assume from this that montage techniques are perceived as interrupting the natural flow of events, and that differential focus fractures our perception of spatial continuity.

Nevertheless, Bazin realised it was necessary to employ some degree of contrivance in order to achieve the full effect of realism. Bazin's examples of 'good practice' included both *Citizen Kane* (US, 1941) by Orson Welles, a movie rife with deceptive set design and camera work, and the films of the Italian neo-realists, such as Roberto Rosellini, who prided themselves on truthfulness. For example, Rosellini's *Paisà* (Italy,

1946), concerned with facts not shots, gives a six-episode account of the Allied Forces' progress through Italy toward the end of World War II. Not only does the film use unobtrusive camera and editing techniques, it also uses non-professional 'actors' in everyday environments. For example, random shots of crowd-scenes were filmed, and one of the heroines in *Paisà* was 'discovered' on a dockside. Rosellini concentrates on social issues, giving them a decidedly observational treatment: 'My purpose is never to convey a message, never to persuade, but to offer everyone an observation, even my observation' (Andrew, 1978: 120). According to Bazin, the qualities of the medium itself make it suitable for the representation of reality, and it is the 'facts' represented that are to be given primary emphasis. Another way of putting this is to say that an overriding pursuit of realism is preferable to a concern with the 'formal' characteristics of the medium.

Despite the rationale and arguments for cinematic realism outlined in this section so far, the form (as opposed to the content) of the medium stubbornly remains. Attempts may be made to suppress it, in order to gain a more transparent view of the subject matter, but the formalist aspects of the medium refuse to go away. Despite the 'real world' origins of the documentary, a shift of emphasis away from objectivity and toward the form of the medium and the ways that images are positioned in a temporal structure is detectable as it develops. As John Grierson put it, 'we pass from the plain (or fancy) descriptions of the natural material, to arrangements, rearrangements, and creative shapings of it' (Hardy, 1946, 70).

The Scope of the Medium and Formalism

> The white explorer may wish to see a world as it was before the white man came; but he can only see it as it reacts to the coming of the first white man. He is looking for the rainbow's end, unless he can imaginatively reconstruct what things would have been like if he had not been there.
>
> Calder-Marshall (1963, 22)

It can seem convenient to make a distinction between 'form' and 'content', but in practice the two remain inextricably linked. A movie-maker can decide to place a special emphasis either on the subject, or on the recording medium, yet in the lens-based media in particular, form and content are mutually supportive. With reference to painting, the tendency to separate form from content was criticised by Russian formalist theorist Viktor Shklovsky. In his *Literature and Cinema* (1923) he notes that 'people who try to "solve" paintings as if they were crossword puzzles want to take the form off the painting to see it better' (Erlich, 1955, 187). This practice automatically arises from the 'window on the world' theory of visual representation, which holds that the only purpose of the medium is to give us access to the represented world – if we puzzle hard enough, the *window* might begin 'to melt away, just like a bright silvery mist' (Lewis Carroll, 1872, 11). Technical developments in cinema still strive to make the medium less and less apparent, in order to achieve a total interactive immersive experience intended to make the representation of human activity more and more like 'real life'.

The tension between the formalist and realist approaches to representation highlights one of the essential differences between lens-based media and the more traditional graphic arts. In contrast to cinema's quest for ever greater verisimilitude, for the last 160 years or so of the second millennium, painting pursued non-representational goals. Indeed, it may be considered possible to produce a painting that is entirely self-referential – one that makes no external reference to an outside world, but displays exclusive concern with the properties and activity of painting. Although digital technology and animation techniques have the potential to bring moving image media closer to painting in this respect, in the conventional use of lens media at the same period, there is usually an expectation that the image will be 'of' something; and in cinema, no matter how expressionistic or distorted the final outcome may appear, the underlying expectation is usually that the image projected on the screen will be fundamentally representational.

An alternative strategy to the transparent realist approach is to be 'up front' and honest by making the film-maker's process very clear to the viewer. By emphasizing the 'terms of engagement' between the subject, the movie, and those who have made it, the movie-makers make viewers aware of the extent of the artifice employed to represent the subject, so they can compensate accordingly. It is only one step further to taking the view that there is no need to even attempt to reproduce 'reality'; the world 'out there' may have provided the audio-visual source material for the movie – but the movie, by its very nature, has been constructed, and departs from its reallife origins the moment the film is exposed. Movie-maker and viewer are left with mere shadows of events that have passed, which they cannot reach or respond to: a world that is accessible only through its screen projection.

3. The Motivation Behind The Camera

> ...if he swam the river, how did he preserve the film? How did he really take the pictures? Why isn't there any trace of camera shake? He'd been drinking, he was balancing on tiptoe; they're long enough exposures, you know, time exposures ... Why did he risk his life at all, taking those photographs?
>
> John le Carré *The Looking Glass War* (1965, 77)

Apart from a tendency to ask questions about the movie-makers' process, there is another dimension to the viewer's questioning – what is the movie saying? In addition to recording the subject of the movie (realism) and, at the same time, revealing evidence of the movie-maker's process (formalism), the movie also tells us something about those who made it and the circumstances under which it was made (expressionism). In this context, the movie may express the movie-maker's particular point of view, and also express something about the culture for which it was made. Even an automatic surveillance camera, with no camera operator, remains expressive, in suggesting the type of culture in which it belongs. It might express criminal activity, the alienation of modern society, or the powers of state control. Recognizing this may draw upon the viewer's experience of the literary tradition of dystopias such as George

Orwell's novel *Nineteen Eighty-Four* (GB, 1948), or a knowledge of the tragic case of the killing of two-year-old James Bulger in Britain in 1993. Jon Venables and Robert Thompson (both aged 10) were captured on closed-circuit television, abducting the toddler from a Liverpool shopping centre before they battered him to death on a railway track. The image of the child being led away by the two boys was regularly broadcast on British television news as part of the hunt for the killers.

However, returning to the sliding scale of low to high control in documentary and ethnographic movie-making, it is possible to propose that this scheme is equally applicable to the audience. From this perspective, the essential difference between, at one extreme, the propaganda movie, which consciously directs viewers' interpretation, and at the other, the so-called 'fly-on-the-wall' approach of 'direct cinema' (or indeed the surveillance camera), which purport to leave interpretation to the viewers themselves, is more clearly emphasized.

Here, low and high control approaches may be compared with realism and formalism, through contrasting the views of Bazin and Eisenstein on the use and qualities of the medium. Briefly summarizing, where Bazin propounds minimum intervention both of the medium and on the part of the film-maker, Eisenstein advocates the direction of the film's meaning through the precise arrangements of its elements. In his theory of montage, Eisenstein (1943, 14 & 19) finds that 'two film pieces of any kind, placed together, inevitably combine into a new concept, a new quality, arising out of that juxtaposition ....In such cases the whole emerges perfectly as "a third something"'. Eisenstein cites the Gestalt psychologist Kurt Koffka in support of his theory – the Gestalt movement was responsible for coining the catch-phrase 'the whole is more than the sum of the parts'. The aspiring documentary movie-maker is faced with the choices between directly informing viewers, facilitating their vision, or adopting a strategy that runs somewhere in between these positions. The directorial propagandist approach represents an obvious danger, but an approach that gives the viewer too much autonomy may be equally, if not so obviously, dangerous. As documentary editor Dai Vaughn puts it, 'We cannot boast of leaving our films open-ended and at the same time complain if people draw from them conclusions we dislike' (Barbash & Taylor, 1997, 51). There is a narrow course to be steered between 'spoon-feeding' information and giving the audience such a free rein that they become disoriented.

Narrators, Guides and Informants

... Then to me
The gentle guide: "Inquirest thou not what spirits
Are these which thou beholdest?"...

Dante Alighieri, 1321 (Inferno, Canto IV)

There is a long literary tradition, which depends upon a guide who escorts the reader or the author through strange lands inhabited by strange beings. The guide is usually a marginal figure with a foot in both camps. In the world of moving image media, the

Figure 8. Illustration for Dante's Inferno. Gustave Doré (1832-83).

role of the narrator often adopted by well-known British documentary-maker and TV presenter David Attenborough, in wildlife adventures and ethnographic movies alike, is akin to that of Virgil in Dante's *Divine Comedy* of the early 14th century (Figure 8). Taking on an intermediary role, Virgil acts as an informant or ethnographer as he guides, informs and educates Dante (and listeners or readers) about the inhabitants of the *Inferno,* while maintaining a safe distance between observers and observed. The narrator is a pivotal figure, who has a place in 'our world', yet also appears at home in the world we are visiting.

In the filmed documentary, we have become accustomed to accepting a disembodied voice which informs us about the events we see on the screen. This omniscient spectral presence can belong to a trusted, reliable and enthusiastic 'friend' – as in the case of Attenborough's voice-overs – or can be used to create an anonymous persona, which stands for a Western 'authority' on the subject in question. Nonetheless, the voice-over does not have to adopt a patronizing tone, and can be used more creatively. For example, Jean Lydall's film of the Massai, *Two Girls Go Hunting* (BBC 2 TV, GB, 1991), relies upon a narrator with an African accent. Although she does not appear in the film, the voice-over imparts the knowledge of a local informant speaking to us, offering a very different impression to that made by the accents of a Western tourist, tour-guide, explorer, scientist, teacher or presenter, who acts on our behalf.

Many have felt it preferable to dispense with the voice-over narrator altogether. Such was the spirit informing the British 'direct cinema' movement of the 1960s, when certain changes in film-makers' style can be partly attributed to technological changes. Newly developed lightweight hand-held cameras with sync sound, fast film stock that could operate in natural light, zoom lenses able to record from an unobtrusive distance – as could directional microphones – led to a change in emphasis, away from the film-makers' controlling the elements of the movie in post-production (after the shoot) – their 'telling' the audience – and toward the viewer's choice of perception of the action within the frame. The evolution of this style of documentary was paralleled by the contemporary cinéma-vérité movement in France, although this differed stylistically from direct cinema through the inclusion of the film-maker's questioning of the subject to elicit a 'truthful' response. In *Chronique d'un été* (France, 1961), film-makers Rouch and Morin even include open discussion with the subjects of their film, about the film-making enterprise and their experience (Figure 9).

To de-emphasize the technological determinist standpoint, it should not be forgotten that these new documentary forms arose through social and political changes during the period, and that the general cultural climate also had a part to play in the emergence of a direct, authentic and non-interventionist approach to the subject. However radical the movements in film-making of the 1960s may seem in providing alternative narrative strategies, which refrain from comment in favour of allowing viewers to see and explore for themselves, they too had their forerunners. Returning to Dante's *Divine Comedy*, at the end of *Purgatory*, Virgil is able to relinquish his duties, leaving Dante to rely on his own direct experience:

> ...No longer expect word or sign
> from me. Free, upright and whole is thy will and
> it were a fault not to act on its bidding; therefore
> over thyself I crown and mitre thee.

> Dante Alighieri, 1321 (*Divine Comedy, Purgatorio, Canto XXVII*)

Sullivan, writing on the direct-cinema style of the film-maker Frederick Wiseman, summarizes: 'We find ourselves *there*, with the camera. We are observers, but there is no handy guide' (1979, 453)[iii].

4. Ethnographic Movies – the 'Avant-Garde' of Documentary?

> Ethnographic film is the documentary's avant-garde... more than conventional documentarians, visual anthropologists are compelled to consider the relation of the film-maker (and the film process) to the filmed.

> J Hoberman (Barbash & Taylor 1997, ix)

Figure 9. Chronique d'un été (France 1961). Film-makers Rouch and Morin reflect on their film-making exercise in the galleries of the Musee de l'Homme, Paris.

The majority of mainstream documentary movie-makers would probably find Hoberman's point of view extremely controversial. He proposes that it is in the very nature of ethnographic film that, in addition to concern for recording the subject, strict attention must be paid to the film-makers' process, and to their motivations. This standpoint includes echoes of the 'realist' concern for the subject, the 'formalist' preoccupation with the movie-makers' process, and of the 'expressionist' aspects of movie-makers' motivations. However controversial Hoberman's assertion, in the ethnographic field, issues of movie-making do become highlighted and can be extremely sensitive. For example, the power relationships between movie-maker(s) and subject(s) become highly questionable. Who is being observed and why? Are the subjects to be regarded as unusual specimens of mankind; are they being exploited for popular entertainment? Is it expected that the representation of these 'others' will cause viewers to reflect on their own lives? Are these 'other' subjects given an opportunity to voice their own opinions? If so, how do we overcome the language differences? Subtitles, dubbed translation or voice-over narration give different perspectives to 'our' (the viewers) understanding of 'their' (the subjects') life experiences.

Late 20th-century attempts to avoid the traditional us/them dichotomy have revolved around the role of the anthropologist or movie-maker as a facilitator. This role enables subjects to compose the representation of their own lives, not necessarily as seen by an outside observer. Such movies may be used to reaffirm traditional cultural values, to break down stereotypes or to perform the political function of promoting a culture's aims and aspirations, as well as broadcast real and potential threats to its way of life – as in the case of the Kayapo of Central Brazil, who in 1985 began to use video in their protest against a hydro-electric dam-building project. The protest, involving their use of video, became the subject of the *Disappearing World* documentary film *The Kayapo* (Granada Television, 1989). This development not only impacts upon the actuality of the situation by creating new perspectives, it can also enrich the formal properties of the medium, whereby dominant Western modes of representation become permeated with indigenous visual schemes and narrative strategies (Worth and Adair, 1972; Turner, 1992).

The 'Docu-Stars': Big Men and Good Women

> In front of the lens, I am at the same time: the one I think I am, the one I want others to think I am, the one the photographer thinks I am, and the one he makes use of to exhibit his art... I am neither subject nor object but a subject who feels he is becoming an object.
>
> Roland Barthes (1982, 13)

How are the subjects of documentaries chosen? In a written account there is always the luxury of generalization. An author can write about 'the French' or 'the Inuit', implying that the account refers to the 'typical' French or Inuit person. However, as soon as the camera and sound recorder are rolling, it is with specifics that it deals: this is no longer a matter of 'a' French woman, it is 'Madeleine' or 'Nanook'. As individuals, these subjects may not be found to fit the stereotype of their national culture, nor act as a fair representative of a definable group. They may have been chosen because they would be 'good' on camera – because they have an extrovert character, are eloquent or possess an attractive appearance or personality.

In the Charlie Nairn's Granada TV *Disappearing World* film *The Kawelka: Ongka's Big Moka* (GB, 1974), the central character, Ongka, was chosen as protagonist because of his skill in oration and persuasion. He made 'good television' and indeed soon became a 'star' in ethnographic circles. In fact, at the Royal Anthropological Institute film festival in 1996, a line of Ongka T-shirts was available for purchase. In Ongka's case, we see a merging of the tribal role as a *Big Man* with an on-screen presence (Figure 10).

The anthropologist Maurice Godelier provides a list of the attributes of a Big Man. This is worth quoting in its entirety:

> He is shrewd, cautious, calculating, a good speaker, convincing.
> He pursues a strategy of gifts and countergifts.
> He is a great producer, but above all a great accumulator and redistributor of wealth.
> He is polygamous, with many wives and children.
> He receives help from those whom he has helped, particularly young men in search of a wife, but wanting the pigs and other forms of wealth needed for a dowry.
> He represents first and foremost his lineage, his village, and clan as well as his entire tribe in certain circumstances.
> His name and reputation are known far and wide.

Figure 10. Ongka, 'star' of Charlie Nairn's The Kawelka: Ongka's Big Moka (GB, 1974).

He stands apart from ordinary men, and particularly from those young warriors with 'bloodshot' eyes whose impetuous violence can be a nuisance in peacetime.
He intervenes in affairs relating to kinship between lineages and in political relations between clans, arbitrating disputes.
He bequeaths to his children wealth, a name, and partners in other tribes whom they may use in turn to aggrandize themselves within the network of ceremonial ex-changes.
If he turns this reciprocity into exaction, he will gradually become a despot. Sooner or later his faction will abandon him, and he will fall. Or he may even be murdered.
(Godelier, 1986, 175)

There are strong resonances within this 'job description' with a host of established feature-film roles, from the heroes of *The Magnificent Seven* (John Sturges, US, 1960), a Western adaptation of Akira Kurosawa's *Seven Samurai* (Japan, 1954) – or indeed nearly all of Kurosawa's protagonists – to Orson Welles's *Citizen Kane* (US, 1950), Francis Ford Coppola's *Godfather* (US, 1971) or the Wachowski Brothers' Morpheus in *The Matrix* (US, 1999). And Ongka is portrayed as a man with a quest, having to use all his skills of oratory and persuasion to achieve the Herculean task of assembling six hundred pigs, eight cows, twelve cassowaries[iv], $10,000, one truck and a motorbike as a massive presentation for a rival Big Man.

By way of contrast, Dennis O'Rourke in his *The Good Woman of Bangkok* (Australia, 1991) (Figire 11) chose to portray his subject in the role of a tragic heroine, at the same time as raising issues of reflexivity and exploitation. Described by O'Rourke as 'a documentary fiction film', the movie's main constituent themes neatly demonstrate a Levi-Straussian scheme of binary oppositions (Levi-Strauss 1987, pp. 75-77 *et passim*):

West/East
Male/Female
Wealth/Poverty
Observer/Observed

It seems that O'Rourke is recognizing his own position in a lineage of exploitation of the East by the West. After all, the Bangkok sex industry flourishing at the end of the 20th century owed its origins to the moment in 1965 when the city was the designated venue for R & R (Rest and Recreation) for US troops recuperating from tours in Vietnam. *The Good Woman of Bangkok* opens with shots of naked, or near naked, women dancing erotically in a Bangkok bar. The soundtrack is of a female voice singing a Mozart aria. Has this sequence been constructed so as to distance the viewer from the scene and allow reflection on the activity, or has the music been added to give an aura of respectability to images that could be described as gratuitously voyeuristic?

The Good Woman of Bangkok has a 'plot'. O'Rourke himself picks up a girl in a bar, takes her to a hotel room, and asks her if she will agree to his making a film about her life. She does agree, and relates her tragic life-story to camera. It transpires that all she wishes to do is earn enough money to buy a rice-farm in her home village in the country. Finally, O'Rourke intervenes, and provides the money to buy the farm. The epilogue caption informs the audience that on his return a year later, O'Rourke found that she had given up the farm, to return to Bangkok and her former lifestyle. Whatever reflections there may be to be made on O'Rourke's method, the film does raise a number of complex questions concerning the nature of movie-makers and the relationship between the documentarist and the subject. For example, in making the movie at all, buying the services of a subject whose assets are her female sexuality in order to do so, is O'Rourke himself contributing to her exploitation? Prostituting her for the camera?

A 20th-century development in documentary is the sub-genre of the 'docu-soap'. In 1974 Paul Watson's *The Family* was shown on BBC TV as a 13-part 'fly-on-the-wall' serial. The episodes provided a regular insight into the goings-on of an actual British working-class family, and might be said to be in the spirit of 'mass observation': producing a popular anthropology 'at home' for a mass audience. Indeed, the viewing figures for this 'real life' family rivalled those of Britain's longest-running television soap-opera, ITV's *Coronation Street* (GB, 1964-). Such programmes as *Driving School* (BBC1, 1997) and *Vets in Practice* (BBC1, 2000) continued to challenge the popularity of the more traditional soaps. *Castaway* (BBC2, 2000), which follows a group of people trying to live on a remote Scottish island, building their own living environment, could be said to approach 'live' ethnography even more closely, with the group on the island acting as a more 'primitive' version of the viewers themselves – a historical rather than geographical 'otherness'. Despite the creation of totally artificial communities operating in situations designed by the television company, this form of explorative

Figure 11. Dennis O'Rourke The Good Woman of Bangkok (Australia, 1991).

anthropology has strong appeal for historical documentary: *The House* (BBC TV, 1999), combining education and information with entertainment, attracted high numbers of viewers by following the attempts of 20th-century people to run a 19th-century household, relearning the arts of managing domestic affairs without electricity or gas.

However, the questions of representation and manipulation such programmes raise are not in themselves new – they are essentially those discussed throughout this section. Should documentary observe, or should it re-enact, or tailor for entertainment? Should the subject be selected and the camera placed for optimum didacticism, realism, formalism, expressionism? The danger with docu-soap productions is that the story can take over from the actuality – life does not occur in story format, with such clean-cut and defined edges, or a cast that is manageable for the audience; it is considered that the action has to be contained (for example, in the episodic format) to facilitate the audience's comprehension of events.

As John Corner points out (ed. Rosenthal 1999, 45): 'The charge is made that the viewers are encouraged to give truth status to unsubstantiated or purely imaginary elements, and furthermore, that the communicative, affective power of the dramatic treatment is likely to install accounts in the minds of the viewer with force and depth.' While this genre centralizes factual content, the treatment and style is that of the soap-opera – it focuses on a range of definable characters and a narrative storyline, and the participants rapidly start to perform in the mode of the soap-stars with whom they are familiar. Does this brand of documentary provide a bold interpretation of Grierson's 'creative treatment of actuality'?

The surveillance camera has given birth to another television format, which brings together docu-soap with a form of ethnographic filming. In shows like *Big Brother* (C4, GB, 2000), which started to appear on European TV in the middle of 2000, volunteer

186

groups of people are sealed into an intimate living environment, where every part of the dwelling is under surveillance. In some cases, cash prizes are offered to the subject who can survive these living conditions the longest. At specified times (or in some cases at any time) viewers can observe the human subjects in their cage, at the most intimate and normally private moments of their lives. Viewing figures can be very high, though audiences seem to show little follow-up interest after the run is over. This format combines docu-soap with ethnography with wildlife observational programme with game show. It is a form of live social experiment for the entertainment of the mass audience. The practice, over time, has formal and ethical repercussions on other types of documentary and ethnographic movie-making.

Further, related, perspectives will develop with the growth of interactive Webcam situations, where groups of people or individuals can observe and interact with each other over vast distances in real time, independently of the editing of broadcasting or netcasting companies. As in the case of direct cinema and cinéma-vérité, the technology that facilitates the growth of new content forms develops in the context of social and political changes.

The general cultural climate in the 21st century favours the democratization of knowledge, information and power. The role of interpretative viewers, when they can select between the pictures transmitted by different cameras in different rooms in a house full of subjects, for example, becomes proactive. The producer or movie-maker(s) can hand control over to them, putting them in the position of the editor, or the vision-mixer of TV sportscasts and other live transmissions. Viewers can then choose their own individual and unique pathway through the available material, participating in a kind of ongoing director-less improvisation, and drawing their own conclusions, based on the narrative they construct themselves. When this happens, the choice and placing of the cameras, the selection of the available viewpoints, are all that is left in the control of the producer, cinematographer, or director.

Eventually, if viewers start to record live Netcasts and digital broadcasts in electronic form, they are able to edit material from different sources together, using appropriate software on the domestic computer, which receives the e-cast, into personalized 'documentaries' or essays. At this point, awareness of the practices, aesthetics and ethics outlined in this section becomes as important a part of cultural equipment as a knowledge of the alphabet is to reading and writing.

5. The Interactive Documentary

> There are many reasons for the oddity of the knight's move, but the principle reason is the conventionality in art.
>
> Viktor Shklovsky, *The Knight's Move* (Erlich, 1955)

The earlier discussion of the narrative structure of *Pond Inlet* refers to the analogy of the knight moving across the chessboard. Needless to say, this was only a simple analogy, implying no essential physical similarity between the chessboard and the film. However, this is not the case with MIT's interactive documentary *Jerome B Wiesner,*

Figure 12. The Keyword Grid in Jerome B Weisner: A Random Walk Through the Twentieth Century (MIT Media Lab Web hyperportrait, US. 2000).

where a chessboard-like structure, a 'Keyword Grid', is displayed on the Web page to enable the viewer to map out the 'hyper-portrait' of Wiesner (Figure 12).

The Grid marks out the 'time periods' of Weisner's life; the central themes of his life's activities and the most significant people that affected him (family, friends and colleagues). The viewer, by clicking the mouse on the Keyword Grid, activates the 'Material Listing' of video clips and text documents. The Weisner hyper-portrait not only enables the viewer to steer their own course through the documentary, but it has the facility for viewers to add their own personal contributions to the piece.

My own experiment in interactive documentary was *The Batwa 1905*, part of the *From Silver to Silicon* CD-ROM (Wright, GB, 1995). This CD project aims to explore photography, culture and the digital technologies by examining the social role of the photographic image, from the family snapshot to the surveillance photograph. It comprises a visual essay accompanied by seven multimedia 'chapters', including *The Batwa, 1905*. The Batwa chapter, belonging to the surveillance section of the production, explores the possibilities, and addresses some central issues concerning the re-use of archive images, in the context of multimedia and digital processing. It also questions the Western preoccupation with staging and representing members of 'other' cultures.

The viewer of *The Batwa, 1905* is first presented with one particular photograph from which they can begin to uncover more information about the subject, the broader historical context, and a variety of ways of interpreting the image. In essence, the *Batwa* programme can be explored through two main 'routes' entitled 'The Stage' and 'The Study' (Figure 13). These can be accessed by two tinted 'buttons' which, on the first click of the mouse, appear superimposed on Sir Benjamin Stone's original photograph of the Batwa. If you choose 'The Stage' you can examine the photograph from the contexts of the appearance of the Batwa on the stage of the London Hippodrome. If you choose 'The Study', you can follow the anthropological investigation set up by The Royal Anthropological Institute. These routes give the viewer access to a wide range of primary sources – additional photographs, press-cuttings, scientific reports, extracts from academic papers, theatre reviews and playbills, sound recordings and eye-witness accounts.

One reason for choosing Stone's image of the Batwa is that the subjects have been arranged in a photographic style that is immediately recognizable. Its formal composition is that of a family group, yet on taking a closer look the subject matter proves puzzling and this, in itself, invites further investigation. As the mouse explores the screen, it activates a soundtrack outlining the biographical details of the subjects. Thus the viewer moves through from initial background information – biographical and other descriptive detail – to uncover greater depths of theoretical context. For example, from the photograph the viewer can see that the Batwa had been dressed in the period clothing for children. As Stone himself put it, 'they wore the less picturesque raiment of civilisation, the men being in boys' sailor suits' (1905, 18). Further

Figure 13. 'The Pigmies' by Sir Benjamin Stone (1905) with the addition of tinted buttons 'The Stage' and 'The Study' superimposed on the original (The Batwa, 1905, Terence Wright, 1995).

exploration connects this with press reports which described the Batwa as children. Yet further, the programme aims to link these observations to contemporaneous theories of recapitulation: whereby the 'primitive people' were identified, according to psychologist GS Hall (1904, 49), as representing the 'childhood stages' of the 'higher races', a view he shared with Freud. Both theorists had sought evidence for 'archaic' traits and, in doing so, were indebted to theories of evolutionary biology prevalent at the turn of the century. As for the archive and the museum, the evolutionary model was not only applied to the categorization of cultures, but was also evident in the arrangement of the artefacts they had produced (Chapman, 1985).

The presentation of *The Batwa, 1905* was designed to overcome two limitations of language. It avoids structuring in the form of linear progression and does not rely upon a narrative text, or third-party voice-over narration, to contextualize the images. This helps to suppress the didactic elements of the piece so that the form of presentation can make ambivalent attitudes self-evident, with little suggestion of external mediation or opinion. Although an initial aim had been to overcome the problem of prioritizing information, in practice it became difficult to avoid this particular characteristic of the linear narrative. Nonetheless, the information could be presented in a series of parallel strands, thus allowing for the inclusion of many more visual images than would be possible in 'conventional' publishing. The result is a visual essay, with a strong emphasis on spatial layout.

As the programme is explored additional photographs are uncovered, which not only include images from the press and some anthropometric images (commissioned by the Royal Anthropological Institute), but also those taken by James Harrison, the explorer who 'found' the Batwa in the Congo Free State and brought them to England (Harrison, 1901; 1905). The presentation of this information is accompanied by sounds of the Batwa singing and conversing. The discovery of the soundtrack in the National Sound Archive was especially fortuitous. A recording of the Batwa, made in 1905, was transferred from its wax-cylinder original to a CD-ROM digital sound file – a technological jump of some 90 years.

Each of the two 'routes' ('The Stage' and 'The Study') draws reference from a wide range of sources. In one case, a section of 'The Stage' route refers back to the *Egyptian Book of the Dead* (Budge, 1895) of the 18th dynasty (1570-1293 BC) for its description of how pygmy peoples were brought to entertain at the court of the Pharaohs (Figure 14). These hieroglyphics form a procession, which scrolls across the bottom of the screen.

This reflects the Victorian/Edwardian preoccupation with ancient Egypt and the prevailing *diffusionist* view of history: promoting the idea that the Batwa had been uncontaminated by external influences since the dawn of Western civilisation. In common with museum artefacts, they were considered to be worthy of attention, as Dominguez (1986) has put it, 'not because of their intrinsic value but because of their

Figure 14. 'The Pigmies came to him from the lands of the South, having things of service for his palace' (Egyptian Book of the Dead) The Batwa, 1905, Terence Wright 1995).

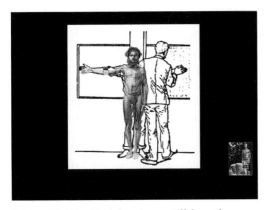

Figure 15. 'The Study' route – a still from the animation illustrating the relationship between ethnographic photography and Bertillon's anthropometric method (The Batwa, 1905, Terence Wright, 1995).

perceived contribution to our understanding of our own historical trajectory'.[v] In another instance, 'The Study' includes a short animation sequence of Bertillon's (1893) diagrammatic prescriptions for obtaining anthropometric information. These have been superimposed on to an anthropological 'subject' (Figure 15).

At another level of consideration, if we adhere to the metaphors employed by the 'Director' computer -program, which supports the interactive treatment of the material, the archive photographs have become 'cast members' and have been placed on a 'stage'. This, in itself, suggests an updating of the 1905 story. In the case of the Batwa pygmies, there is the risk of adopting the modern-day equivalent of putting them on the Hippodrome stage – where the design of the multimedia production fails to distinguish between the two forms of exploitation: entertainment and study. In addition, Benjamin Stone's own photographic method, fuelled by his realist aesthetic, developed an unforeseen potential in the reuse of his images: :

> My method is to shoot successively, so as to show details and changes. If necessary, I take a dozen pictures of a ceremony or custom, recording the whole thing from beginning to end with a clearness that leaves little or nothing for the imagination to supply.[vi] (Stone, 1905)

This method, aided by Stone's use of a tripod, which has had the result of standardizing the background in the photographs of his 1905 Batwa shoot, results in an accumulation of images containing sufficient information to enable digital processing to create quite easily rudimentary animations of his subjects. They can be made to move slightly giving an impression of their repositioning – as if posing before the camera.

I considered it important that *The Batwa, 1905* project should not be strictly limited to the archive, but that it should include reference to the contemporary plight of the Batwa. Each of the routes is supplemented by a 'postscript' that contains up-to-date information and refers the viewer to the Internet's Rwanda Crisis Web. Furthermore, it suggests that the Batwa have remained 'media victims'. As the 'third class' of Rwandese society, their plight has been largely ignored by a press that prefers to focus its attention on two-sided conflicts. In the course of the genocide of 1994, it is estimated that up to 75 per cent of Rwanda's 'third tribe' were murdered.

In contrast to their commonly-assumed conventional roles, the contemporary archivist as well as the multimedia producer face many of the decisions and dilemmas of anyone that fulfils an editorial role, who must focus on such issues of representation as visual narrative, contexts, ethics and the estimation of audience response. Responsible review has the positive consequence of concentrating the mind on the editorial frameworks and theories of reception adopted by those aiming to represent 'other' cultures. Furthermore, it opens up an additional role for digital imaging. While colonial history can be rewritten, it cannot be re-photographed; yet the multi-referential nature of the photograph allows, through new technologies, the scope to reinterpret the photographic record through the reorganization, access and re-contextualization of images.

Conclusion

> ...I shall take great care not to accept into my belief anything false, and shall so well prepare my mind against all the tricks of this great deceiver that, however powerful and cunning he may be, he will never be able to impose on me. (Descartes, 1641, 100)

Fixed to the rooftops overlooking the town square in Krakow, Poland (said to be the largest Mediaeval town square in Europe) is a video camera. It captures an image every 10 minutes, feeding it into a computer, from which it is transmitted around the world via the Internet. By the end of 2000, there were 150 such Webcams cited worldwide, from Antarctica to Zagreb, with the number growing almost daily. One has been placed in the Southern Californian living room of the Wright family (no relation!). The family activities are open to anyone who wants to 'look in' – they can be surveyed 24 hours per day (www.generationXfamily.com).

The advent of the computer age has radically changed global communications. Innovations in digital technology have had a major impact not only in the areas of animation and feature movies, but also within the media which are concerned with transmitting factual information. In this arena, the traditional distinctions between such discrete areas as documentary, news and closed-circuit TV or camera surveillance, have become blurred. Indeed, the surveillance camera has found a unique role in public entertainment by providing television audiences with the uncritical spectacle of people's bad driving habits in Carlton Television's *Police, Camera, Action* (GB, 1999) programmes.

The use of digital Webcams, which transmit whatever they 'see' directly via the Web to whoever is able to access them, amounts to a further undermining of the fact/fiction dichotomy discussed earlier. A merging of rumour, gossip, opinion and fact emerges, perhaps the inevitable result of technological innovation. There are two main technological accelerators of this blurring effect: the democratization of hardware, and instantaneous communication. With the proliferation of cheap computers, digital cameras and Webcams, and easy access to worldwide networks, in effect virtually everyone can get hold of a camera and have instant access to worldwide media. Video footage of uncertain origin as well as more traditionally gathered and edited news and information can be distributed around the globe in seconds. Audio is faster than video, and at the end of the 20th century Israeli security forces began to encounter problems from 'phone-home' soldiers, who used their cellular phones to give real-time, first-hand accounts of action in the field to friends and family.

It is increasingly hard for television producers from fiercely competing companies to find the time, or possibly the inclination, to check the authenticity of all their sources when these are not camera teams hired by the station. But lack of responsible editing is not just a simple matter of (non-) reaction – programme-makers have also been proactive in this regard. At the end of the 20th century, a media row erupted concerning faked chat-show participants, and untruthful television documentaries (Gillard & Flynn, 1998). Instead of being drawn from the public at large, it was revealed that some chat-show guests had been supplied by entertainment agencies. This means that the participants are able to take on far more dramatic and entertaining roles than ordinary people, and because their personas are in fact fictive, do so without the reticence or embarrassment. Given the audience-ratings war, created by an explosion of satellite television channels at the close of the second millennium, competition grows increasingly fierce, and the demand for 'good television' starts to outstrip the demand for veracity. It is necessary to make sure you bring home the honey, when viewers will flip to another channel if you do not.

As for 'official', edited documentaries, for example, apart from using stock shots to add more lively footage, in BBC's *Driving School* (GB, 1997) some scenes were re-enacted; Channel 4's *Daddy's Girl* (GB, 1998) had to be dropped when it was revealed that a couple purporting to be father and daughter were not so at all; Carlton's award-winning documentary *The Connection* (GB, 1996) on the Colombian drug cartels relied upon subjects who were acting. The *Guardian* newspaper claimed that a scene that involved a 'drug courier' swallowing packets of heroine, to be smuggled into the UK, featured packages which did not contain drugs at all. It was also claimed that the television producer paid for the courier's flight. The result was a £2 million fine for Carlton Television (Gillard & Flynn, 1998). It would seem that although the 'new media' are quite able to deceive through technological trickery, the greater threat to veracity comes from the age-old techniques of the actor and creative producer, and the perennial demand to make documentary entertaining.

Although ethical considerations are, of course, central to making a documentary, as they are to the making of all ethnographic movies, it is most likely that in practice it is impossible to find the perfect solution, and give a fair and accurate representation to all concerned. However observational we think we may be being, as soon as we choose a point of view for the camera, we are creating a point of view on the subject. The most important factor is to be aware of the work of those who have trodden the path before, and consider the subject, the medium and the intention carefully, not making the naïve assumption that film or video is a transparent medium, in order to make an informed choice of action.

Notes

i   *Sight & Sound* April/May 1954

ii   For further discussion of this phenomenon, see Pirenne, 1970, 121-23

iii (1979) "'What's All the Cryin' About ?' The Films of Frederick Wiseman" *The Massachusetts Review* Vol. 13, No. 3, 453.

iv   A dangerous wild bird capable of causing serious injury, a great cassowary hunter wins considerable renown.

vi   Unidentified press cutting (1905) in The Benjamin Stone Collection, Birmingham Reference Library

Screenography

Films

Screenography

Screenography

Movies Based on Games

Television

Interactive titles

Other titles

Wright, Terry (1995) 'The Batwa 1905' in Lister, M. and Dewdney, A. (eds.) *From Silver to Silicon*, CD ROM. London: Artec (Mainz & Berlin: 1995) 188–191

There's No Simulation Like Home (Virtual Living Environment)(1999) (Paul Sermon/BNI/Lighthouse - Fabrica Brighton) GB 1

Think (22 screen presentation at New York World's Fair) (1964/1965) (Charles and Ray Eames) US 149

Web Sites

http://www.intac.com/PubService/rwanda/index.html Rwanda Crisis Web 191

http://ic.media.mit.edu/JBW/ *Jerome B Wiesner: a Random Walk Through the Twentieth-Century* n.d. (a hyper-portrait) 187-8, 188

Bibliography

Books

Aarseth, Espen J *Cybertext: Perspectives on Ergodic Literature* (Baltimore/London: Johns Hopkins University Press, 1997)

Adorno, Theodor and Horkeimer, Max *Dialectic of Enlightenment* (London:Allen Lane, 1973)

Alighieri, Dante *The Divine Comedy of Dante Alighieri II: Purgatorio* (trans. Sinclair, John D) (Oxford: Oxford University Press, 1939)

Alighieri, Dante *The Vision of Hell* (trans. Cary, HR and illus. Doré, Gustave) (New York: AL Burt, c. 1890)

Andrew, D *André Bazin* (New York: Oxford University Press, 1978)

Barbash, L and Taylor, L *Cross-Cultural Filmmaking* (Berkeley: University of California Press, 1997)

Barthes, Roland, *S/Z* (trans. Richard Miller) (New York: Hill and Wang 1974)

Bazin, A *What is Cinema?* Vol. I (trans. H Gray) (Berkeley: University of California Press, 1967)

Belton in Geoffrey Nowell-Smith (ed.) *The Oxford History of World Cinema* (Oxford: Oxford University Press, 1997)

Benjamin, Walter 'The Work of Art in the Age of Mechanical Reproduction', Arendt, H (ed.) *Illuminations* (London: Fontana, 1973)

Benton, Tim *The Villas of Le Corbusier, 1920-30 with photographs in the Lucien Hervé collection* (New Haven: Yale University Press, 1997)

Bergson, Henry *Essai sur les donneès immédiates de la conscience* (Paris: F Alcan, 1889)

Bergson, Henry *L'évolution créatrice* (Paris: F Alcan, 1907)

Berque, Augustin *Les Raisons du Paysage* (Paris: Hazan, 1995)

Bertillon, A 'Relève de Signalement Anthropométrique', *Identification Anthropométrique; Instructions Signalétiques* (Paris, 1893)

Bettelheim, Bruno (ed.) *The Uses of Enchantment* (Harmondsworth: Penguin, 1991)

Bruno, Giuliana *Atlas of Emotion: Journeys in Art, Architecture and Film* (Paris: Cerf, 1958)

Bullock, Nicholas 'Imagining the Post-War World', Penz, F and Thomas, M (ed.) *Cinema and Architecture* (London: BFI, 1997)

Bullock, Nicholas *Building the Post-war World* (London: Routledge, 2002)

Calder-Marshall, A *The Innocent Eye: the Life of Robert J Flaherty* (Harmondsworth: Pelican, 1963)

Campbell, Joseph *The Hero with a Thousand Faces* (Princeton: Bollingen, 1949)

Campbell, Joseph *The Inner Reaches of Outer Space* (New York: Alfred van der Marck, 1986)

Cassells, Justine and Jenkins, Henry (ed.) *From Barbie to Mortal Kombat: Gender and Computer Games* (Cambridge Mass: MIT Press, 1998)

Chapman, W 'Arranging Ethnology: AHLF Pitt Rivers and the Typological Tradition', *History of Anthropology*, Vol. 3, *Objects and Others* (Madison: University of Wisconsin Press, 1985)

Coates, Stephen and Stetter, Alex (ed.) *Impossible Worlds* (Basel-Boston-Berlin: Birkhauser/ London: August, 2000)

Cook, Pam (ed.) *The Cinema Book* (BFI: London, 1985)

Corner, John 'British TV Drama Documentary', Rosenthal, Alan (ed.) *Why Docudrama?* (Southern Illinois University Press, 1999)

DeCordova, Richard, 'From Lumière to Pathé', Elsaesser, Thomas (ed.) *Early Cinema* (London: BFI, 1990)

Descartes, R (trans. Sutcliffe, FE) *Discourse on Method and the Meditations* (Harmondworth: Penguin, 1968)

Eisenstein, SM *The Film Sense* (trans. and ed. Leyda, Jay) (London: Faber & Faber, 1943)

Eisner, Lotte H *The Haunted Screen: Expressionism in the German Cinema and the Influence of Max Reinhardt* (London: Thames and Hudson, 1969)

Elsaesser, Thomas (ed.) *Early Cinema* (London: BFI, 1990)

Elsaesser, Thomas 'Germany, the Weimar Years', Nowell-Smith, G (ed.) *The Oxford History of World Cinema* (Oxford: Oxford University Press, 1997)

Erlich, V *Russian Formalism: History – Doctrine* (New Haven & London: Yale University Press, 1955)

Fear, Bob (ed.) *Architecture and Film II* (Wiley-Academy, 2000)

Georgiadis, Sokratis *Sigfried Giedion; eine intellecktuelle Biographie* (Zurich: Aumann, 1989)

Giedion, Sigfried *Building in France, Building in Iron, Building in Ferroconcrete* Georgiadis, S (ed.) (Santa Monica: Getty Center, 1995)

Godelier, M *The Making of Great Men: Male Domination and Power among the New Guinea Baruya* (trans. Swyer, R) (Cambridge: Cambridge University Press, 1986)

Gunning, Tom, 'The Cinema of Attractions', Elsaesser, Thomas (ed.) *Early Cinema* (London: BFI, 1990)

Hall, GS *Adolescence* (New York: Appleton, 1904)

Haraway, Donna J M*odest_Witness@Second_Millenium.FemaleMan(c)_Meets_OncoMouse* (New York: Routledge 1997)

Hardy, F (ed.) *Grierson on Documentary* (London: Faber & Faber, 1946)

Harrison, James J *Life Among the Pygmies* (London: Hutchinson, 1905)

Heim, Michael *Virtual Realism* (New York/Oxford: Oxford University Press, 1989)

Jansen, Andres, 'Only Film Can Make the New Architecture Intelligible', Penz, F and Thomas, M (ed.) *Cinema and Architecture* (London: BFI, 1997)

Jones, Alan *Lara Croft Tomb Raider: The Official Film Companion* (London: Carlton Books, 2001)

Kandinsky, W 'Concerning the Spiritual in Art' (1911), Harrison, Charles and Wood, Paul (eds.) *Art in Theory 1900-1990: an Anthology of Changing Ideas* (Oxford: Blackwell, 1992)

Karcauer, Siegfried, *From Caligari to Hitler: A Psychological History of the German Film* (Princeton NJ: Princeton University Press, 1947)

Katz, Stephen D *Film Directing Shot by Shot* (Los Angeles: Michael Weise, 1991)

Kirkham, Pat *Charles and Ray Eames: Designers of the Twentieth Century* (Cambridge, Mass: MIT Press, 1995)

Konstantarakos, Myrto (ed.) *Spaces in European Cinema* (Bristol: Intellect, 2000)

Kuenzli, Rudolf E *Dada and Surrealist Film* (New York: Willis Laker & Owens, 1987)

Kuper, A *Anthropologists and Anthropology: the Modern British School* (London: Routledge, 1983)

Lamster, Mark (ed.) *Architecture and Film* (Princeton: Princeton Architectural Press, 2000)

Landow, George P *Hypertext – the Convergence of Contemporary Critical Theory and Technology* (Baltimore: Johns Hopkins University Press, 1997)

Laurel, Brenda *Computers as Theatre* (Reading, MA: Addison-Wesley, 1993)

Le Corbusier *Vers une architecture* Etchells, F (ed.) (Oxford: Butterworth Architecture, 1993)

Leavis, FR 'Mass Civilization and Minority Culture', in Storey, John (ed.) *Cultural Theory and Popular Culture, a Reader* (GB, 1994)

Leavis, QD *Fiction and the Reading Public* (London: Chatto & Windus, 1932)

Le Diberder, Alain & Frederic, *L'Univers des Jeux Video* (Paris: Editions La Découverte, 1998)

Levin, GR *Documentary Explorations* (New York: Anchor, 1971)

Lévi-Strauss, Claude *Anthropology and Myth: lectures 1951-1982* Willis, Roy (trans.) (Oxford: Basil Blackwell, 1987)

Leyda, Jay (ed.) *Eisenstein on Disney* Upchurch, A (trans.) (London: Methuen, 1988)

Bibliography

Maltin, Leonard, *Of Mice and Magic: A History of American Animated Cartoons* (New York: New American Library, 1997)

Manevich, Lev, *The Language of New Media* (Massachusetts: MIT Press, 2001)

Marey, Etienne-Jules *La Machine Animale: locomotion terrestre et aérienne* (Paris: Ballière, 1873)

Marey/Muybridge Pionniers du cinéma (Conseil Régional de Bourguogne, 1995)

Mast, Gerald *Film, Cinema, Movie, a Theory of Experience* (New York: Harper Collins, 1977)

Mitchell, William J *City of Bits* (Cambridge, Mass.: MIT Press, 1996)

Moholy-Nagy *Painting, photography, film* (Cambridge, Mass.: MIT Press, 1969)

Murray, Janet H *Hamlet on the Holodeck: The Future of Narrative in Cyberspace* (Free Press: New York/London/Toronto/Sidney/Singapore)

Muybridge, Edward *Complete Animals and Locomotions* (New York: Dover, 1979)

Negroponte, Nicholas *Being Digital* (London: Hoddder & Stoughton 1995)

Neumann, Dietrich (ed.) *Film Architecture: Set Designs from Metropolis to Blade Runner* (Munich: Prestel, 1996)

Newhall, B (ed.) *Photography: Essays & Images: Illustrated Reading in the History of Photography* (London: Secker & Warburg, 1981)

Noguez, Dominique 'Paris-Moscou-Paris', *Paris vu par le Cinéma d'Avant*-Garde (Paris: Paris Experimental Editions, 1985)

Parker, Philip *The Art and Science of Screenwriting* (Bristol: Intellect, 1998)

Penz, François 'The Architecture in the Films of Jacques Tati', Penz, F and Thomas, M (ed.) *Cinema and Architecture* (London: BFI, 1997)

Pirenne, MH *Optics, Painting and Photography* (Cambridge: Cambridge University Press, 1970)

Poole, Steven *Trigger Happy* (London: Fourth Estate, 2000)

Propp, Vladimir *Morphology of the Folktale* (trans. Scott, L) (Austin: University of Texas Press, 1928, 1968)

Pym, John (ed.) *Time Out Film Guide* (Harmondsworth, Penguin Books, 1998)

Romanyshyn, Robert *Technology as Symptom and Dream* (London: Routledge, 1989)

Rosenthal, Alan (ed.) *Why Docudrama?* (Carbondale, Ill.: Southern Illinois University Press, 1999)

Samsel, Jon and Wimberley, Darryl *Writing for Interactive Media: the Complete Guide* (New York: Allworth Press, 1998)

Stone, Sir JB *Sir Benjamin Stone's Pictures: Records of National Life and History* Vol. II, 'Parliamentary Scenes and Portraits' (London: Cassell & Co 1905)

Stone, Allucquère Rosanne *The War of Desire and Technology at the Close of the Mechanical Age* (Cambridge, Mass/London: MIT Press, 1996)

Talbot, WHF *The Pencil of Nature* (London: 1844)

Turkle, Sherry *Life on the Screen: Identity in the Age of the Internet* (New York: Simon & Schuster, 1996)

Vogler, Christopher *The Writer's Journey: Mythic Structure for Storytellers and Screenwriters* (Los Angeles: Michael Wiese Productions, Studio City, 1992)

Wallis Budge, EA *The Egyptian Book of the Dead* (London: 1895)

Warner, Marina *From the Beast to the Blonde* (London: Vintage, 1994)

Wells, Paul *Understanding Animation* (London: Routledge, 1998)

White, J *The Birth and Rebirth of Pictorial Space* (London: Faber & Faber, 1957)

Woodhead, L *A Box Full of Spirits: Adventures of a Film-maker in Africa* (London: Heinemann, 1987)

Worth, S and Adair, J *Through Navajo Eyes: An Exploration in Film, Communication and Anthropology* (Bloomington: Indiana University Press, 1972)

Wright, Terry 'Photography: Theories of Realism and Convention' in Edward, E (ed.) *Anthropology and Photography, 1860-1920* (Yale: Yale University Press, 1992)

Wright, Terry (1995) 'The Batwa 1905' in Lister, M and Dewdney, A (eds.) *From Silver to Silicon*, CD-ROM. London: Artec (Mainz & Berlin: 1995)

Periodical Articles

Arago, F. *The London Globe*, 23 August 1839

Ashbee, Brian 'There's no Place Like Home', *Art Review Magazine*, March 2000

Banks, M 'Talking Heads and Moving Pictures: David Byrne's *True Stories* and the anthropology of film', *Visual Anthropology*, 3, 1990, pp. 1-9

Bassett-Lowke *Artwork*, 1930

Dominguez, V 'The Marketing of Heritage', *American Ethnologist* 13 (3), 1986, pp. 546-555

Frith, F 'The Art of Photography', *The Art Journal* 5, 1859, pp. 71-72

Futurist Manifesto *Le Figaro*, 20 February 1909

Gillard, MS and Flynn, L 'Carlton fined £2m over documentary' *The Guardian*, 19 December 1998

Godard, Jean-Luc *Cahiers du Cinéma*, December 1962

Heath, Stephen 'Narrative Space' *Screen* (Society for Education in Film and Television), Vol. 17, No. 3, 1976

Harrison, James J 1901 'A Journey from Zeila to Lake Rudolf', *Geographical Journal XVIII*, pp. 258-75

Russell, Erica 'Animation and the Post Modern', *Art & Animation*, *Art and Design Profile*, No. 53 (GB, 1997)

Turner, T 'Defiant Images: the Kayapo Appropriation of Video', *Anthropology Today*, Vol. 8, No. 6, 1992, pp. 5-16

Video and PC Games Industry Trends Survey (Video Interactive Digital Software Association), No. 4 (US, 1998)

Wright, Terry 'Systems of representation: towards the integration of digital photography into the practice of creating visual images', *Visual Anthropology* Vol. II, 1998, pp. 207-220

Postgraduate Theses

McGregor, Helen, *James Joyce's Dublin* MPhil Dissertation (Dept. of Architecture: Cambridge University 2000)

Drama

Aeschylus (525-456 BC), *The Oresteia*

Shakespeare, *Hamlet* (1603)

Shakespeare, *Romeo & Juliet* (1597)

Fiction

Austen, Jane *Northanger Abbey* (GB, 1818)

Barrie, JM *Peter Pan* (GB, 1911)

Bronte, Charlotte *Jane Eyre* (GB, 1848)

Burroughs, William *The Naked Lunch* (US, 1959)

Carroll, Lewis *Through the Looking Glass and What Alice Found There* (GB, 1872)

Chandler, Raymond *The Lady in the Lake* (GB, 1943)

Conan Doyle, Arthur *The Land of Mist* (GB, 1926)

Conan Doyle, Arthur *The Lost World* (GB, 1912)

Conan Doyle, Arthur *The Poison Belt* (GB, 1913)

Dickens, Charles *Bleak House* (GB, 1853)

Dickens, Charles *Great Expectations* (GB, 1861)

Du Maurier, Daphne *Rebecca* (GB, 1938)

Fleming, Ian *Casino Royale* (GB, 1951)

Fleming, Ian *Goldfinger* (GB, 1964)

Gibson, William *All the World's Parties* (US, 2000)

Goonan, Kathleen Ann *Crescent City Blues* (US, 2000)

Goonan, Kathleen Ann *Queen City Jazz* (US, 1994)

Hoban, Russell *Riddley Walker* (GB, 1980)

Homer, *The Iliad* (Greece, C8BC) (Faglos, R. (trans) London: Penguin Books, 1991))

Isherwood, Christopher *Goodbye to Berlin* (GB, 1939)

Joyce, James *Ulysses* (GB 1918, Paris 1922) (Gabler, HW [ed.] London: Bodley Head, 1986)

Kesey, Ken *One Flew Over the Cuckoo's Nest* (US, 1969)

le Carré, J *The Looking Glass War* (GB, 1965)

Melville, Herman *Moby Dick* (GB, 1851) (Tanner, T. [ed.] Oxford: OUP, 1988)

Neal, Stephen *Snow Crash* (US, 1992)

Noon, Jeff *Pollen* (GB, 1995)

Orwell, George *Nineteen Eighty-Four: A Novel* (GB, 1948)

Pavic, Milorad *Dictionary of the Khazars, a Lexicon Novel in 100,000 Words* Pribicevic-Zoric, C. (trans.)
    (US, 1988)

Pelevin, Viktor *Clay Machine Gun* (USSR 1996, GB 1999)

Piercy, Marge *Body of Glass*, (US, 1991)

Proust, Marcel *À la Recherche du Temps Perdu* (France, 1913-27)

Radcliff, Ann *The Mysteries of Udolpho* (GB, 1794)

Rider Haggard, H *King Solomon's Mines* (GB, 1885)

Rider Haggard, H *She* (GB, 1887)

Saltern, Felix *Bambi* (Austria 1923, English trans. US 1928)

Shelley, Mary *Frankenstein* (GB, 1818)

Stevenson, Robert Louis *The Strange Case of Dr Jekyll and Mr Hyde* (GB, 1886)

Stoker, Bram *Dracula* (GB, 1869)

Sullivan, Tricia *Someone to Watch Over Me* (GB, 1997)

Tepper, Sheri S *The Family Tree* (US, 1997)

Thompson, Hunter S *Fear and Loathing in Las Vegas* (US, 1967)

Tolkein, JRR *The Lord of the Rings* (GB, 1954/5)

de Troyes, Chrétien *Perceval* (France, 1188) Bryant, N. (trans.) (Cambridge: DS Brewer, 1982)

de Troyes, Chrétien *Yvain, the Knight with the Lion* (France ,1175) Owen, DDR (trans.) (London/Melbourne:
    Dent, Everyman's Library, 1987)

Walpole, Horace *The Castle of Otranto* (GB, 1764)

Wharton, Edith *The Age of Innocence* (US, 1920)

Wilkie Collins, William *The Moonstone* (GB, 1868)

Willis, Connie *Bellwether* (US, 1996)

Woolf, Virginia *Mrs. Dalloway* (GB, 1925)

Graphic Novels

Aliens: Female War (Titan Books, US, 1997)

Adventures of Tintin (Hergé, Belgium, 1955)

Thorgal Rosinski/Van Hamme (Journal Tintin, 1985 –)

Index

Index

Index